TELL HALAF

The Great Front Façade of Kapara's Palace (restored)

TELL HALAF

A New Culture in Oldest Mesopotamia

BY

DR. BARON MAX VON OPPENHEIM

TRANSLATED BY

GERALD WHEELER

*With Maps, Text Figures and 68 Plates
in Colour and Half Tone*

LONDON AND NEW YORK

G. P. PUTNAM'S SONS

913.358

PRINTED IN GREAT BRITAIN BY ROBERT MACLEHOSE AND CO. LTD.
THE UNIVERSITY PRESS, GLASGOW

Foreword to the English Edition

THE present English edition is a translation from the German edition which was published by F. A. Brockhaus at Leipzig in 1931 under the title *Der Tell Halaf, eine neue Kultur im ältesten Mesopotamien.* In the English text, however, additions have been made in some places.

The dates given for the historical events, kings, dynasties, etc., as well as those given to the works of art at Tell Halaf are in this English edition brought into agreement with the Langdon-Fotheringham scheme.

Foreword to the German Edition

ON the discovery of Tell Halaf in 1899 I have already written in the *Zeitschrift der Gesellschaft für Erdkunde zu Berlin*, Band 36, and afterwards in an essay with the title 'Der Tell Halaf und die verschleierte Göttin' (*Der alte Orient*, 1908). A combination of unfortunate circumstances—the War and the conditions arising out of it—have so far hindered me from publishing the looked-for report on the excavations.

In 1927 and 1929 I was able to carry out needful further researches in my old field, and I am at last in a position to publish the first book on my excavations and their scientific results.

This book is only meant as the forerunner of a definitive scientific work on Tell Halaf and its culture. That it may fit into the popular series of which it is to form part, I must here leave on one side any learned disquisitions.

My heart is filled with thankfulness to the many who have helped on my work, and supported me by counsel and action. First of all my thanks are owing to the self-sacrificing co-operation of the gentlemen who accompanied me on my researches, above all to Dr. Felix Langenegger, *Regierungs- und Baurat*, who was the chief architect for the excavations of 1911-13 and 1929, as also to Dr. Karl Müller. My thoughts turn reverently to the dead who gave their lives in the service of the excavations—Paul Löffler, State Architect (*Regierungsbaumeister*), and Josèphe Darrous, the Director of the Department for Antiquities in Northern Syria.

To Professor Hubert Schmidt I am truly thankful for the long years of work devoted to examining and cataloguing the smaller objects, expecially the pottery, found at Tell Halaf.

The two former scientific assistants of the Max Freiherr von Oppenheim Foundation, Dr. Anton Moortgat and Dr. Adam Falkenstein, have admirably supported me.

Valuable services have been given by the sculptor, Herr Igor von Jakimow, and by the certificated engineer, Herr Hans Lehmann, in the arrangement of the Tell Halaf Museum in Berlin at 6 Franklinstrasse, where such finds as fell to my share are for the present shown in the original, and the others in plaster casts; Herr von Jakimow's services were particularly valuable for the reconstruction of the façade of the temple-palace.

There are three men of learning whom I have especially to thank; I look upon myself as their pupil, and their views are those I have mainly followed. They are Professor Arthur Ungnad for history, Professor Bruno Meissner for the dating of inscriptions, and Professor Ernst Herzfeld for the classification of the sculpture on stylistic grounds.

I have also to thank the publishers for their readiness always to meet me in every way.

Of the illustrations in the text of this book those on pp. 80, 82, 97, 98, 136, 221, and 284 are after drawings by Dr. Felix Langenegger; those on pp. 22 and 78 after drawings by Dr. Karl Müller; that on p. 242 after a drawing by the certified engineer, Hans Lehmann; and those on pp. 296, 298, 300 and 301, after drawings by the architect Otto Streu. The map of the surroundings of Tell Halaf on p. 4 was made by Major Ludloff on Tell Halaf on the occasion of his passing through. The ground plans on pp. 240, 241 are taken from Humann and Puchstein's book, *Reisen in Kleinasien und Nordsyrien*.

Finally I must not omit to express my thanks here also to the Franco-Syrian Mandatory government, as also to the former German consul in Beirut, Dr. Schwörbel, for the friendly support they have given me in these last years in my work of excavation.

Contents

List of Illustrations

COLOUR PLATES

Text Figures and Maps

TELL HALAF

I

The Discovery and Excavation of Tell Halaf

I HAD already spent many years in the Nearer East, and had ranged over the Islamic world from Morocco to India and East Africa. For over six months in the native quarter of Cairo I had shared in the life of the dwellers, who have kept themselves wholly Arab, and especially of the religious sheikhs. I often spent whole months in Northern Arabia, Syria, and Mesopotamia with the Beduins, the free sons of the desert, in their tents. I had a full knowledge of their soul, their speech, and their customs. I had come to love these people, and everywhere I was welcomed with open arms.

I had been since 1896 in the service of the German diplomatic mission in Egypt. From Cairo I made fresh journeys for discovery; and in 1899 I once more started on one of these, which was to take me from Damascus into the Land of the Two Rivers. I had been asked by Georg von Siemens, one of the founders of the Deutsche Bank, to determine the best line for the proposed Bagdad railways in the stretch between Aleppo and Mosul. It has been a great joy to me that my proposal to take this through the middle of the desert by Jerablus and Ras el Ain was accepted. This line was much further to the south than the course taken up to then by the usual caravan road, which followed the big towns of Birejik, Urfa and Mardin. This desert had till then only been crossed by nomadic Beduins; but I had found in it countless hills of ruins bearing witness to a great culture of long ago. In 1902 and 1904 I was attached to the German embassy in Washington ; among other duties, I was to study, in the interest of the development of the Bagdad railway territory, especially in Syria and Mesopotamia, the lessons learnt in the United States when areas

A

hitherto unopened or only slightly opened were brought to
the highest pitch of prosperity through new railways.
I have delightful memories of the important lessons
learned, and of the friendly welcome and the great hos-
pitality I met with on this occasion all over the United
States.

Travelling in Mesopotamia, especially between the two
tributaries of the Euphrates, the Belikh and the Khabur,
was at that time (in 1899) not without its dangers. I took a
zigzag course again with my caravan through the desert
tracts along paths hitherto untrodden by any European, so
that I might find the remains of old culture. A Beduin chief,
Ibrahim Pasha, the sheikh of the great tribal group of the
Milli, consisting of Beduins and Kurds, was then all-
powerful in these parts. Ibrahim Pasha had his residence
in Veranshehir, an old ruined site south of the Kurdish
mountains, in the Mesopotamian plain between Urfa and
Mardin. It was founded by the Emperor Constantine the
Great; and to-day the remains are still standing of a magnificent Christian cathedral. Ibrahim Pasha had made of
the deserted spot an important Beduin market centre.
Mohammedan and Christian traders had been attracted
there by him, and had built permanent houses amidst the
ruins. The Pasha himself, however, almost throughout the
year, led in the Mesopotamian plain the life of the Beduins,
who wander about with their tents and herds of camels
from pasture-ground to pasture-ground.

Like other tribal chiefs dwelling on the edge of the
desert, he had been granted by Sultan Abdul Hamid the
right of forming irregular cavalry from his men, known as
the Hamidiye regiments. They were fitted out with good
rifles by the Turks. Ibrahim, thanks to these superior
weapons and his energetic policy, had gradually got the
upper hand over all the tribes between Belikh and Khabur
from the Euphrates in the south as far as the northern rim
of mountains. Even the dwellers in the big towns of Urfa
and Mardin lived in dread of him in spite of their Turkish

I

The Discovery and Excavation of Tell Halaf

I HAD already spent many years in the Nearer East, and had ranged over the Islamic world from Morocco to India and East Africa. For over six months in the native quarter of Cairo I had shared in the life of the dwellers, who have kept themselves wholly Arab, and especially of the religious sheikhs. I often spent whole months in Northern Arabia, Syria, and Mesopotamia with the Beduins, the free sons of the desert, in their tents. I had a full knowledge of their soul, their speech, and their customs. I had come to love these people, and everywhere I was welcomed with open arms.

I had been since 1896 in the service of the German diplomatic mission in Egypt. From Cairo I made fresh journeys for discovery; and in 1899 I once more started on one of these, which was to take me from Damascus into the Land of the Two Rivers. I had been asked by Georg von Siemens, one of the founders of the Deutsche Bank, to determine the best line for the proposed Bagdad railways in the stretch between Aleppo and Mosul. It has been a great joy to me that my proposal to take this through the middle of the desert by Jerablus and Ras el Ain was accepted. This line was much further to the south than the course taken up to then by the usual caravan road, which followed the big towns of Birejik, Urfa and Mardin. This desert had till then only been crossed by nomadic Beduins; but I had found in it countless hills of ruins bearing witness to a great culture of long ago. In 1902 and 1904 I was attached to the German embassy in Washington ; among other duties, I was to study, in the interest of the development of the Bagdad railway territory, especially in Syria and Mesopotamia, the lessons learnt in the United States when areas

A

hitherto unopened or only slightly opened were brought to
the highest pitch of prosperity through new railways.
I have delightful memories of the important lessons
learned, and of the friendly welcome and the great hos-
pitality I met with on this occasion all over the United
States.

Travelling in Mesopotamia, especially between the two
tributaries of the Euphrates, the Belikh and the Khabur,
was at that time (in 1899) not without its dangers. I took a
zigzag course again with my caravan through the desert
tracts along paths hitherto untrodden by any European, so
that I might find the remains of old culture. A Beduin chief,
Ibrahim Pasha, the sheikh of the great tribal group of the
Milli, consisting of Beduins and Kurds, was then all-
powerful in these parts. Ibrahim Pasha had his residence
in Veranshehir, an old ruined site south of the Kurdish
mountains, in the Mesopotamian plain between Urfa and
Mardin. It was founded by the Emperor Constantine the
Great; and to-day the remains are still standing of a magnificent Christian cathedral. Ibrahim Pasha had made of
the deserted spot an important Beduin market centre.
Mohammedan and Christian traders had been attracted
there by him, and had built permanent houses amidst the
ruins. The Pasha himself, however, almost throughout the
year, led in the Mesopotamian plain the life of the Beduins,
who wander about with their tents and herds of camels
from pasture-ground to pasture-ground.

Like other tribal chiefs dwelling on the edge of the
desert, he had been granted by Sultan Abdul Hamid the
right of forming irregular cavalry from his men, known as
the Hamidiye regiments. They were fitted out with good
rifles by the Turks. Ibrahim, thanks to these superior
weapons and his energetic policy, had gradually got the
upper hand over all the tribes between Belikh and Khabur
from the Euphrates in the south as far as the northern rim
of mountains. Even the dwellers in the big towns of Urfa
and Mardin lived in dread of him in spite of their Turkish

PLATE I. THE HUGE TENT OF IBRAHIM PASHA

PLATE IIA. BEDUINS ON A RAID

PLATE IIB. CHECHEN VILLAGE OF RAS EL AIN, WITH THE SOURCE-POND
OF THE KHABUR (1899)
(The volcano of Kbise in the background)

garrisons. Thus, sheltered by the Sultan's good graces, he behaved like an independent ruler.

As I was travelling through his territory, I made my call on him after the custom of the land. I came upon him a day's journey south-west of Veranshehir at the foot of the Tektek mountains in his huge tent (Pl. 1), the biggest one I have ever seen. The men's part would probably hold 2000. For three days I lived with all my men, about twenty-five of them, as the Pasha's guest.

He was a man of extraordinary personality, and it was a pleasure to be with him. As I knew Arabic, I talked with him for hours at a time about his blood feuds and fights with different desert tribes; and in this way I won his trust and his friendship. I was used to living among the Beduins quite in their own way, and also to taking my meals with them, at which the fingers do duty for knives and forks. This way of eating, however, needs much practice. A high mountain of rice or *burgul* (coarse-ground wheat) is brought in on a great dish and set on the ground. On the rice has been put a sheep cut up into small bits; and besides this hot sheep's fat is poured over the dish in the guests' presence. Then ten, twelve or more of the tent-dwellers squat round the dish, and with the right hand only—on no account whatever with the left—a ball is kneaded from the rice and crammed into the mouth. Anything left over in the hand is thrown back into the common dish of rice, in which an ever-growing hole forms before the person eating. Then another lot is taken up, and so it goes on until you are filled and stand up, when another takes your place. Thus up to a hundred or more are fed from one pot. What is left—if anything—of the meal, is at length put a little tidy, and taken off into the women's part of the tent for them and the children to eat. The usual bread of the Beduins is baked thin as paper in a flat round cake 18 inches across on an iron pot upside down heated by camel dung. The smaller loaves shaped like cow's dung, not more than 8-12 inches across, and much thicker and hollow, are found only in the Arab towns, more seldom in villages. These remind us of the loaves that are seen on old Hither Asiatic stone monuments when meals are represented.

In Ibrahim Pasha's camp I was told of remarkable statues said to have been found on a hill by the small

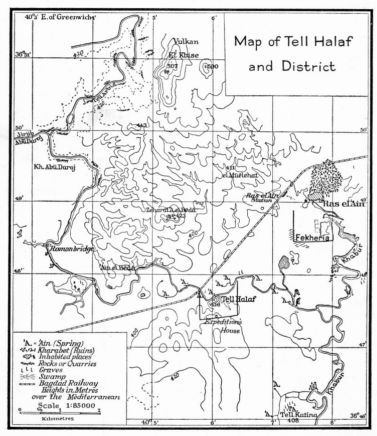

village of Ras el Ain, the 'spring-head' of the Khabur. The village was inhabited by Chechens, Mohammedans coming from the Caucasus and akin to the Cherkesses (Circassians), who after the Russian conquest of their home had fled as religious refugees to an Islamic land, that is Turkey.

The Chechens, I was told, had wanted some years before to bury one of their dead on the hill, and, while doing this they had come upon stone statues of animals with human heads. Filled with superstitious dread, they filled in the hole again and buried the body at another place. In that same year the neighbourhood was visited by drought, locust swarms and cholera. This was attributed by the Chechens to the evil spirits that they believed to have been in the statues, and now set free. As a result they most carefully avoided speaking of the statues, fearing that others might dig out the fabulous beings and thereby bring ill-hap on them once more. I at once resolved to go into the matter.

In five days' march we went by devious ways to Ras el Ain, and at the same time I examined parts of the Tektek mountains. During this time I met with eight *ghazwas*, Beduin robber-bands, who attacked us, but I succeeded always in coming to an understanding with them (Pl. 2a). Our baggage caravan, however, which at first I ordered to march apart, was driven off the road we had arranged, and we did not find it till the third evening. During all this time we had nothing to eat. Luckily, however, we had been once more most plentifully entertained in Ibrahim Pasha's camp when we set forth at early morning; but the little food we carried in our saddle-bags for the road was soon used up. However we found on the way, in some pools, enough water for ourselves and our horses. For the Beduin such privations as these are nothing; he only thinks of a proverb that bids him pull his belt in tighter. The meeting with my caravan again was very dramatic. My excellent servant Tannus, to whom, as always when I separated from my caravan, I had given the line of march beforehand, had for some unexplained reason been brought by the Beduin guide sent with him by Ibrahim Pasha straight to the camping-ground fixed upon for the third day. Here

on account of the dangerous neighbourhood he had built
with camels and the baggage a regular fort covered behind
by a steep cliff. He himself had been attacked many times,
but luckily unsuccessfully. A part of my following that was
marching with the caravan had then ridden to the second
camping-ground I had fixed on, and there found us. They
had, however, themselves eaten up on the way the pro-
visions meant for us. But I still had important scientific
surveys to complete, and only when these were done did I
ride off with my starving men and animals to the camp of
our caravan. Tannus had now almost given us up, just as
we had feared that the caravan was lost. Our joy at meeting
once more was all the greater.

In Ras el Ain (Pl. 2*b*) I dismounted at the house of the
Mukhtar, the village headman of the Chechens. Of the
50,000 or so Caucasians who had settled here thirty years
earlier, only about 200 families were now left. They were
living in close settlements in Ras el Ain and in Safh, a
small neighbouring village. All the rest had perished owing
to the fever-stricken climate of the headwaters region of
the Khabur, or else had gradually worn away in the never-
ending fights with the great Beduin tribes that had pasture
grounds in their neighbourhood. The surviving Chechens
had come to be much-dreaded sharpshooters and high-
waymen, but at that time were kept in dependence by
Ibrahim Pasha. Since we came from his camp we were
hospitably welcomed. The Mukhtar would not hear of our
putting up our own tents; while soon all the people of the
place had gathered in his house to see the strangers.

It was not until we had partaken of the feast that I
started to speak with great care of the remarkable statues.
As I had foreseen, they denied everything. However I did
not give up; I described the stones and promised the
Chechens a good reward if I could get guides to the place
of the finds.

It was all in vain. Then I appealed to the laws of hospi-
tality, and demanded, as the guest, not to be told what

was untrue, but to have my request granted. Thereupon the Mukhtar and the village elders swore on the Koran that they had not lied. I now played my last trump. I stood up, and yelled to my men, the soldiers of my escort and the Beduin guides to come; I hurled a curse at my hosts for having sworn falsely by the Koran. I told them to their faces that they had come upon the statues when burying a body close to Ras el Ain, that in the same year the harvest had failed and that they, for fear of the evil spirits, believed therefore that they must say nothing.

There was then a dramatic scene. All the Chechens stood up. Some drew their long narrow daggers; such a thing as this had never yet befallen the hot-tempered, proud Caucasians. My soldiers ran to my side; the situation grew threatening. I shouted to the Chechens to cap their false oath with the murder of their guest in their own house. At the last moment three old Chechens and the guides sent with me by Ibrahim Pasha came between us. The Mukhtar, who was really a most decent man, was evidently ashamed of their unworthy behaviour. A sudden silence fell on them, and I was getting ready with all to leave the inhospitable house and the village, when the Mukhtar acknowledged his wrong, and asked me to stay; and on this the Chechens most solemnly promised to take me up the hill on which the statues were said to have been found.

Next day, 19th November, 1899, they brought me to Tell Halaf (Pl. 3a). Only the evening before, when we had crossed the Khabur by a ford higher up on our way to Ras el Ain, we had ridden by this hill without any inkling whatever.

I could now have the first digging carried out by Chechens and by Beduins belonging to a small half-nomadic tribe, who happened to be bringing home the harvest from Ras el Ain for the Chechens. Surprises quite undreamt of fell to my lot; it was a turning-point in my life. The spade was first of all applied at the spot where the

Chechens had come upon those remarkable statues when they had tried to bury the dead man.

Here I carried on work for three days only, but even in this short time I was able to lay bare part of the great principal face of the temple-palace (Pl. 10a) and, besides, several large and beautiful relief-slabs, I discovered the remains of some statues in the round; among these was my veiled goddess (Pl. 43). All these statues were of basalt. The uncovering of the veiled goddess was a great event. This large, dark-coloured woman's figure with its retreating forehead, thin lips and mysterious cast of countenance —whose effect was further heightened by the large, black oval eyeball with a very narrow white rim—threw a spell over me.

We had neither the proper outfit, the time, nor any permit to carry out more detailed investigations; we therefore carefully covered in the statues again with earth. It was with a heavy heart that I left the place after so short a time, but just because I was determined to come back later and dig over the ground systematically I had to leave now.

From Tell Halaf I continued my journey of exploration in Upper Mesopotamia, and was the first to cross the Abd-el-Aziz range, so full of legends. I halted finally in the village of Hesseche, where the Khabur is joined by its tributary the Jarjar, coming from Nizibin in the north. Here I joined up with the route I had followed on my journey of exploration in 1893, which had taken me from Der ez Zor to Nizibin, and then eastwards to Mosul and Bagdad. From Hesseche I bore north-west to Mardin and Diarbekir, and then along the ordinary caravan-road by way of the big towns through Siverek, Urfa and Birejik to Aintab, Adana and Konia. This was the stretch that had once been proposed for the Bagdad railway, and which was afterwards quite rightly given up, and the line laid further south in the plain of Upper Mesopotamia. This plain had long since become a desert and a wandering-ground for nomadic Beduins and Kurds, but countless mounds of ruins still bore witness to the possibilities of cultivation and to a numerous population in earlier times.

When, at the end of 1899, I was on my way back to Germany after the expedition which led to my discovery of Tell Halaf, I requested the Turkish government to reserve the hill for me for later investigation. This was most kindly done; but ten years afterwards the Turks declared that they were being pressed by other nations, and could no longer keep Tell Halaf for me. I then took off my diplomatic uniform and turned to digging.

In 1911 the first attack was made with the spade. I was resolved, for excavating Tell Halaf, to have the advantage of the technical experience tested in Babylon and Assur of the well-known archaeological school of Professor Robert Koldewey, and accordingly enlisted the services of one of his best assistants, Dr. Felix Langenegger, who holds to-day an important post as *Regierungs- und Baurat* in the Finance Ministry in Dresden. He became my chief architect for the excavations, and afterwards gave his services permanently to the work carried on at Tell Halaf. The knowledge he had won from many years of earlier excavating was extraordinarily valuable; and I have to thank him especially for an untiring love of work.

Besides Dr. Langenegger, I was accompanied by a younger architect, *Regierungsbaumeister* Paul Löffler, by a physician, Dr. Oswald Seeman, who also undertook the photography, and by a secretary. As the Turkish Government commissioner we had been allotted a young educated Turk named Ahmed Durri Bey, and with him we were always on a very friendly footing. It was most important for me that I was able to have the services again of two capable natives of these parts, whom I had already tested on my earlier expeditions, namely Tannus and Elias Maluf.

Tannus Maluf, a Syrian Christian from the Lebanon, had already been with me on my 1893 journey, and I had taken him on all my expeditions afterwards. He was my body servant, and also in charge of my caravans and the camp. When I was sick he looked after me devotedly; and in times of danger on our journeys he would sleep on the ground at the door of my tent. He always kept his good temper, so that he understood excellently how to handle the Beduins. To him fell the task of distributing the robes of honour among them on my behalf, and it was to him that my men and the Beduins applied when they wished to bring something to my notice.

Tannus could neither read nor write, nor did he understand any European tongue. After my first expedition I had recommended him to the German Consulate in Beirut and ever since then he had been kept there by the consul as *Kavass* (a kind of policeman and messenger). He was a true mountaineer, with all his good nature dauntless and brave, and moreover one of the strongest men I have ever met. One day when two of my horse-boys were fighting, and one was already lying on the ground and the other had picked up a heavy stone to smash in his head, Tannus fell on the two, lifted both of them together, one in each hand, knocked their heads together, and then threw them down. After that the camp was always quiet when Tannus was there.

Elias Maluf, his cousin, the village schoolmaster in an eyrie up in the Lebanon, was my Arabic secretary. His mastery of Arabic was equal to any learned man's. He had been educated in a French monastery school on the coast, and there he had learned spoken and written French, and also European ways of thought. He was moreover, absolutely honest and trustworthy and was painstaking and careful in his work. To him I owe the spelling of all the geographical and Beduin names in Arabic and the European transcription. I had taught him also to help in my scientific observations and note-taking. Moreover he shared with Tannus in looking after the supplies and the equipment at Tell Halaf. Unfortunately this fine fellow died a few days before I came to Syria again in 1927, when he

was to go with me on my new expedition to Tell Halaf.
My faithful Tannus, too, died at the beginning of 1930 at
Beirut.

The preparations for my first season of digging in 1911
were by no means simple. Tell Halaf is many days' journey
from the nearest towns—Der ez Zor, Mardin and Urfa,
and even these at that time could only meet Arab needs.
I had to bring nearly everything needed for the excavating
and for life on Tell Halaf on camel-back from Aleppo: the
heavy expeditionary baggage brought with me from
Europe, the scientific apparatus, the tools for digging, a
field railway with twelve tip-waggons, and nearly all the
materials for building the house for the expedition; it was
only the timber for this that we could buy in Mardin and
Urfa. Taken altogether, nearly 1000 camels were used for
our transport from Aleppo to Tell Halaf, and for safety's
sake a road was used that needed almost twenty days for
the journey.

Myself, I had made of the ride to Tell Halaf with our
party a fresh scientific journey. This time our way from
Aleppo was by Bab, Membij, and the mediaeval Arab
castles of Kala'at el Nejm Bali—Old Meskene—and
Kala'at Jaber to Der ez Zor, and then along the left or
east bank (which I had not followed in 1893) of the Khabur
to Hesseche, and thence to Tell Halaf.

In 1911 I found at Ras el Ain only a few of the Chechens
whom I had known in 1899; the Mukhtar and two of the
old men who at that time had made peace between my
hosts and me were dead. The third old man, Dekkel, who
was, indeed, an insignificant man without influence, I
afterwards employed permanently out of gratitude, together with his sons, on my excavations.

Our reception in Ras el Ain was quite other than I had
looked for, and circumstances were altogether changed.
Ibrahim Pasha, the powerful Prince of the Milli, had
fallen. As late as 1908, just before the Sultan Abdul Hamid
was deposed, he had by order of his lord and friend gone

to Damascus with about a thousand men of his Arab and Kurdish militia, to help to safeguard the building of the Hedjaz railway to the holy towns of Mecca and Medina. On the sudden fall of the Sultan, Ibrahim at once rode back with his men to Veranshehir, And now the hitherto all-powerful ruler of the Milli was regularly hunted down. The new Young Turkish government had demanded from him the handing over of all modern weapons. Upon his refusal Turkish forces supported by the neighbouring tribes marched against him. Veranshehir was bombarded by Turkish guns. Ibrahim Pasha withdrew to Ras el Ain. Here he was attacked by the Chechens too, and in the end the sick man died a fugitive and almost alone in the desert near Tell Hesseche.

But the shadow of his personality had stayed with his house. After his death the political leadership of the family and its closer adherents that were still faithful was taken over at first by his clever and energetic head wife, Sitte Khansa (Pl. 3b). She made her peace with the new Young Turkish government. The Milli soon found the way back to their former well-being, and recovered that respect which had formerly been shown by the Mesopotamian Beduin tribes to the family of Ibrahim Pasha.

Ibrahim's sons were capable men brought up by the father in the old Beduin virtues of generosity and chivalry. When they set up their huge tent quite close to Tell Halaf during my excavations, I rode to see them. I was given a very hearty welcome as an old friend of the family. They called me 'uncle', the name I am still given to-day by all the members of Ibrahim Pasha's family. This term of address ('father's brother') implies a particularly respectful relation among the Beduins, and always betokens great honour.

It was the Chechens who had profited most from the destruction of Ibrahim Pasha's power. Thanks to the moral help and the protection of the Turkish Kaimakam (District Head) of Safh they were enabled to keep their foes

PLATE IIIA. THE KHABUR AND TELL HALAF

PLATE IIIB. SITTA KHANSA, IBRAHIM PASHA'S WIDOW, WITH HER SON MAHMUD
BEY, THE HEAD SHEIKH OF THE MILLI, AND HIS FAMILY

PLATE IVa. EXCAVATIONS ON THE CITADEL HILL (1911)
(The Khabur and Beduin Camp in the background)

PLATE IVb. COURTYARD INSIDE THE EXPEDITIONARY HOUSE

off, above all the Shammar Beduins, and so were in a
position to carry out their deeds of robbery without fear of
punishment.

Ras el Ain was five days' journey from Der ez Zor, the
seat of the Mutesarrif (Government President) concerned
with it. The road to it lies through the desert and is
dangerous. Thus the Kaimakams had gradually become
almost absolute, and many of them had misused this position to make up to themselves for having to live in what
was almost banishment in the desolate village, and to
grow rich. In the time just before my expedition a kind of
regular community of interests had arisen between the
Kaimakam and the Chechens. Complaints of robbery and
violence committed by the Chechens were simply shelved
by him. It was only several months after our arrival that
the Kaimakam met with retribution. His favourite, a
former slave, had once more joined in a *ghazwa* (plundering expedition) against the Yezids living in the Sinjar
range—that remarkable half-Islamic sect, which is also
called a sect of Devil-worshippers. The Chechens had
attacked a peaceful caravan of the Yezids coming back
from Mardin to the Sinjar with winter supplies. In the
attack a good many Yezids had been killed and wounded
from an ambush, and all their belongings carried off to
Safh and Ras el Ain, where the Kaimakam, as the master
of the slave who had led the *ghazwa*, took a third of the
booty. When the Yezids brought this case forward in Der
ez Zor and Constantinople, and my complaints against
the Kaimakam reached there at the same time, he was at
last removed.

Thus the Chechens after Ibrahim Pasha's fall had become a regular affliction for the wide territory between the
Tektek and Jebel Sinjar in spite of their small numbers.
The great Beduin tribes for fear of the government did not
dare to destroy their robber-nests in Ras el Ain and Safh.
The weak tribes around Ras el Ain had become quite
subject to the Chechens, and were made by them to till

the land for them, receiving in return a small share of the harvest. The proceeds of robberies were turned into money by the Chechens, and when needful they made small advances from this to their followers. In this way the Sherabin, Na'em and Harb had come to be to a certain extent dependent on the Chechens, and hence these tribes took part also in their plundering expeditions.

The Chechens in Ras el Ain and the Kaimakam had ridden to meet me. But in spite of the outwardly friendly reception it was very soon clear to me that they were in alliance together to make an extortionate profit out of my expedition. Their object—which they at first darkly hinted at, but very soon quite clearly made known to me—was that I should compensate them as self-styled owners of Tell Halaf for my excavations, and should through them hire workmen, for whom they themselves had fixed extravagantly high wages.

I had pitched my tents on the east side of the Tell Halaf hill. When next morning I set my own servants to work with the first strokes of the spade on my old prospecting-ground, the Kaimakam came riding up to me with a number of Chechens and *zabtiyes* (police) to stop me. He took no heed whatever of the concession for digging which I had been granted in Constantinople, and of the written orders brought with me from his superior, the Mutesarrif at Der ez Zor. As a precaution I had made my call on the latter on my way, and I had been told by him that Tell Halaf was not private property but belonged to the government. But the Kaimakam declared that one of the Chechens, Sogh Ahmed, claimed Tell Halaf and refused leave to dig. There were other Chechens too who claimed the hill.

My Commissioner for excavations, Ahmed Durri Bey, intervened, but without effect. I was to be kept from excavating even by force of arms. Sogh Ahmed demanded a fantastic sum for leave to start work. I had hopes of gradually overcoming the difficulties in a friendly way, but I at

A. KHALIL BEY

PLATE V. IBRAHIM PASHA'S SONS

B. MAHMUD BEY

PLATE VIB. THE MEMBERS OF THE EXPEDITION IN THE CAMP BEDUÍN TENT

PLATE VIA. THE AUTHOR IN HIS TENT

once sent off a messenger to the nearest telegraph station, Veranshehir, nearly two days' journey away, to ask for orders to be sent to the Kaimakam from Der ez Zor and Constantinople. In a few days they came, and the Kaimakam withdrew in a towering rage.

Thus I began the excavations on 5th August, 1911, with a gang of ten men made up of my own servants and of Arabs. My attempts, however, to enlist a greater number at anything like reasonable wages ended in failure. Through fear of the Chechens and the Kaimakam the smaller Beduin tribes in the neighbourhood did not dare to enter my service on their own account. I therefore at once decided to ride off to Mardin to see what I could do with the Christians living around this town. They were Armenians, living in some of the villages and tilling the land.

In Mardin at the same time I made all arrangements for the forwarding thence of supplies of every kind and of money. The wages for the workmen had to be paid out not only in small coin, but also in the smallest there was; consequently I had to have whole sacksfull of small money brought on horseback from Mardin to Tell Halaf. Later on I set a thief to catch a thief and always had these convoys accompanied not only by soldiers or *zabtiyes*, but also by a Chechen.

I succeeded in enlisting about 200 Armenians as workmen, and at the same time a start was made with building a house for the expedition, But we were not yet at the end of our difficulties. The Kaimakam and the Chechens tried to frighten our Armenian workmen and craftsmen with their threats, and it was not easy to quiet the latter down.

We took the utmost possible care of the Armenians; and we had supplies and flour for their bread brought at our own cost from their villages. But they showed no gratitude whatever and made difficulties of every kind for us. They became particularly troublesome when in the dreadful heat, in spite of every precaution taken, the dried-up walls

in one of our deep trial trenches fell in, with the result that
several workmen were buried and one young man killed.
I therefore availed myself of the presence of a Beduin
nomadic tribe, the Baggarat el Jebel, who were not dependent on the Chechens and who usually camp on the
northern slope of the Jebel Abd el Aziz, to enlist workmen
from among them. I discussed with their Sheikh, Mu-
hammed Sultan, the *ghazwas* (raids) he had made lately;
his eyes lit up as he told me of the looted horses and camels.
When I asked him, however, what had meanwhile been
taken from him, it turned out that the winnings and losings
were about equal. Thereupon I made the proposal to him
that he should entrust me with some of his many sons and
daughters to work on a special footing. This example would
then be followed by many of the common people in his
tribe, and they would also work for us. He should take for
himself his proper share of their wages; and besides this I
promised him gifts corresponding to his position as a
sheikh. He understood what I meant. We got from him
first of all quite a number of Beduin workers, who set about
digging along with the Armenians. Soon afterwards I was
able to send the Armenians, who were becoming more and
more troublesome, back to Mardin.

From this time onward our position on Tell Halaf became more and more assured. After the hostile Kaimakam
had been removed, we were successful also in getting
workers from the Beduin tribes of the Sherabin, Na'em and
Harb without the intermediary of the Chechens.

To each twenty workmen or so there were two foremen
with pickaxes, either kinsmen of the Sheikh or especially
good workers; also four or five men using mattocks, who
put the earth into baskets, when it was taken away by the
rest of the gang—youths, boys or girls. The workers with
iron tools earned about 80 pfennig, the other men about
60, and the boys and girls 40 pfennig a day, and had to
find their own food. For these wages they had to work ten
hours daily.

The payment of wages for work done regularly every ten days without any deduction and in good coin had never before happened in those parts. The Beduins used the money they earned above all in buying a new wife. In accordance with old usage and law it is still the custom to-day among the Beduins for the man to give the father horses, camels, sheep or money if he wants the daughter as his wife. Our women-workers bought themselves clothing and ornaments with their earnings. Dr. Seemann gave medical care and remedies without any payment. So far as I possibly could I helped the workmen and their families, and they looked on me as a father. When in 1913 a grievous famine threatened the whole of Upper Mesopotamia, I had stored in good time, in rooms made for the purpose in the house of our expedition, large supplies of corn brought from Mardin and Urfa by several camel caravans; the corn was dealt out to my people and corresponding deductions made from their wages, but they were not charged for the transportation. In this way I was able to stop my Beduins leaving me; otherwise they would undoubtedly have gone back again to their herds and their nomadic life.

At first the Chechens often appeared in great numbers on pay-days, with the object of getting money from their former dependants on the ground of pretended or real advances they had made. I sent them off, and in the end I would not allow a single Chechen on our excavations. As a result we could now get as many workers from the Beduins as we wanted. I engaged more and more; and in the end we had an average of 550 Beduins working for us. They were like children, and were treated as such. From time to time they would strike because the weather was too bad— when the storms that came so often drove too much sand into their eyes, or when some mischief-maker tried to get higher wages for them. However, they were always easy to quiet down and keep in order.

Owing to my good relations with the great nomadic

B

tribes, who often enough made plundering raids also in the neighbourhood of Ras el Ain, I was able to protect my men. From great distances the sheihks of all the big Beduin groups, or their envoys, came to visit me on Tell Halaf; they came from the Shammar, from the 'Aneze, from the Baggarat ez Zor, and of course from my friends, the sons of Ibrahim Pasha. At times there would be a huge encampment of tents belonging to our workers' families and tribesmen around our field of excavations, several thousands being housed there. In the house of the expedition besides the superintendents over the excavations, whom I had brought in from outside, there was always quartered a guard of twelve mounted Turkish soldiers. There were times when the expedition's kitchen had to feed seventy men.

In the middle of 1913 the works for the Bagdad railway had come as far as Tell Halaf. The engineers found all kinds of difficulties in our neighbourhood. Often their gangs were attacked by Beduins, and often they had men killed. Just at this time there were threats of a serious war between the tribes of the Milli, of the Shammar and the 'Aneze. Through my influence I was able again and again to help when in danger the camps of the engineers, and later it was a very good thing for them that I had broken the power of the Chechens and so given the railway-builders in our neighbourhood—perhaps the worst storm-centre in Upper Mesopotamia—the opportunity to engage workmen. I have always had the best of relations with the gentlemen of the Bagdad railway works, who on their side also have often shown me great friendliness in bringing materials.

From the very first our digging operations were favoured by fortune. As I have already mentioned, I had started digging where I had done my first prospecting in 1899. Bit by bit the gigantic front of the temple-palace came into view. At barely 20 centimetres below the surface of the ground the upper part of the sculptured stones could already be seen; it was this that earlier had led to the discovery of the statues when the dead man was being buried. Surprise followed surprise. One after the other we came on colossal animals, gigantic statues of gods, veiled sphinxes, and more parts of the façade. As we felt our way forward along the paved floor on which the statues were standing, we gradually laid bare the remains of the walls and the rooms of the temple-palace. Following the arch of the gateway passage in the great façade, we found ourselves, just like the visitor in old days to the temple-palace, in the first of the inner rooms. Its floor was wholly covered with charred remains of fallen beams. In the east part of the room we found the skeleton, twisted in agony, of a young girl wearing her ornaments, and in a side room a bronze half-moon, which probably had belonged to a standard planted on the roof of the castle.

To our great astonishment, behind the opening of the gate in the main front, in the archway of a second passage to another and larger room, we came again on great stone statues.

Following the outer walls of the palace, we found at the south-west of the building a relief carving about 70 centimetres high, which rested upright below in the masonry near the foot of the wall and on the outside. Relief slabs such as this are called orthostats. On the south the outer wall of the palace had great bastion-like projections, and here to our great joy we came upon an endless number of these smaller orthostats. The temple-palace was found to be built on a huge brick mass. The hill was also attacked from various other directions by means of deep trial trenches, which were driven into the Tell from the level of the ground covered by the town (Pl. 4a). Later on, at the north-east corner of the hill, another great palace was discovered, and more and more buildings from old times came to light. The great art lay in following the line of the remains of the walls. The search for a wall such as this is a science in itself. The walls of Tell Halaf were all of them

built from sun-dried bricks which crumble in quite a
different way to stone or burnt bricks.

It was astonishing to see how our Beduins took to the
work of excavating. They were really no more than nomadic robbers or half-nomadic husbandmen, but their
power of adaptation soon gave them a most satisfactory
skill. The fact that we had women too on the excavations
brought about a pleasant tone over the whole. The women
were never annoyed by the men at work. When the time
came for the midday interval, the sexes rested apart under
the shade of the ruins of a mud wall, and so ate their
scanty meal.

In the work of excavation the men with the pickaxes
first loosen up the ground, whether the object is to dig
trial trenches or to lay bare a definite layer. Then come
the mattock men and rake it into the baskets of the women
and older boys, who carry them away under the arm, on
the shoulder, or on the head, and empty them where they
are told. In this way new hills are made, called 'metrab'.
It is then the overseer's duty to see that the bearers do not
get too little soil put in their baskets through politeness
being shown to the ladies or for some like reason.

When the masses of soil dug away had to be taken some
distance off lest interesting bits of the ruined buildings
might otherwise be buried under them, the field railway
we had brought with us came into use. The Arabs again
quickly learned how to lay the rails, push the trucks, and
tip out the earth.

As a result of the unexpectedly important results of our
excavations I very soon had to think of increasing my staff
of fellow-workers. I had had the great misfortune of losing
Dr. Löffler in 1911; he died a victim of the dreadful
climate on Tell Halaf. We were still living at that time in
tents. I had the sick man, grievously stricken by fever,
brought in a carriage to the coast; but he was beyond recovery and died in Beirut. In this fine man, so full of
promise, I lost a most excellent fellow-worker. Soon after

his death he was replaced by another architect, Mr. Kurt Heinrich Tischer. Not long after his death I myself fell ill with the same symptoms as his, and for several weeks I was at death's door. Dr. Seemann cared for me devotedly until I was well enough again to ride to Urfa, falling several times from my horse through weakness. Urfa is one of the prettiest small towns in the East that I know. Here a Swiss physician, Dr. Vischer, had a hospital for an Armenian mission. It was to his experience in the illnesses of this land and to the change of air that I owed my recovery. After my return to Tell Halaf the fevers no longer had any hold on me.

Meanwhile the house for the expedition had been finished (Pl. 4*b*); I had had it built a little away from the river and at the edge of the old town. With its high walls and great courtyards it looked like a castle, and brought us much credit. Here I lived with my staff and servants like a desert prince.

Life in the house instead of in tents made conditions healthier, too, for the members of the expedition. In spite of all, however, several of them could not stand the climate. Afterwards I had for this reason and to my greatest regret to send back to Germany Dr. Oswald Seemann, the architect Konrad Lehmann (*Regierungsbaumeister*), a photographer, and a secretary. *Regierungsbaumeister* Konrad Lehmann (now *Regierungs- und Baurat*) lay near death, and I was happy indeed that this distinguished man was able to reach Germany in time and so be saved. Afterwards at home, as the representative of the expedition and through his great drawing talent, he has done valuable service for our work of excavation and research.

In the late summer of 1912 I resolved to go myself to Europe for a short stay, partly to compare the scientific results of the excavations with other finds in the museums of Berlin and Paris, and partly to enlist further help. First of all I secured a second pupil of Koldewey, Dr. Karl Müller, and three more architects—*Regierungsbaumeister*

Erich Rauschenberger (who died a hero's death in the Great War), Dr. Th. Dombart, who is now professor of the History of Art in Munich University, and Kurt Tischer. I also found another medical man, Dr. Ludwig Kohl, who before this and afterwards made very successful scientific expeditions, especially in the Arctic regions. In the end we were ten Germans on Tell Halaf; besides myself five architects, a medical man, a photographer, and two secretaries. With the Turkish commissioner Durri Bey, eleven of us made up the mess in the house of the expedition.

THE EXPEDITIONARY HOUSE

We were a lively company. Each had his horse and was armed. Instead of Sunday, Friday was kept as the day of rest owing to our fanatically Mohammedan workers. On this day we often went shooting, or investigated ruins in our immediate neighbourhood.

My German colleagues were untiring in their work— work carried on by them without a break with the greatest self-denial on this isolated spot, in spite of the terrible heat in summer and the evil climate.

The architects, besides carrying through the highly difficult and important excavation work, also made a great part of the drawings on the spot. The principles and rules for excavation of the excellent Koldewey school were carefully followed under the high technical leadership of Dr. Langenegger and Dr. Müller.

The cleansing, sorting and registering of the finds, with in some cases small drawings added, was carried on daily.

The photographers developed their plates on Tell Halaf itself under the most difficult conditions.

The physicians were kept steadily at work with the medical treatment of the sick and watching over health conditions; they also for some time took the photographers' place and made natural history and ethnographical collections. The secretaries were kept busy all the time.

Besides their own excavating work and the journeys for research, the architects also took regular meteorological records. Records of Arab music and songs were also made on phonographic rolls.

The photographers and secretaries, who were working with me during the various periods of excavation were:

1899: Photographer - Mr. O. Moeller.
       Secretary   - Mr. Heinrich Haenichen.

In the long excavating period, 1911-1913:
       Photographers - Dr. Heinrich Franke and Mr. Robert Paul.
       Secretaries   - Mr. Ernst Lehman, Mr. Peter Hoefges, Mr. Hermann Lehne.

1927: Photographer and
       Secretary   - Mr. Alfred Dietrich.
1929: Photographer - Mr. Otto Schotten.
       Secretary -   - Mr. Georg Fischer.

Everyone helped in the great work of excavating and exploring to the best of his ability. Once again I should like here to express my deep and heartfelt gratitude to my assistants and fellow-workers.

I have used the exceptional opportunities which my living with the Beduins and my associations with the sheikhs of so many tribes have afforded me to complete my studies on the Beduins which I began many years ago.

Within a short time I shall publish a large work of several
volumes on the Beduins and other nomadic tribes of
Northern Arabia, Syria and Mesopotamia: on their tribal
divisions and their importance (with statistics), and on
their history, their genealogies and their habits of life.

Starting from Tell Halaf, so far as the state of the excavations and the security of the Tell allowed of it, I carried
out quite long journeys for more distant investigations in
various directions. I was able always to prepare for them
beforehand most carefully, and so they yielded the best
scientific results, especially as I always took with me the
most experienced Beduin guides. Including my earlier
expeditions and the journeys to and from Tell Halaf, I
went zig-zag through the whole of Upper Mesopotamia,
and on the basis of the bearings taken by myself I was able
to make a new map of this area. As I had done earlier, so
now I followed up the remains of old culture, and thus all
the important hills of ruins were visited, and many of them
drawn to scale or photographed. The journeys were sometimes very toilsome and the responsibility great, both on
account of the lack of water and the difficulty of supplies
in the unknown stretches of desert, as also on account of
the danger from the Beduins.

Over and over again we would find dead swarms of
locusts in the wells, which are sunk as much as 90 yards
deep in the limestone ground, and come down from very
ancient times. But this did not hinder us from using the
water. It is a strange fact that dead locusts do not set up
any poisoning. After the water had been drawn from the
well in the Beduin way by means of a leather bucket fastened to a long cord, the dead insects were removed. We
Europeans sucked up the precious moisture through a
cloth laid over it, the other side of which had constantly to
be wiped clear of the clogging filth with the finger. We
first quieted down our poor horses by holding some water
out to them on the plates of our breakfast basket until their
turn came to drink. The time was far too short to use

filters. We never fell ill on our desert rides through drinking the water.

On one of my journeys for exploration I had found some water under an overhanging block of rock, and sheltered by it from being dried up by the sun, water which had been standing for many months and was covered with a thick green scum. Men, horses and camels threw themselves on the pool, which was barely two yards across. Frogs, toads, and two snakes sprang out of the water. What was left of it was poured into the great holders made of goat-skins turned inside out, and we drew on it the whole of next day. This, too, did no harm to any of us. It was, however, by no means pleasant when we had to go thirsty owing to the water-places on which we had reckoned being dried up.

We constantly had to come to an understanding with the smaller or greater Beduin tribes whose pasture-grounds we rode through; while we often met with *ghazwas* (raiding bands), which in many cases came from a great distance.

But in all these journeys good luck stood by us. I explored Jebel Abd-el-Aziz, being the first European to do so, and here I found in 1913 on its western spur the fantastic statues of Jebelet-el-Beda, which I shall describe in Chapter VIII. I also many times visited Jebel Tektek with its buildings above and below ground from the time of the Abgars.

On the plain I followed the tracks of the old Roman roads with their guard-houses, rode along the roads of the Abbasid Khalifs again, by which they had moved from Bagdad to their summer capital at Rakka on the Euphrates. Above all I sought to determine so far as possible all the places in the desert which held water even in the summer, not only on geographical grounds, but also because it is in such places particularly that old ruins may be looked for; and indeed we often found in the midst of the desert Tells and remains of former settlements from very early times whose former water-places or wells had gone to ruin or become stopped up.

On one of these journeys I also visited the station of the *Deutsche Orient-Gesellschaft* at Assur (Kala'at Sherkat) on the Tigris so that I might see how the excavations were being carried on there. In the absence of Professor Walter Andrae I was welcomed in the most friendly way by Dr. Julius Jordan.

Our staff was so composed as to make the work easier on our journeys. The drawings and photographs were made by the architects and professional photographers. The scientific observations at Tell Halaf and on the research expeditions were carried out by me, for which work I had the help of a comparatively big library, archaeological as well as geographical. During my journeys away I was represented on Tell Halaf by the tireless Dr. Langenegger.

At the end of 1913 I broke off our excavations, since they had to a certain extent come to a definite end. The statues had been brought into the expedition's house, which I handed over to the staff of the Bagdad railway constructional works; they set up their headquarters here in January 1914. I had meant to come back again to my Tell Halaf for further digging in the winter of 1914-15, but I was stopped from this by the Great War.

After the War the Khabur headwaters area was the scene of heavy fighting. By agreement between England and France Upper Mesopotamia had become a French sphere of influence; but when the struggle for freedom under Mustafa Kemal Pasha began, the Turks drove out the small French force quartered near Ras el Ain, which withdrew to Der ez Zor beyond the Euphrates. The Chechens in Ras el Ain were friendly to the Turks; while Ibrahim Pasha's sons were held in suspicion by the Turkish government owing to their Kurdish following. They were badly treated, and as a result took sides with the French. Meanwhile Syria had become a mandated territory under the French, who now wished to get back the area about the Khabur head-waters. There was severe fighting with Tell Halaf itself as its centre. The Turks and Chechens had fortified themselves in the house of my expedition, and dug trenches ón the castle hill. The French and the Milli attacked the fortified position, but soon had to withdraw again. The expedition's house was on this occasion utterly destroyed by gun fire. The mud-brick walls, when they fell, covered up the statues that were inside the house, which was a good thing, for now they were buried again and safe from further damage. The situation was left uncertain until the boundaries between Turkey and the Franco-Syrian mandatory area were settled under the Franklin-Bouillon agreement of 1925 at Angora. The Bagdad railway was made the boundary in Upper Mesopotamia between the two states, and the boundary stones stand 100 metres south of the track. The railway crosses the Khabur immediately west of Tell Halaf, then turns north-eastward, and leaves the area proper of the Khabur head-waters almost wholly on the Syrian side. Tell Halaf and the Chechen village of Ras el Ain were left Syrian, and Ibrahim Pasha's sons became Syrian subjects.

Khalil Bey, Ibrahim Pasha's second son and a clever politician, has moved into a house in Ras el Ain, while Mahmud Bey, the eldest son, is leading a nomadic life with the great tribal confederation (Pl. 5). Fortunately for both sides the relations between the mandate government and the Pasha's sons are excellent. It is only quite lately that the youngest surviving son of Ibrahim, Abderrahman, has gone to settle in Turkish territory.

The Chechens, on the other hand, except for three or four families, have left Ras el Ain. Some of them have moved to Tell Ermen, a village formerly occupied by Armenians and south of Mardin. Only the Chechen settlement at Safh is still left. Ras el Ain in the shelter of the French fort now built there has become a rising market. It is here that the Beduins of the Syrian-French zone now get all their supplies instead of, as formerly, at Mardin. Ras el Ain is now even a railway station.

Meanwhile I had sorted and scientifically worked out in Germany the rich results of my first expedition in 1911-13. My hope of going once more to Tell Halaf was at first not fulfilled; it was only when Germany had come into the League of Nations in September 1926, that I could turn my thoughts to a new expedition.

When in the spring of 1927 I called on the French administration with the object of once more taking up my excavation work, I was met from the very beginning with the utmost friendliness. The French Chief Commissioner, M. Ponsot, and the Franco-Syrian central and local authorities gave me their hearty support, above all the then Chief of antiquities in Beirut, Professor Ch. Virolleaud. I had also the unwearying help in word and deed of the exceedingly capable German consul in Beirut, Dr. Herbert Schwörbel. The large city of Aleppo had been the backbone for my excavations during the period of 1911 to 1913. This city was again to serve the same purpose in 1927 and also in 1929. In 1911-13 we had the never-failing support of the German consul in Aleppo, Dr. W. Roessler; and the Dutch consul in Aleppo, Mr. Rodolphe Poche, who belongs to one of the best and most hospitable families of this city, did us the same service in 1927 and 1929.

In 1927 I spent five months in Syria and Mesopotamia; and was in Ras el Ain for two months as the guest of the French military post. I had the great joy of meeting once more my old Beduin friends, above all the Pasha's sons. At Tell Halaf the statues that were buried under the ruins of the expedition's old house had first of all to be dug out again. Unfortunaely many of the relief tablets that had been lying in the courtyard of the house had meanwhile been turned into mill-stones or building stone by Armenian stone-masons in Ras el Ain, and in the process the reliefs on them had simply been barbarically chiselled away. Luckily in 1911-13 I had not only photographed these sculptures, but I had also had casts taken from them by a German plaster-moulder, whom I had sent for then as a

precaution owing to the insecurity of the neighbourhood. Thanks to this foresight they have been saved for
science.

In 1927 I carried out various trips in the neighbourhood
of Ras el Ain, in particular to the Jebelet-el-Beda, and
made all the needful preparations for starting systematic
digging again. The Franco-Syrian mandatory administration most kindly granted me the concession for excavating
in the whole of the Khabur head-waters region (Ras el
Ain to Tell Halaf), and in the Jebelet-el-Beda. The concession was made out in the name of the 'Max Freiherr von
Oppenheim - Stiftung (Orient - Forschungs - Institut) zu
Berlin' which I had founded; and in this way the carrying
on of the work of excavation is assured also after my
death.

I was also allowed to make a division of my finds. Those
from the earlier seasons were mostly brought to Aleppo
already in 1927, for which thirteen railway trucks were
needed. The railway indeed now ran from Aleppo to Ras
el Ain, a stretch which formerly we had to cover with
horses and camels in many days' journeys.

Those objects that fell to my share I had to have
brought in motor lorries from Aleppo to Alexandretta and
thence shipped to Europe. For the finds allotted to the
Syrian state I organized a small museum in Aleppo.

In the beginning of March 1929 the work of my third
expedition on Tell Halaf was started. For this expedition
I had once more been able to secure Dr. Langenegger as
chief architect on the excavations; I also took two younger
architects—Hans Lehmann, a certificated engineer, and
Robert Riedel, a State architect (*Regierungsbauführer*)—as
also a German professional photographer and a secretary.
This time I had also engaged a sculptor, Igor von Jakimow, who was to put together the fragments of statues left
behind in Aleppo, and to make plaster casts of the objects
which had been allotted to the Syrian state under the
sharing agreement of 1927, so far as this had not been

already done. Lehmann and Jakimow afterwards erected the façades of the temple-palace of Tell Halaf again in my Tell Halaf Museum in Berlin, at 6 Franklin-strasse.

Our first task was to examine on Tell Halaf the layers under the palaces uncovered by us on the citadel hill from 1911 to 1913. Secondly, Fekheria, another ruined site belonging to Ras el Ain, had to be accurately measured and drawn. And lastly, systematic excavations were to be carried out on the Jebelet-el-Beda. The new expedition lasted about six months. On Tell Halaf, beside the ghostly ruins of the former expeditionary house, we pitched the old tents I had been using for twenty or thirty years in Egypt, Syria and Mesopotamia. Besides these we had this time a great Beduin tent, one half of which we used as a sitting-room, a mess-room and a work-room, the other half being a reception-room for Beduin guests. I had also brought with me some transportable wooden sheds.

My old friendship with Ibrahim Pasha's sons was now once again particularly useful to me. Their huge tents were pitched for quite a long time in the neighbourhood of Tell Halaf, and I spent much time with them and their distinguished mother, Sitte Khanza, the widow of Ibrahim Pasha (Pl. 3b).

This time I again hired Beduins as workers, 200 on the average, men and women; and there were also some Kurds. Many of the Beduins had been working for us before.

While the work of excavation was going on I first of all, in the beginning of May, made a preliminary expedition alone to the Jebelet-el-Beda from Tell Halaf with a few followers. Our tents were then all moved there, and we stayed a whole month for the systematic exploration of the remarkable hill.

During this time the disturbed state of the Tell Halaf district cost one of my fellow-workers his life. He was the only Frenchman on the expedition, M. Josèphe Darrous,

Director of Antiquities in northern Syria and Mesopotamia. He had brought us arms and supplies from Aleppo to Jebelet-el-Beda, and on his way back he was attacked by a *ghazwa*, near Ras el Ain, and killed and plundered. This most excellent man had already done splendid work in 1927 at Tell Halaf, and then had been in charge of the museum in Aleppo.

After we came back from the Jebelet-el-Beda to Tell Halaf, the work here was resumed. In connection with the excavations I carried out a small but interesting expedition to supplement my earlier explorations by an examination of the scientifically still as good as unknown area south of the Jebel Abd-el-Aziz and the Jebelet-el-Beda as far as the Euphrates. On this expedition I was able to determine several large ancient Tells, and to have them surveyed by one of my architects. The most important was the Malhat ed Deru. This journey was made in two motor cars and a trolley carrying an escort from the Garde Mobile. It is not advisable to travel otherwise than with several cars in the unsafe and unknown stretches of desert, particularly in summer. The breakdown of one car travelling alone would lead to certain death in the pathless desert, where often no water is to be found for days' journeys. During our four days' zig-zag journey we did not come upon nomad Beduins anywhere, and only met several *ghazwas* and a caravan of salt smugglers.

I was remarkably pleased in 1929 also with the results of the excavations. The depth digging on Tell Halaf had above all brought to light an immense amount of painted pottery from the fourth and third millenia B.C.

Before I went back to Aleppo I made two other trips to the towns of Mardin and Urfa in Turkish territory, to supplement earlier investigations there.

In this year too I experienced the utmost readiness to help from all the French civil and military authorities. In Aleppo the expedition was disbanded. I then made my farewell calls on the Franco-Syrian authorities in Beirut and

Damascus. My journey back to Europe was by railway through Aleppo and Constantinople. I rode in the excellent sleeping-car which runs since 1929 as far as Tripolis and Rayak in Syria. What a contrast it was to that life in the desert which lay behind me!

II

The Khabur Headwaters Region and its History

TELL HALAF lies in the headwaters region of the Khabur, the only permanently flowing tributary of the Euphrates in Mesopotamia. During the winter great volumes of water are brought down from the slopes of the Kurdish mountains in the north along by Veranshehir in the deep-cut bed of the Jirjib Abu Daraj to a depression lying about half-way between the Kurdish mountains and the western spurs of the Jebel Abd el Aziz. Near the depression the course of the Jirjib Abu Daraj, which has hitherto been to the south, is bent in a right angle to the east by a barrier of rock. In the summer the Jirjib Abu Daraj carries no water.

On the other hand hundreds of springs rise in this depression, particularly at two places. One of these is near the village of Ras el Ain (that is, 'spring-head'); here a pond has formed with an outlet to the south known as 'Khabur'. The other place is in the bed of the Jirjib east of the bend. Its first spring, Ain el Beda, rises about five kilometres south-west of Ras el Ain. It is followed to the east by a great many other springs in the channel of the Jirjib and near it. The waters from these make up the second arm of the Khabur, which joins the Khabur proper running north to south. The river at first keeps to the southern course of the main arm, and only makes a bend to the east-south-east some way lower down, keeping this course as far as Hesseche.

Tell Halaf lies two kilometres east of Ain el Beda on the south bank of the Khabur. Already at this spot the river, even in summer, is some 30 yards broad, and so deep that it can be crossed only at two fords, one just above and one just below the site of the old Tell Halaf town. It abounds

in small, well-tasting fish; and now and again a species of
the carp family (Cyprinidae), about the length of a man
swims up as far as this from the Euphrates, and is hunted
by the natives with harpoons. It was always a great event
when a huge fish of this kind was brought to us in the
expedition's house; the first time we ate so much of it that
we all got ill.

The Khabur headwaters region lies in a triangle formed
by a line between Ain el Beda and the two arms of the
Khabur. In this depression there are more spring-ponds,
one of which is highly charged with sulphur, in which the
remains of a Roman bath are still intact.

About five kilometres north-west of Ras el Ain, there lies
a low extinct double volcano, whose highest point bears
the name El Kbize (Keppez in Turkish).

The many springs and the volcanic character of the
ground are the reason for the extraordinary fruitfulness of
the Khabur headwaters region, which furthermore owing
to its geographical position, is an important junction for
the roads leading from west to east in Upper Mesopotamia.
Thus the territory seems made, as it were, to hold a ruling
position in the wide areas around it and to be the capital
of a great kingdom.

Near Ain el Beda and Ras el Ain there are extensive
remains of two towns from pre-Hellenic times. The southern town is our Tell Halaf; the northern one lies in the
field of ruins known to-day as Fekheria, that is, "rich in
sherds'. Both town sites are surrounded by walls and
quadrangular. Fekheria is somewhat larger than the Tell
Halaf town, and covers over a square kilometre. Both
towns were once of very great importance for the Upper
Mesopotamia of olden times. They also had extensive suburbs outside their walls. By Tell Halaf, particularly, there
are a great many small and big hillocks, pointing to old
settlements with fairly large mud-brick buildings long
fallen to ruins.

The origin of these Tells needs a special explanation.

In the whole of Middle and Upper Mesopotamia, in Syria, and in many other regions of the Nearer East, the houses have been built from very earliest times down to our own day only from unbaked mud bricks dried in the sun. This way of building the Spaniards took with them to America. In California and other southerly states they are to-day still called adobe houses, corresponding to the old Spanish word for the sun-dried brick, which comes from the Arabic word *dob*=dust, dirt, earth. The roofs were flat, and made from the wood of poplars, date-palms, and so on. The earth laid upon this wood is, from time to time, especially after rain has fallen, rolled hard again with cylindrical stones. When a place has been destroyed or left, the upper part of the walls gives way and fills up the rooms and the ground about what is left standing of the walls. The bricks perish as time goes on and become earth again. In this way a kind of rise is formed on the earth's surface, and on this rise new settlements have then been made; these again have perished in the same way, and then once more have been used as the foundations for new buildings, always built from the same material of mud bricks. For the sake of security especially new settlers loved to make use of somewhat raised sites. Thus fresh layers of dwellings were always forming one on top of the other, often during thousands of years.

Tell Halaf holds within it the oldest settlement in the area of the Khabur headwaters. First of all the upper layers on it were systematically examined by the expedition of 1911-13. Immediately under the palaces and temples, belonging to the twelfth century B.C., and at other places also we found in the deeper layers great quantities of painted pottery in the area of the citadel and town wherever we dug down to the living rock: baked clay vessels decorated with glazed painting, or fragments of them, always together with flint and obsidian implements. Also the lower layer of painted pottery was mingled with coarse, self-coloured earthenware, which at the very bot-

tom appears also by itself without the painted sherds. The
deepest layers of Tell Halaf are therefore neolithic and
belong to pre-history.

A painted pottery like this has also been found at the
deespest layers in other places excavated in Syria and Asia
Minor; so also in Tepe Gaura, Tell Billa and Nuzi near
Khorsabad and Kerkuk, in Nimrud, Assur and Samarra,
as also in Lower Mesopotamia (cp. below, p. 43), but above
all in Elamin, its capital Susa, and in Tell Mussian—where
it can with certainty be dated as far back as about 3000 B.C.
Myself I have been able when on my journeys of investigation to determine the existence of the painted pottery in
Upper Mesopotamia in a great many Tells. But nowhere
is it found in such quantities as on Tell Halaf.

The painted pottery found in West Persia lately by Ernst
Herzfeld, and earlier by Hubert Schmidt at Anau in Tur-
kestan, is very much akin to ours. A similar earthenware is
found in Western China and north-western India, and also
in Europe, in the Balkan lands.

Furthermore in the lower layers of Tell Halaf here and
there we have come upon small quantities of copper and
bronze, fragments of basalt without any sculpturing and
remains of broken basalt bowls, but strange to say never
whole objects. There were also terra cotta statuettes of
women; these are painted over and very like those that
have been found in southern Mesopotamia, likewise along
with painted pottery under the Sumerian layers from historical times. The Hither Asian painted pottery is rightly
for the present still styled prehistoric.

As to the remains of buildings, in the Painted Pottery
layer of Tell Halaf during the last season (1929) we opened
out in the north of the temple-palace parts of very thick
mud walls belonging to very old palace buildings.

It is unfortunate that up to now we do not know the
name of the Painted Pottery town of Tell Halaf; nor do we
know how long this settlement lasted, I rather think that it
did not disappear earlier than about 2000 B.C. Anyhow

painted pottery seems to have lasted on Tell Halaf down to a much later time than it did, for instance, in Susa and in the towns of south Mesopotamia, such as Ur and Kish, where as early as about 3000 B.C. it was succeeded by the Sumerian pottery of quite a different make.

On Tell Halaf, immediately above this oldest layer, are the palaces which I uncovered in 1911-13, whose beginnings may perhaps be placed some 1000 years after the end of the Painted Pottery period. Some of the stone statues of the temple-palace bear the cuneiform inscription of one Kapara, son of Hadianu; both names are Aramaic. Professor Bruno Meissner (cp. Appendix IV) supposes on linguistic grounds and from the form of the cuneiform characters that these inscriptions belong to the twelfth century B.C. With this the small finds from the Kapara layer and the Aramaic names are in agreement; for it is only from the twelfth century on that there is any certain proof of the Aramaeans being in Mesopotamia. According to the readings of Professor Meissner, the name of the country of which Kapara was king was 'Pa-li-e'.

From the circumstances of the finds and on archaeological and stylistic grounds it would seem to be an impossibility that the statues were made under Kapara and belong to the end of the second millenium. Rather they were, as we shall see below, used over again by Kapara and belong to the third millenium. As often happened in ancient times, Kapara simply put his own name on the old sculptures. The inscriptions, indeed, are no more than building ones, in which Kapara does not call the statues his own work at all.

If we ask whence the statues could have been brought here, only two answers can be given: either from Tell Halaf itself, and from the Painted Pottery layer below, or else from some hill near. But for far around the district of the Khabur headwaters there is no ruined site that is at all important enough to warrant a belief that it may have held within it palaces with such great statues and so many.

Fekheria, the hill of ruins that lies, indeed, within this head-waters district, cannot come into question here, since the flourishing period of the old Fekheria town, Vashukani, lies in the middle of the second millenium (cp. below, pp. 60 ff.), and since we see from the style of our Tell Halaf statues and reliefs that they must come down from a far earlier time.

In 1929, through excavations at several spots around the temple-palace, I established the fact that the Painted Pottery layer had been thoroughly dug over. Evidently the citadel hill, which in course of time had become uneven, had been smoothed down by Kapara or his father. It was just where the temple-palace was standing that great terraces were made by the Aramaic rulers, and on these they then put up the new buildings. For this purpose the soil of the lower layers had to be taken away at some places and at others the ground had to be raised; and when this was done the sherds and the flint and obsidian implements lying there were all mixed up together; we found, for instance, bits of a large beautifully painted pot scattered many yards apart. It was on that occasion evidently that our statues came to light and were dug out, unless perhaps at that time they were still partly standing out from the ground. Along with the statues all the other objects not past use were also taken out from the Painted Pottery layer including the basalt bowls and copper implements that could still be used, so that in the old layer we could only find small and worthless fragments of them.

It is evident that not only were the undamaged statues and reliefs taken away out of the old ruins of the town, but also all the fragments that were of any size at all. Whatever could be put together again from these sculptures was taken along with the undamaged statues for the new palace. The rest of the larger fragments may have been used to make mill-stones, mortars, bowls, or missiles by knocking away any sculptured surface; I found many remains of such in the Kapara rubbish. The vanished palace of the Painted Pottery must have held far more statues than the later one of Kapara uncovered by us. As on Tell Halaf, so in other places of old Hither Asia, statues have been found which have been used again later.

All the statues in the round on Tell Halaf and the greater part of the reliefs on the Kapara palace were of basalt. This had been brought in old times from the Kbize volcano near by, on which I could still make out the old quarries.

Above the Kapara buildings was a layer from later Assyrian times; and to these times belong a set of fairly large buildings on the citadel and a great temple in the town area, also a great number of Assyrian sarcophagi, which had been lowered into the Kapara layer from inside houses belonging to these times. In this later layer we found a good many clay tablets with cuneiform and Aramaic writing. In many of the texts the name Guzana occurred; from which it may be gathered that this Tell Halaf town was the capital of the Assyrian province of Guzana.

Above the Guzana layer we then found remains of settlements from Graeco-Roman times, and above these again those from early Arab times.

In Fekheria so far we have not undertaken much systematic digging. Painted pottery sherds, which on Tell Halaf lay in masses on the surface of the ground, I was not able to find either on the citadel hill nor in the town area; nor have they been brought to light by any of the sporadic predatory excavations of these latter years. Thus we cannot assign the Fekheria town to the Painted Pottery period of the 4th or the 3rd millenium; rather it was undoubtedly the capital of the district *after* the fall of the Painted Pottery town on Tell Halaf in the 2nd millenium B.C. The part enclosed by walls lay south of the northern main source of the Khabur. I am inclined to think that in Roman times the military camp of Resaina stood here, while the great Arab town of Ras el Ain grew up more to the north of the main source. The Ras el Ain of to-day stands on the old Arab ruins.

Both archaeologically and historically for the area of the Khabur headwaters the oldest times of all are the most important. To them belongs the Painted Pottery town of Tell Halaf; to them belong the stone statues. Unfortunately we could not find any inscriptions whatever from those times on Tell Halaf itself, nor on other sites of Upper Mesopotamia have any written documents come to light having any relation to the area of the Khabur headwaters or the rest of Upper Mesopotamia. For these oldest times we have nothing but the statements in documents from other areas, and these are yielded for us by Lower Mesopotamia alone, but unfortunately only very sparingly.

Our knowledge, therefore, of the history and culture of the very oldest times in the upper part of the Land of the Two Streams was more than scanty—we were groping almost wholly in darkness. Luckily for the knowledge of those olden times the archaeological results of the excavations I have so far carried out yield new and valuable information, which fits in with the little we know from the literary sources of south Mesopotamia.

In astrological soothsaying texts, which mostly are known to us from the clay tablet library of the Assyrian king Assurbanipal (668-626 B.C.), but go back to very old Babylonian originals, the world is divided into four lands: 1. Akkad (Sumer) in the south; 2. Elam in the east; 3. Amurru in the west; 4. Subartu in the north. It is to be noted, however, that the main direction for the geographical orientation of the Babylonians runs not from north to south, but from north-west to south-east, so that Akkad (Sumer) must be put in the south-east, Elam in the north-east, Amurru in the south-west, Subartu in the north-west.

This picture of the world does indeed rightly give the geographical relations between the lands named. Akkad in the cuneiform literature is usually joined with Sumer in the one concept 'Sumer and Akkad'. This corresponds to

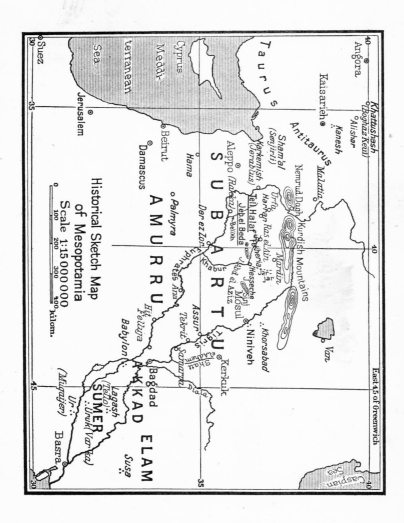

Historical Sketch Map
of Mesopotamia
Scale 1:15 000 000

'Babylonia' and embraced Lower Mesopotamia,[1] that is, the old Turkish Irak (not the much bigger Irak state of to-day under King Faisal). East, or north-east, of it lay Elam in the Persian border districts; this was joined on the west and north-west by Subartu, while Amurru lay to the south and south-west. The area of the Khabur headwaters belongs according to this division beyond all doubt to Subartu.

Subartu.   Elam.

Amurru.   Akkad (Sumer).

But before we deal more in detail with Subartu, we must turn to the other three lands, particularly to Sumer-Akkad, that is, south Mesopotamia.

The geographical name 'Akkad' first arose when a Semitic ruler, the great Sargon, in the second quarter of the 3rd millenium conquered Lower Mesopotamia, that formerly had belonged to the Sumerians, and made the town of Akkad his capital. From then on the inhabitants of Babylonia of Semitic descent, who had certainly come into the land later than the Sumerians, called themselves Akkadians. But before both the Sumerians and the Akkadians there was an older aboriginal population there.

[1]South Mesopotamia, or Lower Mesopotamia, is the name I give to the Land of the Two Streams south of the line running more or less between where the Shatt el Adhem flows above Bagdad into the Tigris and Felluja on the Euphrates; this area is alluvial land. All the rest of the Land of the Two Streams is Upper Mesopotamia. This last can further be divided into Middle Mesopotamia and Upper Mesopotamia. Upper Mesopotamia proper is the area north of a line drawn from Mosul-Niniveh on the Tigris to where the Khabur flows into the Euphrates, while Middle Mesopotamia lies south of it. South Mesopotamia corresponds to Babylonia, Sumer-Akkad; the whole of Upper Mesopotamia once belonged to the land of Subartu.

In Ur, the home of Abraham, Woolley in the most successful excavations of the joint expedition of the British Museum and the Museum of the University of Pennsylvania, came upon older layers under the Sumerian ones with their well-known splendid objects in gold and ivory, these older layers being separated from the Sumerian by a bank of alluvial clay; a mighty flood, which Woolley brings into relation with the Biblical 'Flood', must once have poured over the land and left the clay bank behind it. In these lowest layers were found wholly un-Sumerian objects, especially the painted pottery corresponding fully to that of Tell Halaf and Susa. The same thing is true of Kish, Varka and other south Mesopotamian sites excavated.

Who now were the dwellers in Lower Mesopotamia in this Painted Pottery period? They cannot have been the Sumerians or the Semitic Akkadians, and this because of the wholly different style shown in the objects made by their craftsmen. The uniformity of the finds, particularly of the pottery of the oldest layers, leads us rather to conclude that anyhow in a great part of Hither Asia there was a homogeneous and settled aboriginal population. Now the representations on the old scupltures, statues, and cylinder seals of west Persia (Elam), Mesopotamia, Syria and Asia Minor of the time of the painted pottery, show a characteristic racial type, into which that big, broad nose enters which we find very markedly on the Jebelet-el-Beda and Tell Halaf. This racial type is known as the 'Hither Asiatic', and seems to be near akin with the type of the Dinaric race, remains of which can still be shown to-day, particularly in eastern Europe, in Albania, Dalmatia, and also in the eastern Alps. The Hither Asiatic racial type has also survived in our day among the mountain folk that have remained Christian in certain parts of Asia Minor, such as the Armenians, the Jacobites of Mardin, and so on, as also in parts of Syria, such as the Lebanon folk, while owing to Islam there has been more and more racial mingling among the Mohammedans there. The Jews are a mixed people of the old Subaraic race and the Semitic immigrations, of which Abraham's was one. The true Semitic type, as, for instance, that of the Arab Beduins of to-day, is quite other than the old Hither Asiatic-Subaraic. In the Bible itself this origin of the Jewish people is affirmed. In the Book of Ezechiel, xvi 3, and xvi 45, it is said of Jerusalem: 'Thy father is an Amorite (that is, Semite), thy mother a Hittite'. The Bible, which originated only much later, in the 1st millennium B.C., after the Hittites had in the 2nd millennium B.C. been predominant in Syria also, is wont to call the aboriginal population of Palestine, that is, the Subaraic, simply 'Hittite'. This may be explained in the following way. Soon after the return of the Jews from Egypt, which is said to have been in the middle of the Second Millenium B.C., during the eighteenth Egyptian dynasty, the Hittites had become the dominant nation in the western parts of the Near East, thus also in Syria and Palestine. Consequently, the various peoples of this Hittite state, among which also were the Subaraic inhabitants of Palestine, were merely referred to by the writers of the Bible as Hittites.

The origin of the Sumerians is not known; presumably they are an Asiatic people. For the present their tongue cannot be brought into any of the known groups. Their oldest settlements lie in the extreme south-east of Mesopotamia.

The home of the Semites, who were already settled together with the Sumerians in Babylonia before 3000 B.C. and who, as we said above, were later called Akkadians, is on more or less valid grounds held to be Arabia.

Politically southern Mesopotamia in the oldest times was divided up into a set of city princedoms with their own dynasties, one of which usually held lordship over the whole land. We have information about these dynasties from the so-called lists of kings that have been found in old clay tablet archives in various places. But often they give dynasties of different cities as ruling one after the other, whereas in reality they must to some extent have been ruling contemporaneously. Furthermore only those dynasties are given that could claim to be overlords of the whole of south Babylonia; thus, for instance, we do not find the two art-loving dynasties of Lagash (the Telloh of to-day), the second of which has become famous through its prince Gudea (end of twenty-fourth century B.C.). The dating of the older period in Babylonian history is not yet definitive. It depends on the astronomical determination of the revolution of Venus, for which the calculations differ. Thus it is that the earlier periods are by English scientists, for example, Langdon-Fotheringham, set much further back than they are by other Assyriologists, the Germans, for instance. Hence, C. L. Woolley, following the English dating, puts the Ur finds far back into the 4th millennium, while in Germany they are usually put at about 3000 B.C.

The lists start with the kings 'before the Flood', who of course are legendary. There are ten kings, whose period of rule is set at 456,000 years. In the oldest time after the Flood the dynasties are purely Sumerian. It is only in the twelfth dynasty after the Great Flood, the dynasty of Akshak (2943-2851 B.C.), that a ruler is found with a Semitic name. The first undoubtedly Semitic dynasty is the fifteenth after the Flood, that of Akkad (2751-2568 B.C.); as was said above, it was founded by the great Sargon, and to it belonged also the much-spoken-of Narâm-sin. Then follow mainly Sumerian dynasties again until in the twenty-second, that of Amurru or of Babylon (2169-1870 B.C.), Semites again won the over-lordship, and that not only over Babylon but also over the whole of the Nearer East. These Semites, however, are no longer the so-called Akkadians, to which the older Semitic layer in south Mesopotamia belongs, but the Amurrites, new-comers, who are also known as East Canaanites. The most important ruler in this dynasty is Hammurabi. It was over-thrown through the invasion of the Hittites, who, coming

from the north-west, conquered the land, but had to withdraw again immediately afterwards. In the seventeenth
century there started in south Mesopotamia a rule by
foreigners that lasted many centuries, the rule of the Kassites (1642-1176 B.C.), who came in from the north. After
them comes the later Babylonian period, which ends in
539 B.C. under Nabonid the Chaldaean with the conquest
of Babylonia by Cyrus.

How much of the culture and art of the aboriginal population was taken over by the Sumerians in south Mesopotamia cannot yet be fully determined. Anyhow they are
the inventors of cuneiform writing, which developed out
of an older picture writing. Not only was it adopted by the
Semites of Babylonia, but gradually it spread throughout
the Nearer East. On the other hand the Sumerian tongue
was driven out by the Akkadian of the immigrant Semites.
As early as 2000 B.C. Sumerian disappears as a living
tongue; from this time onwards it was kept up essentially
only for religious worship, like Latin in the Catholic
Church. For this purpose it was still cultivated long after
the fall of the Babylonian empire and right into the first
century before our era.

We do not know what cultural elements the Semites
themselves brought beyond their tongue; probably, indeed,
they brought little else. Before they came into south Mesopotamia they were undoubtedly nomads. In Babylonia
they accepted the Sumerian culture, and developed it perhaps by adding elements of their own. They took over the
Sumerian religion too, with all its gods and its ideas, while
themselves contributing but little of their own.

The second land of which we find mention in the geo-
graphy of the 3rd millennium is Elam. For the Sumerians
and the Akkadians it lay to the east or north-east, and
corresponds more or less with Luristan, Arabistan and
Fers in south-western Persia. The Akkadian name Elamtu,
like the Sumerian Enima, means 'Highland'. The capital
was Susa (Shushan), where the painted pottery already

mentioned has been found in great quantities; this points to an original population of the same kind as was settled in southern Mesopotamia before the coming of the Sumerians. At times, for instance under Sargon and Naram-Sin, Elam belonged to the kingdom of Akkad. On the other hand the Elamites often invaded Babylonia, and there were times when they held it in subjection. Indeed in the time of the Kassites (in the 2nd millennium) an Elamite conqueror succeeded in bringing away Hammurabi's celebrated stele of the law from Babylon to Susa, where it was found again in 1901 by the French expedition under De Morgan. In the 1st millennium B.C. Elam was conquered by the Assyrians; and in 640 B.C. Assurbanipal plundered the capital, Susa. At a later time Elam came, like southern Mesopotamia, under the Persian dominion.

Amurru—the Western Land—was known to those times especially through the area between Palmyra and 'Ana-Hit, that is, the Syrian desert. This is a Semitic area from of old. It is from here, perhaps, that the Akkadians, and undoubtedly the Amurrites (Eastern Canaanites) came into south Mesopotamia.

To the Amurru tribes belonged also probably the nomadic peoples of Sutu and Akhlamu; they are forerunners of the later Aramaeans and other Beduin peoples who broke from Arabia, the 'cradle of nations', into the civilized land of Mesopotamia in the north.

The fourth area, Subartu, forms the north-west of the then known world. A cuneiform text found in Assur gives a description of the kingdom of Sargon the Great. According to it the land of Subartu stretched from the district of Anzan in Elam (the south-west Persia of to-day) as far as the Cedar Mountains (the Amanus or Anti-Taurus). Elam and Subartu were next one another, as is to be seen from an inscription of Naram-Sin which speaks of his conquests.

For the Akkadians Subartu was the whole of the huge area west of the southern part of western Persia, and em-

braced Middle and Upper Mesopotamia, as also Syria.
Moreover it included in the north the great mountain loop
that stretches from near Kirmanshah through Kurdistan
and Armenia in Asia Minor as far as the Mediterranean,
and in the south it included Palestine.

There is much that points to the aboriginal population
of Subartu having been homogeneous, namely, the above-
mentioned Hither Asiatic race; while in historical times,
owing to immigrations from outside, states grew up here
with a mixed population. A. Ungnad was the first (*Kultur-
fragen I*, 1923) to bring in the name 'Subaraeans' for the
old population of Subartu, as also the terms 'Subaraic
speech', 'Subaraic culture'. The geographical concept of
Subartu handed down to us by the Akkadians more or less
coincides also with the area of Subaraic speech. In the
west of this area the term Hurrians for the Subaraic population and Hurritic for the Subaraic speech became the
usual one in the 2nd millennium. On this account the name
'Hurrians' (German: 'Hurriter') instead of 'Subaraeans',
has with some justification been adopted. It can be shown
that Subaraic was the tongue spoken in the district of the
Samarra, Altun Köpri, Kerkuk, Erbil and Niniveh of
to-day, that is, in what was later Assyria. Also the oldest
historical city rulers of Assur—Ushpia and Kikia—bear
Subaraic names. Although about 3000 the Sumerians became supreme in Assur, where they founded a Sumerian
colony, in the time of Ushpia and Kikia the native Subaraic elements were probably again stronger here. But
outside the area assigned to old Subartu there are also
many traces of Subaraeans. Thus in the 3rd millennium we
find a great many people with Subaraic names settled in
various parts of south Mesopotamia. We do not yet know
whether they were living in Lower Mesopotamia for trading or whether for other purposes. It may be that they
were, as it has been already suggested by others, remnants
of the old aboriginal population of Lower Mesopotamia,
belonging to the Hither Asiatic race.

In southern Syria and in Palestine we also find Subaraic names, though not until the 2nd millennium.

Monuments of the Subaraic speech have only come down to us in small numbers. The most important is a letter from Tushratta, the King of the Mitanni (about 1420-1380 B.C., cp. below, p. 62) to the Egyptian king Amenophis III. At Boghaz Keui, the capital of the Hittite kingdom, there was found a Subaraic fragment of the Gilgamesh epic. Among the Boghaz Keui texts are several rituals, in which whole sections are written in Subaraic. If at Boghaz Keui this language was still preserved in the 2nd millennium in the cult, this seems to point to its having been formerly the general language spoken hereabouts. That in Syria, too, Subaraic was still spoken in the Amarna period (about 1400 B.C.) is shown by the many glosses in a letter to Pharaoh coming from mid-Syria.

The area of the Subaraic speech, therefore, stretched from east Tigris-land and Assyria to Asia Minor and Syria. Subaraic was also certainly spoken in the area of the Khabur headwaters in the 3rd millennium B.C. and later.

As to the political conditions in Subartu in the 3rd millennium we have no information from this land itself. We may presume that it was made up of a set of smaller states. Thus in a victorious report of King Naram-Sin of Akkad (2671-2634 B.C.), preserved to us in a later Hittite form, a whole list is given of the names of rulers in Mesopotamia and Asia Minor, that is, belonging to Subartu, and among these the kings of Khatti, Kanesh, Amurru, Arman and of the Cedar Mountains. Unfortunately we are still in the dark as to most of these kingdoms, so that we cannot arrive at the name of the area of the Khabur headwaters from this victorious report of Naram-Sin.

I believe it to be probable that in this ancient time the Painted Pottery town of Tell Halaf was the capital of anyhow a great part of Subartu. This is pointed to not only by the importance of the Khabur headwaters area through

D

its geographical position and its fruitfulness, but above all by the quantity of artistic objects found there.

Between Subartu and Lower Mesopotamia there were undoubtedly close relations from earliest times. There were no natural hindrances standing in the way of the intercourse between these neighbouring lands. Caravans went to and fro; and besides the friendly exchange of wares, which undoubtedly was at work then just as it is to-day, there must have been warlike expeditions, especially from the richer Lower Mesopotamia—at times, anyhow, politically more unified and therefore probably the stronger— against Subartu and far into the land.

These relations are reflected in the sagas from the oldest times, though they must not at once be given the weight of historical documents, while undoubtedly having an historical foundation.

This is true in the first place of the Gilgamesh saga, that magnificent epic describing the heroic deeds, adventures and travels of Gilgamesh, and containing also the saga of the Flood. The action lies partly in Subartu, though this name is not itself mentioned. Gilgamesh is two-thirds god, and one-third man. His city is Uruk, the Varka of to-day in Lower Mesopotamia. According to the old Babylonian lists of kings he is the fifth king of the first Sumerian dynasty of Uruk, the second dynasty after the Flood. On one of his journeys the hero with his fighting comrade Engidu reached the Cedar Forest (Anti-Taurus), 'which stretches 10,000 miles', and there overcame the monster Khumbaba. This fight has naturally appealed particularly to the Subaraic culture area. In the Hurritic (Subaraic) version the Gilgamesh epic is known as the Khuvava epic. On one of the Tell Halaf orthostats is represented the binding and slaying of Khuvava by Gilgamesh and Engidu. The Cedar Forest was within Subartu territory, but Huvava may have been a hateful monster for the Subaraeans just as much as for Gilgamesh, the king of Uruk, but perhaps also an intruding stranger, whence we know not, in the dim and far past. It is evident that the Subaraeans, had reason to celebrate the defeat and death of Khuvava in the same way as was done in the Sumerian Gilgamesh epic. In any case not only on Tell Halaf (see p. 176), but also in other Subaraic representations Khuvava is treated as an object of detestation, and his death hailed with joy.

For a second time Gilgamesh goes, after the death of his friend Engidu, through Subartu to the coast of the Mediterranean, to learn from the goddess Siduri the way to Utnapishti, the Babylonian Noah, from whom he hopes to get the Herb of Life.

The origin of the Gilgamesh epic is not determined for certain. We do not know whether it really belonged to the Sumerians from the first. Already the question has been raised by others whether the name 'Gilgamesh' has not some connection with that of the Subaraic town of Karkemish (to-day Jerablus, below Birejik on the Euphrates). In the Sumerian version Uruk (the Varka of to-day) is the town of Gilgamesh. According to the old lists of kings, Gilgamesh is the fifth king of the first dynasty of Uruk, which for the present we must still look on as legendary. It is only the following Sumerian dynasty in the lists of kings, that is, the first dynasty of Ur, that has become a matter for history through the excavations of Mr. C. L. Woolley, the leader of the joint expedition of the British Museum and the Museum of the University of Pennsylvania. We shall see whether the German excavations in Uruk-Varka now being carried on under Dr. J. Jordan, the Director of the Bagdad Museum, are to bring to light any traces pointing to Uruk having really been the town of Gilgamesh.

The land of Subartu is explicitly named in a mythological text dealing with the Sumerian king Lugal-anni-mundu (about 3100 B.C.) of Adab (now Bismaya), but written long after his time.

The first really definite information as to the relations between Subartu and Lower Mesopotamia does not come to us from earlier than the time of the first Semitic dynasty of Akkad. Its founder, the great Sargon (2751-2796), informs us in an inscription that the god Dagan has given him the 'Upper Land': Mari, Yarmuti and Ibla as far as the Cedar Forest and the Silver Mountains (Taurus). The land Mari lies on the Euphrates, below the mouth of the Khabur, somewhere near the Hit of our day. It is from Mari that there come several life-size statues of kings from the end of the 3rd millennium, which reached Babylonia as loot, and were there dug up by Robert Koldewey.

The Ibla mentioned in the Sargon inscription is probably to be looked for in the neighbourhood of the Mardin of to-day, that is not far north of Tell Halaf. Yarmuti is identified by B. Landsberger with north Syria. The conquest of Subartu by Sargon is also referred to in a later chronicle, now in the British Museum. In it we read: 'He laid defeat on them (the Subaraeans), cast their wide-flung army to the ground, and brought their goods and chattels to (his capital) Akkad'. Reference has already been made to a second conquest of Subartu by Naram-Sin (2671-2634).

We are better informed as to the economic relations between south Mesopotamia and the northern lands than we are as to the political. Gudea (about 2550-2500 B.C.), King of Lagash, the Telloh of to-day, brought wood from the town of Ursu in the Ibla mountains and stone out of Mari. Of particular importance for the knowledge of the wide ramifications of the bonds of trade in Hither Asia of the 3rd millennium are the so-called Cappadocian cuneiform tablets of Kül-Tepe by Kaisarieh. In this part of Asia Minor and south of it there were trading colonies at that time of the city of Assur. The most important were evidently Kanesh, the Kül-Tepe of to-day, and Ursu. The clay tablets found in Kül-Tepe give us an interesting insight into the business life of these colonies and of the whole world of that day. Thus in Kanesh the colonists had been granted by the rulers of the land self-administration and their own laws; but they also were in close relations with the natives.

Trade was very definitely organized. Clay tablets have been found with business letters that read quite like modern ones; they were exchanged between merchants in Assur and their employees and also bankers and traders in Kanesh. Gold and silver of different alloys and purity were given in payment by Assur, while the traders in Cappadocia supplied the native products, especially copper, lead (or tin), and alloys of copper, tin, or arsenic, stuffs and clothing, hides and oil for their mother-city of Assur and the Great Kings of south Mesopotamia.

The goods were sent on pack-animals. Carts also were used, as we see from a seal. The roads taken by the trade between Asia Minor and Assur or Lower Mesopotamia cannot as yet be exactly determined from the inscriptions. The nearest and best way of communication between Kanesh and Mesopotamia led over the passes of the Taurus and Antitaurus through northern Syria, and then through the fruitful and (judging by the hills of ruins) thickly populated Seruj plain to Harran. From here it undoubtedly went on to the Khabur headwaters region, to the old town of Tell Halaf, followed the Khabur as far as Hesseche, and then ran south of Jebel Sinjar eastwards to Assur.

The Tigris was also used by ships as a trade route to Assur, and thence to Babylonia. Goods that had to go from Kül-Tepe straight to Lower Mesopotamia could be put on to ships in the town of Tell Halaf; we proved beyond doubt the former existence of a port there. From here they went down the Khabur and then down the Euphrates. In the Arabian Middle Ages also the Khabur river was used for trading intercourse, and for carrying the cotton, which in those days was grown especially in the Khabur district, and on whose yield was based the great revenues from taxation enjoyed by the Abbasid khalifs in Bagdad. Even to-day at certain places on the Khabur between Ras el Ain and Hesseche and further down barges are used for crossing it. During the expedition under the English Colonel Chesney, in 1837, to examine into the possibilities for navigation of the Euphrates, a small steamboat, one of the first, moreover, in the world, went a long way up the Khabur.

Whether the whole huge territory of Subartu ever made up a political unit we do not know; but anyhow there was an independent, homogeneous Subaraic culture-complex. The whole of the land of Subartu in the meaning of the Old Babylonian geographical conception belonged to this culture-complex. The Subaraic culture is undoubtedly just as important as the Old Babylonian and the Old Egyptian. Through the discovery of Tell Halaf and of the statues of Jebelet-el-Beda the proof is given for Upper Mesopotamia also of the existence of this third culture in Hither Asia, independent and rooted in the land, and stretching back into the earliest prehistoric times.

The relations between Upper and Lower Mesopotamia have naturally resulted in influences from the Old Babylonian (Sumerian) culture, on the Subaraic, and conversely many elements of Subaraic culture can be found again in Old Babylonia as also in Elam. From the original dwellers in South Mesopotamia, who, to judge by facial features (beak-nosed faces) and their artistic productions, belonged to the same Hither Asiatic Subaraic race, the incoming Sumerians, as was earlier stressed, undoubtedly borrowed much. On the other hand the influence later exerted on Subaraic art and culture by southern Mesopotamia was stronger than the converse Subaraic influence; this is to be above all attributed probably to the greater wealth, the more firmly established political unity, and the better weapons and greater skill in war of the Old Sumerians.

From times of old, too, there have been relations between Egypt and Hither Asia; the influence of these cultures, however, on one another in the very earliest times has not been so fruitful a one. It was not till the 2nd millennium B.C. that the political conditions and the better communications with Egypt lying so near brought about in places a quite strong Egyptian influence on Syrian art.

The homogeneousness of the motives in the products of Subaraic art that have come down to us, and of their handling, is at once to be seen. We find the same motives on the statues of Tell Halaf and on those of Jebelet-el-Beda, in Tell Akhmar on the Euphrates, in Karkemish and Senjirli, in Sakchegözi, in Hama and Katna, in Mar'ash, in numerous places of Asia Minor and in Assyria. The representations on the statues agree in many cases exactly with those on seal cylinders and seal impressions from Palestine, Syria, Kül-Tepe (from the 3rd millennium), Kerkuk and Assur. It was not without grounds that G. Contenau dealt with these latter under one head and set them beside one another. On Tell Halaf, too, there are like cylinders. We find throughout the Subaraic culture-complex the same way of representing gods, symbols of gods and demons or godlings; the same liking for hybrid beings; hunting scenes, chariots and pictures of riders; sphinxes, in some of which the lion's head is found besides the woman's; we find the same racial type and the same treatment of the hair and beard. In many cases gods are standing on beasts, and always on the same, those, namely, belonging to each god. From the oldest times of all down to the 1st millennium B.C. the motives of Subaraic art kept remarkably true to themselves. The best proof of this is yielded by the stone statues of Jebelet-el-Beda, which go back to the 4th millennium. One of them shows a god standing on two persons exactly in the same way as we see in the rock relief of Yazylykaya by Boghaz Keui, which may be dated shortly before the middle of the 2nd millennium. In another a god is standing on a bull.

Household stones, too, and ornamental objects, also architectural characteristics, are found spread over the whole of the Subaraic cultural area as a common possession. Most striking of all is the kinship running through the very ancient painted pottery on the various sites of finds in the old Subaraic land. Some of the motives in the painting on the pottery are found again on the sculptures, particularly on those of Tell Halaf.

Thus a homogeneous Subaraic culture with its own particular style in art once existed in that area which from the Babylonian inscriptions bears the name of Subartuland. This culture had long been fast rooted here as a self-sufficing, unified whole, when at the beginning of the 2nd millennium Indo-European tribes calling themselves Nasians broke into Hither Asia from the north-west and in the end settled on the plateau of Asia Minor as lords in the land of Khatti. Gradually they were successful in extending their rule over a great part of the west of the Subaraean land. From their first conquest, Khatti, they took the name of Khattiland for the state they founded, and their rulers henceforward called themselves 'Kings of Khattiland'. As was said earlier, we meet with the name Hittites in the Bible for the aboriginal Subaraic people settled in Palestine and found there by Abraham and the other Semitic immigrants. This name in the end had come to be applied to all those dwelling in the Khatti Empire, whatever their race and tongue.

Until a short time ago it was the general custom to give the name 'Hittite' to the art we find represented in the statues from the excavations of Senjirli, Jerablus-Kar-kemish, Sakchegözi, Iyik, and so on, all of which are places that at times anyhow were under the dominion of the Hittite kings.

Thus the idea arose that the ancient art and culture found always in Palestine, Syria, and southern Asia Minor from time beyond memory originated with the Nasian or Indo-European Hittites so-called, although they did not make their conquest of the Khatti kingdom until the 2nd millennium. This mistaken assumption has had much to do with the works of Subaraic art being looked on as much younger than they really are.

Still more complicated is the question of the so-called Hittite picture-writing. We do not know when it arose. Its invention is—I believe, wrongly—ascribed to a time not earlier than about the twelfth century, and attributed to the Hittites. Some of the statues on which we find it have a remarkably archaic look, as for instance the hunting scene from Malatia or the Teshup from Babylon. They undoubtedly belong to the 3rd millennium. Along with others I am of the opinion that it is going against the probabilities to set down the invention of such a complicated writing, which so far has not been deciphered, to the Indo-European Hittites, who had knowledge of the so much easier cuneiform writing, which had long been in fairly general use in the Nearer East. For the Cappadocian sources make use of this writing as early as the 3rd millennium, before the coming of the Hittites into Asia Minor. The Hittite picture-writing in my opinion was already in use before this time, that is, at latest in the 3rd millennium. Then, owing to the appearance of cuneiform writing, the hieroglyphs came to be almost forgotten. The revival of picture-writing in later times was perhaps a form of reaction that strove to bring back old times after overcoming a foreign rule.

It is much to be regretted that we have no written documents of any kind from Jebelet-el-Beda or the Painted Pottery layer of Tell Halaf. In the oldest times to about 2000 I am inclined to think that statues on Tell Halaf and in other Subaraic districts also, such as Senjirli and Karkemish, had no inscriptions. On the other hand it may be that here and in other parts of the Subaraic area the writing was done in those times on a perishable material, which could not withstand the dampness of the soil, or on a substance, such as lead strips, which lent itself easily to further use, and so was lost. It seems to me quite impossible that in a so advanced age, an age which yielded our painted pottery and the old statues, there should have been no writing whatever, especially if we take into reckoning the highly developed stage of the applied arts and the intellectual life in those early centuries, as also the fact that in the neighbouring Lower Mesopotamia and Elam, in the Sumerian colony in Assur and in Egypt, written monuments are known to have existed as early as about 3000 B.C.

The origin of the Indo-European Nasians, who after settling in Khattiland give themselves the name of Hittites, is wrapped in darkness. We know from their written monuments that they belong to the Indo-European family of languages, and to the so-called Kentum group. That they were of Nordic race is shown, too, on archaeological grounds: statues which originated at the time of their dominion, such as the limestone relief of the god of the Gate at Boghaz Keui, show Nordic racial characteristics.

The oldest capital of the Hittite Empire was Kushshar, which about the middle of the 2nd millennium was changed for Khattushash not far away (the Boghaz Keui of to-day). In the nineteenth century B.C. the Hittite king, Murshilis I, took Aleppo. In an unbroken triumphal march he went on to Lower Mesopotamia, where in 1870 B.C. he took Babylon and overthrew the Hammurabi dynasty. The Hittites, however, could not hold Babylon, and streamed back to Asia Minor. On the march both outward and homeward they came through Upper Mesopotamia, and must have also touched the Khabur headwaters region; but here, too, they were unable to make a settlement.

In this connection we cannot help asking when and by whom the old Painted Pottery town of Tell Halaf was finally destroyed, and when Tell Halaf was left and Fekheria became the capital. It has already been pointed out that Kapara brought out the statues from the Painted Pottery layer on Tell Halaf. Now, between certain finds from Tell Halaf and others from Lagash belonging to Gudea's time (about 2300 B.C.) there are likenesses which lead us to conclude that they are of about the same age. This is ground enough to warn us against putting the final destruction of Tell Halaf and the new period with no painted pottery, flint or obsidian so far back as, say, the wars of conquest of the kings of Akkad (2751-2568), or the not much later ones of the Gutaeans. On the other hand it is not wholly impossible to set down the fall of Tell Halaf to the wars of the Hammurabi dynasty (2169-1870). Unfortunately we know but little about the wars of conquest of the Sumerians, since their inscriptions mostly do not deal with historical events, but above all perpetuate the building of palaces and temples. The final revolution—the removal of the capital and the wholly new trend in the applied arts in the Khabur headwaters area—was probably not brought about by these wars of conquest. From the historical sources, anyhow, we do not gather that the Sumerians settled for any length of time in Upper Mesopotamia. And revolutions within can hardly have produced changes such as these.

Since from history we do not get the guidance we need, we have to seek it from the arts and crafts; and I hope to find light from the later excavations in Fekheria. Already the finds made in the Kapara town, that is in the later layer at Tell Halaf, which was followed by the Mitanni capital of Fekheria in the twelfth century b.c., are yielding important indications. The objects of useful art from the Kapara layer, particularly the pottery, have a great likeness to finds made in Assur from the second half of the 2nd millennium. This leads us to conclude that in the older Fekheria like productions from the first and second half of the 2nd millennium will be found.

The following line of development seems at present to me to have the greatest claim to probability:—Down to 2000, perhaps down to 1870 b.c., that is to the time when the Indo-European 'Hittites' destroyed the Painted Pottery town of Tell Halaf on their victorious march to south Mesopotamia, it was only painted pottery and flint and obsidian tools that were in use on Tell Halaf and in the neighbourhood. The Hittite expedition turned everything upside down in Upper Mesopotamia; and this was used to its own advantage by a second wave of Indo-European immigrants. These were Indo-European Aryans, who in the middle of the 2nd millennium B.C. first come within the range of history, and play a great part as rulers in Mitanni-land with its capital Vashukani in the Khabur headwaters region. But as early as about 2000 they penetrated gradually from the north-east through Asia Minor into Mesopotamia and as far as Syria and Palestine. The question is not yet cleared up whether it was only after the conquering expedition of the Hittite king, Murshilis I, that is after about 1870 B.C., that they reached the Khabur headwaters region, or whether it was perhaps they who already before this had destroyed the old Painted Pottery town of Tell Halaf. From Niniveh, Assur and the neighbouring areas, where they had settled for a while, the Mitanni rulers and their followers came anyhow to know the style of the crafts belonging to these places, and then brought it to the Khabur headwaters region. This, however, must have been not much later than 2000 B.C., or immediately after the invasion and the withdrawal afterwards of the Hittite bands of Murshilis I, certainly not so late as the eve of the flourishing period of the Mitanni kings in the middle of the 2nd millennium B.C. We must also bear in mind that about 2000 B.C., during and after the time of the trading colonies founded by the Assyrians in Asia Minor and probably in Upper Mesopotamia also, the peaceful and the warlike spread of Assur may well have brought the Assyrians of that time as far as the area of the Khabur headwaters. The Aryan Indo-Europeans were the inheritors of these efforts by those Assyrians they overcame. During their sojourn in Niniveh, that is, in the neighbourhood of Assur—we do not know whether Assur city itself was ever subject to the Mitanni kings—the Aryan immigrants became accustomed, anyhow, to the Assyrian arts and crafts of the 2nd millennium. Here, on what was once Subaraic territory, there was then flourishing an applied art that was very strongly influenced by Babylonia, but which to a certain extent had developed independently. The pottery was self-coloured and no longer painted, but it was not without beauty. Its forms were now different. The metal instruments, however, were certainly better and more practical than the old ones of stone.

After the Mitanni rulers had settled in the Khabur headwaters area, it may be that, when the last rulers (as yet unknown to us) of the Painted Pottery town of Tell Halaf had been driven out, these Mitanni rulers, to give expression to the beginning of a new period, but perhaps also on strategic grounds, removed their new capital to the Fekheria of to-day. They brought new arts and crafts with them. The example given by the ruling class must have led to a fundamental change in the applied arts. The painted pottery was superseded by self-coloured, for tools and implements flint and obsidian was replaced by bronze and copper, which last was imported in greater abundance than hitherto from Asia Minor, especially from the rich copper mines of Arghana Maden not far away in the neighbourhood of Diarbekir. These mines are to-day still among the most important in the world.

Although the Mitanni were Indo-Europeans themselves, they had nothing in common with the Hittites. Their tongue belongs to the so-called Satem group, and to the Aryan branch; they were therefore East Indo-Europeans. As late as about 1400 B.C. a ruler of the small state of Kelte, near Jerusalem, is known to us who, judging by his name, Shuvardata, is to be looked on as a descendant of these immigrants. About the earliest times of the East Indo-Europeans in Hither Asia we have but a slight knowledge; for history they do not make their appearance till the fifteenth century. About this time a princely family among them had raised itself to the rulership over a great part of the land of Subartu. Numerous princelings were subject to it. In all probability the Hyksos, who about 1700 B.C. conquered Egypt and occupied it for some 100 years, were Subargic peoples led by the Mitanni rulers. Under the

dominion of the Mitanni princes there is for the first time
an important unified empire seen on Subaraic soil. It bears
the name Mitanniland, and undoubtedly comprised, at
times anyhow, Syria, Upper Mesopotamia, a great part of
Assyria with Niniveh, and districts in Asia Minor. One
part of Mitanni was called Hurriland, from which the
Subaraic tongue got the name of Hurritic. The capital of
the Mitanni Empire—the Fekheria of to-day—bore the
Aryan name Vashukani. The dynasty of the Hurrites' land
was related to the Mitanni dynasty of the fifteenth and
fourteenth centuries. Mitanniland in the north reached far
into Asia Minor, on the north-west the Hittites were its
neighbours, on the south-east it touched the boundary of
Babylonia, on the south it came as far as the Euphrates.
On the flat land along the Euphrates there dwelt Semitic
tribes: the Aramaeans.

Among the oldest sources of information as to the Mitanni rulers and the extent of their sway is a clay tablet
letter of the founder of this dynasty, Shaushatar (about
1450 B.C.) to the ruler of Nuzi near Kerkuk, from which
we gather that the latter was in dependence on him.

In the same way as the Hittites the Mitanni ruling class
took over the culture, the art, and the gods of the conquered
Subaraeans. In Mitanniland Subaraic (Hurritic) went on
being spoken.

The best-known king in the Mitanni dynasty is Tushratta, a great-grandson of Shaushatar and a contemporary
of Amenophis III and IV. The capital of his state was
Vashukani, whose position is still a matter of dispute.

I had long believed that Vashukani was to be looked
for in our Khabur headwaters area, and at first I had had
Tell Halaf itself in my mind. Leading cuneiform scholars,
on philological and geographical grounds, seek for Vashukani in the neighbourhood of Guzana, of which to-day we
know that it stood on the ruins of the old Tell Halaf town.
Basing myself on this acertained fact and on our work in
1929, I have come finally to the belief that Fekheria holds

the ancient Vashukani. But this place is certainly far older than the fifteenth century.

At the beginning of the Aryan invasion the newly founded state was undoubtedly greater in area than in Tushratta's time, whose rule already brings with it the decline of Mitanniland. But notwithstanding his empire was still a power to reckon with in Hither Asia. The Egyptian Pharaohs kept up a close friendship with him and his predecessors, probably mainly with the idea of keeping them as allies against the ever-growing power of the Hittite kings of Khattushash-Boghaz Keui.

In cuneiform tablets from Tell Amarna there has been preserved to us a lively correspondence between Tushratta and the kings of the eighteenth dynasty. Three Mitanni princesses came to the Pharaohs' court at Thebes as queens. A sister of Tushratta, Giluhepa, was married to Amenophis III, and his daughter Tatuhepa to Amenophis III and IV. The wife of Tut-enkh-amun, son-in-law and successor to Amenophis IV, was a niece of this Tatuhepa.

But in the relations with Egypt the Mitanni state was the weaker side. The Mitanni kings did not receive any wives from the Pharaohs. We read of their sending rich gifts, especially chariots, to Egypt, but always we find them begging for gold and money. These close relations explain the influence exerted on the Egyptian art of that time by the Subaraic art of the Mitanni.

After Tushratta's death begins the decay of the Mitanni state, brought about probably in the first place through the ever-growing strength of King Shuppiluliuma of Khattushash, who brought over to himself many of the vassals of the Mitanni state in the borderlands. Already in Tushratta's life-time Shuppiluliuma in a campaign against Mitanni had taken Vashukani without striking a blow, since Tushratta avoided a battle. Shuppiluliuma, however, withdrew again from the Mitanni capital. When Tut-enkh-amun died about 1357 B.C., the widow of the young Pharaoh turned not to the Mitanni king but to Shuppiluliuma with the request to send her one of his sons as a husband. But the Hittite king wavered mistrustingly, and before he had granted the prayer the widow's power was already broken.

Tushratta's son Mattiuaza was married to a daughter of Shuppiluliuma's. After Tushratta's death disputes as to the throne had arisen, in which Shuppiluliuma intervened to support his son-in-law. In the Boghaz Keui texts we find treaties between Shuppiluliuma and Mattiuaza of extraordinary importance for cultural history and history in general. But soon after Mattiuaza's death (about 1360 B.C.) the Hittites destroyed Vashukani, and so dealt a deadly blow to the Mitanni state.

The wreck of a state that was left, whose capital became Taidi lying not far north, wedged in as it was between the Hittites on the west and the Assyrians just rising on the east, could not last. Taidi was taken and destroyed in 1308 by the Assyrian king, Adad-nirari I (about 1310-1281); and so the Mitanni state disappears from history.

Just as the basic population and the tongue of Mitanni-land were Subaraic, so too were and remained its culture and its art. It is true that, as we saw, in the smaller arts and crafts new Assyrian-Babylonian stylistic forms were brought in, but the old Pantheon and the old religious conceptions went on living. The Mitanni on their side probably brought little with them, if we leave aside their knowledge of horse-keeping and everything to do with horses. The knowledge of driving they found already there; in South Babylonia it already existed in the time of the Old Sumerian Ur. Their word-stock enriched the Subaraic, and together with the new ones which they took over native to Subartu, they kept their own 'Indian' gods, namely Mitra, Indra, Varuna and the Nasatya, who, probably as being household gods of the Mitanni royal family, are also brought in as witnesses in Mattiuaza's treaties with Shuppiluliuma.

After the fall of the Mitanni state the interests of the

three great powers of that time clashed against one another in Syria and Upper Mesopotamia: those of Egypt, of the Hittite Empire, and of the military state of the Assyrians, ever growing in strength. The latter in spite of their capture of Taidi could not as yet permanently hold their own in Upper Mesopotamia. The successor of Adad-nirari I, Salmanassar I, and other kings were fighting in the following period with Subaraeans and Hittites on the west. The Egyptian kings of the nineteenth dynasty sought with ever growing determination to get a foothold in Syria, but in 1308 the Battle of Kadesh (Tell Nebbi-Mindu, south of Homs) fought against the Hittite king Muvatallu put an end to the advance of Ramses II into northern Syria and Mesopotamia, although he hailed the day as a great victory. The Hittites, too, had been greatly weakened by this battle. They in turn could not keep their hand on Upper Mesopotamia. At length, towards the end of the thirteenth century, owing to the forward movement of fresh Indo-European tribes in Asia Minor—the Thracians, Phrygians and Armenians—their empire came to an end, and these tribes carved out new homes here for themselves. Thus the road to the west lay open for Assyria, when a new power came on the scene: the Aramaeans.

These are Semitic nomads, but we know not whence they came. B. Moritz looks to southern Arabia for their home.

The accounts of the earliest history of the Aramaeans take us back to the Old Testament. It must have been an old usage to reckon Jacob and his forefathers among the Aramaeans (cp. 5th Moses xxvi, 5, where Jacob is called a 'degenerate Aramaean'). Abraham's father, Terah, wandered with his family about the beginning of the 2nd millennium out of Ur in Chaldaea to Harran. From there Abraham when seventy-five years old went at God's bidding to Canaan. In Harran the memory of Laban and his sister Rebecca is still alive. In Urfa not far away, I was able to gather many new tales dealing with Abraham's

E

relations with the Assyrian king Nimrud of the legends. According to one of them Nimrud dwelt as a mighty ruler on the citadel hill of the town of Urfa. Abraham preached the holy faith where the finest mosque in the town, Jame Khalil er Rakhman, now stands. Nimrud with a catapult mounted on the citadel on the great pillars of Abgar times, still there to-day, then hurled glowing charcoal against Abraham. Instead of this burning the holy man, a pond arose where the charcoal fell. The glowing bits of charcoal turned into fishes swimming about in it. They are deemed holy down to our day and may not be eaten. In another version Nimrud had had Abraham shot with the catapult from the citadel into the town and a mighty charcoal fire that was burning where the mosque Khalil er Rakhman stands to-day. But when Abraham fell into the middle of the flames, the fire was put out by a great stream of water, and the glowing bits of charcoal became fishes. God then brought death upon Nimrud by sending a bug that went up his nose. After Nimrud's death Abraham built the mosque to call upon the world to believe in the true God.

Thus in Mohammedan tradition, but with unbelievable historical distortion, Abraham has here become an Islamic saint.

Another legend tells us that Abraham swam from the holy pond in Urfa through an underground stream of water to the place known as 'Ain el Khalil, some 40 kilometres south of Urfa, and where the Belikh river takes its rise. I found in a hamlet here native Mohammedan peasants who declared themselves to be direct descendants of Father Abraham.

The non-Biblical sources, such as the Tell Amarna letters, from the fourteenth century, know the nomadic tribes of the Syrian desert under the name Akhlamu. The Akhlamu gave much trouble to the great powers of Hither Asia, and often stood in the way of communications between the Hittite empire and Babylonia. The Assyrians from the end of the fourteenth century were always at feud with them. Under the Assyrian king, Tiglat-Pilesar I (about 1100) Aramaic Akhlamu are mentioned, so far, for the first time in a way we understand; they were dwelling south of the Euphrates in north-western Babylonia. 'Akhlamu' was probably, like the later word 'Beduins', the general term for nomads.

After the fall of the Mitanni state an unhappy state of things must have arisen in Upper Mesopotamia. Since the nomad peoples have always made use of such times of political decay, when neither townsmen nor countrymen can be properly protected, to push northwards with their herds out of the steppes of Arabia, it is probable that from the thirteenth century Aramaic Beduins were penetrating into the Khabur area and its neighbouring cultivated lands. From oldest times the district between the Belikh and the Khabur south of Jebel Abd el Aziz and its western spurs—as also south of the Sinjar mountains—had been nothing but pasture land. Although on my journeys of exploration I have crossed these districts, I have not found here any Tells of even the slightest importance as remains of old towns of any size, except in the immediate neigh- bourhood of the Belikh and the Khabur, while the innu- merable ruined sites on the southern slope and north of the Abd-el-Aziz and the Sinjar mountains as far as the Kurdish mountains show that this area has always been cultivated land. While there were powerful rulers in the Khabur headwaters region, the nomad peoples of the steppes along the Euphrates could not stir. But after the fall of Taidi it must have been easy for them to penetrate gradually into the northern cultivated land. Among them it may be that the Aramaeans gradually won the upper hand; it is they, anyhow, who in the end took over the in- heritance of the Mitanni kings.

From the earliest times down to the present day we have examples showing that nomads take to a sedentary life in cultivated regions where they are able to make themselves the rulers, and gradually mingle with the true natives. We need only think of what happened with Abraham and his first descendants. The state of things described in the account of the blood-bath of Sikhem (1st Moses, xxxv) reminds us exactly of Beduin life, and the life of the Aramaeans must have been the same. In Islamic times, too, a number of smaller or greater Arab dynasties were founded by Beduin sheikhs that had led the life of nomads.

In the same way, in the twelfth century B.C., an Aramaic sheikh built up a state from the ruins of the Mitanni kingdom, whose centre once again was the Khabur headwaters region. But he did not this time choose the former Mitanni capital, Vashukani, for his own, but the very ancient Painted Pottery town of Tell Halaf, now a hill of ruins, probably meaning in the old Eastern way to express the fact that a new era had begun. He made use of the mounds, which were certainly still to be made out, of the walls to build his new city wall on them. A beginning was made by the founder of the new town with the building of palaces on the earlier citadel hill. Not long after that—this can be seen from the archaeological finds—one of his successors continued his work, and completed the buildings we excavated in 1911-13. He was Kapara, son of Hadianu. He engraved his inscriptions on some of the old statues he brought up out of the Painted Pottery layer and used to adorn the temple-palace.

Professor Bruno Meissner on philological grounds holds that Kapara's inscriptions are to be assigned to the twelfth century. With this the smaller finds in the Kapara layer are in conformity, as also is B. Landsberger's view that the appearance of the Aramaeans in Mesopotamia can be put back into the twelfth century but not farther. According to this Kapara or his father would seem to have been the first Aramaic king in Upper Mesopotamia. As already stated above, the land of Kapara was called 'Pa-li-e'; but so far we know nothing of its extent.

Kapara's dynasty is shown by the inscriptions to have been independent, for they contain nothing that points to his being dependent on a foreign ruler, as happened, for instance, later in the case of the Aramaic ruler of Senjirli, who was much farther away from the Assyrian king's capital, and who calls himself the servant of this king.

Like the Hittites and the Mitanni rulers, these Aramaic intruders, too, took over the old-rooted Subaraic culture, art and religion from the native Subaraeans. It was by these Subaraeans that they had their great buildings and above all the temple-palace of Tell Halaf carried out, and this temple-palace is therefore naturally in the style of the old Subaraic Hilani building. So, too, native craftsmen would have trimmed the old statues used over again, and put them in their places, and would have set the huge figures of gods up again on the colossal animals of the front façade to carry the timber work of the roof.

In the layer from the Kapara times we find Assyrio-Babylonian pottery of the kind that had already been made by the Mitanni folk in Fekheria. On the other hand implements of daily life—stone bowls, mortars, clubs, fighting projectiles, and also goldware—are often still Old Subaraic. Partly we find that individual objects, such as the stone implements, have been taken up out of the old Painted Pottery layer and used over again, and partly the craftsmen have made new objects in the old style, which had not been broken off even by the Mitanni period.

The Aramaeans kept their Semitic speech. For their writing they probably mainly used cuneiform, but also the Aramaic system. On the statues Kapara has left behind only short cuneiform inscriptions, which were doubtless cut by native stone-masons. Since also in the Kapara layer we found nothing written as to the happenings of daily life, nor any letters, it may be assumed that the Aramaeans, like those before them in the Khabur headwaters region, made use of perishable materials, perhaps parchment or papyrus, for writing. As we said above, they also scratched their inscriptions in their own tongue on lumps of clay, as is shown by the clay olives of the later Guzana period found on Tell Halaf (see Appendix V). In the Kapara layer we found a small limestone altar with a few Old Semitic written characters, that were unfortunately unreadable.

The Aramaeans were nomads, or rather half-nomads, but undoubtedly unexhausted and with all their primitive strength. Of the culture they brought with them they were not able to impress anything on the native population— the Subaraeans—but their tongue. The Aramaeans, it is also evident, kept none of their former gods, but took over the whole Subaraic pantheon.

The Aramaeans were able about the end of the 2nd millennium B.C. to settle down not only in Upper Mesopotamia, but especially in northern Syria also, where the Hittites of Boghaz Keui had formerly been the rulers. Here also they founded their own princedoms in the capitals of former small Subaraic states.

Aramaic gradually came to be the main tongue of the peoples subjugated by the Aramaeans, and besides this spread in the first half of the 1st millennium B.C. over Syria as far as the borders of Arabia, while in the east it spread over Mesopotamia to Babylonia, where in the Persian period it stood without a rival. Thus Aramaic had come to be the general speech of a great part of the old Nearer East, and this was brought about in peaceful ways, in contrast with Arabic, which, however, afterwards drove Aramaic out again.

After the destruction of Jerusalem by Nebuchadnezzar in 586 B.C. Aramaic became spoken in Palestine also. And thus some portions of the Old Testament—parts of the Books of Ezra and Daniel—are written in Aramaic. Aramaic was also the tongue of Jesus Christ and the Apostles.

Hebrew, the true language of the Jews, lived on after its disappearance as the speech of a nation only rather as an ecclesiastical form of speech, and as such it has been preserved among the Jews down to our own time.

Later Aramaic, especially since the beginning of the Christian era, is known as 'Syriac'. In it was written an extensive Christian literature down to and beyond the first thousand years of our era. Syriac is still kept alive as an ecclesiastical language in certain forms of Eastern Christianity—the Nestorians and Chaldaeans, the Jacobites and the Maronites. To-day it is also still the everyday speech in Syria in a few villages of the Anti-Lebanon, in Mesopotamia among the Jacobites of Tur Abdin near Mardin, and in the mountains south of Mosul among the Nestorians and Chaldaeans.

But let us now come back to Tell Halaf. The power of the Kapara dynasty can only have been short-lasting, for its city and splendid palaces were very soon destroyed, probably about 1100 B.C. by Tiglat-Pilesar I, the mighty king of Assyria. He speaks in his war reports of long struggles against the Aramaeans, whom he has driven back from the Khabur as far as Karkemish 'in one day'. His conquests, however, in our area were only fleeting ones. In the time of the Assyrian king, Adad-nirari II (911-891), we are told again of an Aramaic state in Upper Mesopotamia under a ruler called Abi-salamu (Absalom); its name is 'Guzana'. This is the first time we meet this name for Tell Halaf and its district. Then in the course of the ninth century the Khabur headwaters area, like the rest of Upper Mesopotamia and north Syria came once for all under Assyrian rule. In 808 Semiramis, the mother of Adad-nirari III conquered Guzana for her son, a minor, or rather conquered it once more, after it had been able to make itself independent again.

Thus the Khabur headwaters area under the name of Guzana had become an Assyrian province. It now no longer had any ruler of its own, but an Assyrian governor stood over it. In the Assyrian archives a governor of Guzana appears for the first time as the eponym for the year 793 B.C. his name being Mannu-ki-ashur. For in Assyria each year was named after some high functionary, the so-called eponym. Lists giving these names in order are called eponym-lists. They make it possible for us to date exactly all the events of the time, and so too, to date the governorship of Mannu-ki-ashur in Guzana.

Unfortunately Tell Halaf only yielded us a small number of cuneiform tablets. The oldest—from the eighth century—were found in a pot. For us they are of peculiar importance as giving the name Guzana for the last, the pre-Hellenistic Tell Halaf town. Several of the tablets bear orders from the royal court to Mannu-ki-ashur, who is explicitly called the governor of Guzana.

A second and later find belongs to the seventh century. It consists of cuneiform tablets likewise and some Aramaic clay olives, such as were found in Assur also (cp. Appendix IV).

On these cuneiform and Aramaic clay tablets the proper names are in part written in Assyrian, in part in Aramaic. In many cases they correspond exactly with the names in the census lists of the town of Harran and its neighbourhood from the seventh century. From the clay tablets we see also that—and we should not have expected otherwise —Assyrian ways of thought had also come into Guzana. The chief gods, however, were left: the head god Teshup, in Assyrian 'Adad', who dwells in Guzana, and the Sun god Shamash. The goddess Hepet, too, who corresponds to the Assyrian Ishtar, is mentioned on cylinder seals of this time.

The old Subaraic inhabitants had been so far Aramaicized that they had gradually taken over the Aramaic speech and Aramaic names along with Assyrian. This is not to be wondered at, for from oldest times conquered peoples have often given their children the names of their conquerors. The Christian sectarians of the Kurdish mountains are to be looked on as the last remnants, driven hither, of the primitive Subaraic population of the Upper Mesopotamia plain, above all those on the southern slopes near Mardin; they are the survivors of the old native population who have kept their stock much purer than have the Mohammedans there. The shape of the head and the cast of the countenance in these Christians often remind one of the oldest representations at Tell Halaf; they often, too, still bear to-day Assyrian names such as Sanherib and Nimrud. The Greek names which we also find among them come from the later Hellenistic times.

Towards the end of the eighth century the Khabur headwaters area was already so well incorporated in the Assyrian empire that it was felt possible to transfer to it foreign peoples that had been carried away from their own homes. The Old Testament tells us that Sargon, the Assyrian king, after laying Samaria waste (722 B.C.) settled Israelites on the Khabur, on the river of Gozan (Guzana) and in the towns of Media.

But now Guzana no longer had the former importance of Kapara's city. Only a part of the city and citadel had buildings on it in the Guzana period. We found the statues of his temple-palace 3000 years afterwards just as they had fallen at the time of their destruction. The mud-brick walls that had collapsed still cover them. The surface of the ground lay only a few centimetres above the remains of the statues of the front of the temple-palace. The main buildings of the later settlers were on another part of the hill.

Vashukani-Fekheria, not far away, also stood into Assyrian times. Under Adad-nirari II, about 900 B.C., it appears under the name Sikari.

The fortunes of the Khabur headwaters area henceforward are bound up with those of the Assyrian state. This state fell in 612 before the combined troops of the Medes and the New Babylonian kingdom. The attempt of the last Assyrian king, Assuruballit II, to make a settlement in Harran in Upper Mesopotamia ended in failure. With the year 606 the once so powerful Assyria wholly disappears from history. The north of Mesopotamia became part of the Median, and then of the Persian world-empire founded by Cyrus.

The Persian period did not leave any real traces on Tell

Halaf. This cannot be said of the period of Alexander the Great and the Diadochi. On the citadel we find houses with baths, a great number of so-called Rhodian wine-amphorai with Greek inscriptions on the handles, and in the town many graves with coffins.

It is not until later Roman times that the Khabur head-waters area has once again any historical importance. Its chief town grew up by the northern sources of the Khabur and is now known as Resh Aina. On the ruined sites of Vashukani-Fekheria I believe I can recognize the traces of a Roman military camp and an amphitheatre. By the pool filled by a strong sulphur-spring not far from where the two arms of the Khabur meet we found the remains of a wall of a Roman bath. Not far west of Tell Halaf and of the first southern spring of the Khabur, Ain el Beda, there are still standing bits of the masonry of a Roman bridge over the Jirjib Abu Daraj. We know from a late Roman road map, the *Tabula Peutingeriana* that Ras el Ain was the meeting-point of a great number of old roads. During my journeys of exploration I found out many of these roads and of the Roman military posts set up for their protection.

As a result of the disgraceful treaty concluded by the Emperor Jovian in A.D. 363 with the Parthians, the eastern frontier of the Roman Empire was withdrawn from the Tigris as far as the Jaghjagh, the tributary of the Khabur that flows down from Nisibin. From now Resh Aina be-came the most important place on the frontier. In 373 it was raised to the rank of a city by the Emperor Theo-dosius and strongly fortified; henceforward it was known as Theodosiopolis. The fortress was held by a strong garri-son, as is seen from the *Notitia Dignitatum*, a list of the civil and military official establishments of the late Roman Empire.

The Khabur headwaters district also played its part in Christian Church history. In it the two newly arisen Syrian churches—the Nestorians and the Jacobites—met one another, each having a bishop in Resh Aina. The Syrian writers give the names of many churches and monasteries in the district between Jebel Abd el Aziz and the Kurdish mountains, and I was able to find many of them.

When later the armies of Islam under the Khalif Omar, the second successor to the Prophet (A.D. 634-644) started on their victorious march through Mesopotamia, they found nothing to oppose them in the Khabur area. Resh Aina seems to have been peacefully occupied. An Arab town now grew up mainly north of the Roman town. It kept the old name, but in the Arabic form Ras el Ain, and always held a strong Christian population. Under the Abbasids Ras el Ain was an important caravan station between Bagdad and the summer residence of the Khalifs in Rakka. But it would seem that the Khalifs also sometimes spent the summer in Ras el Ain; we even find that coins were struck here in this period. The memory of those flourishing times is kept alive for us to-day in the name 'Abbasiye' for what is left of the old Islamic town.

Ras el Ain had a second summer under the rule of the Ayyubites, Saladin's dynasty (1169-1250), and of the art-loving Ortuḳids of Mardin (1108-1408).

The Khabur valley in the Arabian middle ages was highly important for growing cotton, which yielded the raw material for the spinning and weaving works of Mosul and Armenia. The name 'muslin' for its cotton stuffs brought by the Crusaders to Europe comes from the town of Mosul (Arabic Musil). The word 'cotton', too, which has become part of most European languages, is Arabic, but comes originally from an old Assyrian word.

The golden times of Ras el Ain lost much after A.D. 1259 through the Mongol invasion. Under Timur Lenk the town was utterly destroyed. In his rage at the long siege of the little mountain town of Mardin (1400-1401), which put up a desperate defence, Timur laid waste the fruitful plains of Upper Mesopotamia with its many flourishing villages and towns, and had the whole population slaughtered. The biographers of the Tatar ruler write of the pyramids of death which here too he set up from the skulls of the slain.

Since this time the fruitful plains of Upper Mesopotamia have become desert steppes without any fixed settlements, and a wandering pasture-ground for nomad Arabs who broke in from the south. In the north, at the edge of the wilderness, there settled half-sedentary, half-nomadic Kurds.

Osmanic rule brought no change to this state of things. Only quite lately has there grown up by the northern Khabur springhead the small Chechen village already referred to, and since the World War the French military post with the market place Ras el Ain.

III

The Old Tell Halaf Town

I

THE old Tell Halaf town comprises the town area, the citadel, and the outskirts. The town proper is shaped as a rectangle, whose longer sides run west to east and are about 1000 metres long. The breadth is about 600 metres, so that we get an area of about 60 hektars (that is, 150 acres) for the town. On the north, somewhat towards the western corner, and immediately on the Khabur, rises the mighty citadel hill, Tell Halaf proper. To the west and the east stretch great suburbs.

The highest point on the citadel hill to-day lies more or less in the middle. It rises 26 metres above the assumed zero point, the surface of the main spring of the town, which comes out at the foot of the citadel hill. This level is only slightly higher than that of the river in summertime. From east to west the citadel hill is some 330 metres long. The width taken over the highest point is about 200 metres; taken along the east wall it is about 280 metres. On the west the hill is now only about 150 metres broad, since the Khabur in the course of thousands of years has on the north-west worn away great bits of it and the adjoining floor of the town. But taken all together the river must have taken the same course then as to-day, since the bed is fixed by the springs which lie in and by it.

At the time of my first visit in 1899 the mud-houses of the Chechen Sogh Ahmed were standing on the north-east corner of the hill. He settled himself later on grounds of security on the other side of the Khabur, nearer to Ras el Ain.

On the highest point of the hill there was at that time the grave in which the Chechen had in the end found his rest

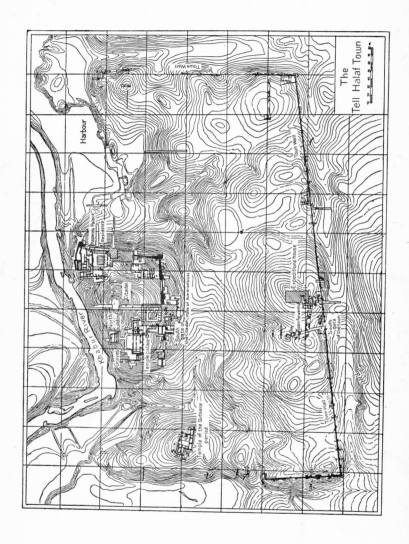

The
Tell Halaf Town

whose first burial above Kapara's temple-palace had led
to the discovery of the statues of Tell Halaf.

Between 1899 and 1911 many Chechens and Beduins
had been buried by this grave, so that on religious grounds
there could be no excavating work on the top of the hill.
We dug, however, broad and deep trial trenches from the
north and the south as far as the top, and we determined
the summit to have been formed only in comparatively
late times. In olden times the highest points of the hill were
on the north-east, by Kapara's palace residence, and on
the west, where the temple-palace stood, under which the
painted pottery lies in such abundance.

In our first excavating expedition, 1911-13, we mainly
dug out the buildings belonging to the second period of
Tell Halaf, when the Aramaic ruling house of Kapara
built its capital here.

Citadel and town are bounded on the north by the
Khabur, which here made a natural protection. The three
other sides are protected by the walls of the citadel and the
town. These walls are planned at right-angles to one
another, and run more or less according to the main points
of the compass. The citadel wall was pierced by three gates,
the south gate in the west of the south wall, and two gates
in the east of the north wall by the river.

Through the south gate, underneath which there was
an older gateway, probably built by Kapara's father, the
temple-palace was reached. It is the most important building from the Kapara period—the government palace and
at the same time the temple of its principal gods. The approach was along a rising way ending at the gateway of
the temple-palace.

The entrance was flanked by two stone sculptures—
hybrids of man, scorpion and bird, and we therefore called
it the 'Scorpions' Gate'. Behind this gate the way rose
once more, then bent to the left, that is, to the west, and
led to a small open place. Here you turned south, and by
way of a small fore-court and a flight of steps reached a

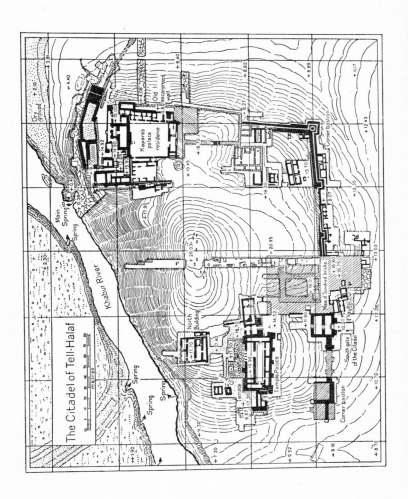

The Citadel of Tell-Halaf

great terrace. Here rose the mighty part of the north façade of the temple-palace that was adorned with relief-slabs. On both hands it was bounded by an outstanding tower, and in it was the broad main entrance, in which stood three gigantic statues of gods on colossal animals and carried the timberwork caryatid-wise.

Through this entrance you came first to a comparatively narrow cross room, and then through a second gateway, likewise flanked by stone sculptures along the sides, to the main apartment of the temple-palace, the Middle Hall, which also ran crosswise. Smaller rooms adjoined at the sides and behind.

The temple-palace stood high above the town on a sub-structure that was supported on the south by five massive buttresses. At the foot both of the south front and of the south part of the east and the west front of this sub-structure there was a line of small upright relief slabs. The walls of Kapara's temple-palace stood on the remains of the old building with the same out-line that rose upon the Painted Pottery layer. The older builder was probably the first king of the Aramaic dynasty, perhaps Kapara's father, for Kapara writes in his in-scriptions: 'What my father did not do (to this palace), that I have done!'

On the terrace before the main front sacrifices were made to the gods. In the middle hall the king probably transacted his administrative business. Here we found a low bronze vehicle, which was perhaps a movable hearth or had a religious use. This great building thus served at the same time both as temple and as the king's govern-ment palace. That is why we have called it a 'temple-palace'. It is a so-called *hilani*, an architectural form be-longing to the Subaraic culture, and which has been found especially in Senjirli and Karkemish. The characteristic of the hilani lies in two broad rooms one behind the other and linked by a gateway, of which the first is entered from the open space in front through a remarkably large gate-

F

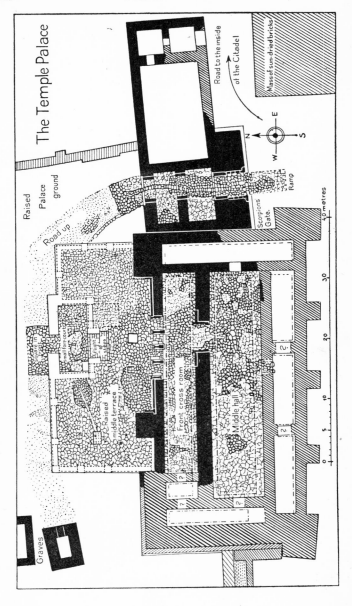

The Temple Palace

way. This gateway is elsewhere divided up by only one or by two pillars carrying the lintel. Alongside and behind the broad rooms are other smaller ones.

The Assyrians used the architectural style known as 'hilani' for small, avowedly foreign buildings: so in Khorsabad and Kuyunjik (Niniveh). In an inscription of the Assyrian king Sargon we read of such a building: 'Set up after the pattern of an Ekal of the Hittites' land, which in the speech of the Western land is called an Hilani'.

Nowhere is the gateway in the front façade of the hilani designed on so monumental a scale as on Tell Halaf.

The hilanis which till now we have known of from the Subaraic culture-complex belong to the tenth and ninth centuries, and thus are all later than the Kapara building, which is from the twelfth century.

The most primitive type of the hilani is to be seen already in the archaic temple of Ishtar at Assur (about 3000 B.C.). We need not wonder at this, since Assur, which at that time was under Sumerian influence, was in the land of Subartu—that is to say, within the area of the old Subaraic culture.

North-west of the temple-palace lie two graves. The older (southern) one went down into the Painted Pottery layer; it was covered over by Kapara's great terrace, and perfectly preserved. In it gold, ivory, copper, and other objects were found. The later one had been plundered.

On the north towards the Khabur there lay a fair-sized building, the 'North Building'. In the gypsum-concrete floor of its courtyard there was a line of roundish pits dug near one another, probably for planting trees, like what we know from Assur. This building was also part of the temple-palace, which seems to have had its own boundary-wall and only one gateway, the Scorpions' Gate.

Immediately east of the south citadel gate there rose a great, high massive structure of mud bricks in two storeys from the time of Kapara, which with a salient stretched itself beyond the citadel wall into the town itself. On the platform, paved with burnt bricks, of this southern portion were two limestone poles supporting some wooden religious symbol. On Tell Halaf it is in this way that the winged sun's disk is held by bull-men by means of the feet of a stool. On the Kassite kudurrus we are always finding religious emblems exhibited on great poles. Perhaps on this massive structure there were sacrifices made before an idol, that could be fastened to masts such as these and seen from a great part of the town.

In this fore-part of the massive mud-brick structure there were two walled-in goddesses seated on thrones, gigantic basalt statues, set up over shaft-graves sunk into the rock. Between the brick structure and the citadel gate we found some more graves, but they had been plundered.

Before the Scorpions' Gate a way forks off to the east of the citadel. Here in the north-eastern corner, likewise on a raised terrace, lay the second castle, Kapara's residential palace. It contained smallish rooms grouped round two courtyards. These made separate dwellings, and were for the harem and the servants of the king. North of these were larger rooms, where the king himself probably lived.

From the main spring of Tell Halaf, whence we, too, drew our water, a path climbed in a narrow corridor into the palace interior. The palace was guarded by gates in several places. Furthermore from the Khabur, outside the residential palace and along its west wall which had bastions, there went a broad way from the Khabur to the second, the northern citadel gate, which we called the 'Spring Gate'.

Along the whole east front of the palace there came to light a cyclopean layered and sloped wall, before which was a ditch hewn out of the rock. This wall was partly overlaid by the platform on which Kapara's castle stood. This old wall construction belonged to the Painted Pottery layer.

On the north side of the palace were stone sub-structures for protecting the lofty buildings against the stream of the

Khabur, and at the same time to lead the river into a harbour that lay near eastwards of the citadel, and ran far into the town.

On the south-east of the citadel hill some smaller buildings from the Kapara period were also uncovered. Here, too, we found in the upper layers the largest building of the Assyrian period on the citadel hill; it was probably the palace of the governor of Guzana. In a small house near by clay tablets with cuneiform and Aramaic writing belonging to this late Assyrian period were found.

All over the hill the ground close under the buildings of the Kapara time was interspersed with painted pottery, obsidian, and flint, and still further down to some extent with self-coloured pottery also. This fact was established not only during the actual digging, but also through trial sections reaching down to the rock, trial shafts, and very extensive depth-digging in the north-west of the temple-palace. The whole citadel area must therefore have been inhabited in oldest times by the Painted Pottery folk.

In the Kapara times also the citadel hill was used to the full. When, however, in Assyrian times Tell Halaf was only a provincial capital—Guzana—only a small part of it may have been built on. This is true also of Greco-Roman and Arab times. In these last periods of settlement the middle of the hill was preferred. The simple mud buildings soon fell to decay, and on their ruins new buildings of the same material were raised. These rubbish heaps grew with the centuries, and thus formed what is to-day the highest point on the citadel hill.

The town came up to the citadel hill on the east, south and west. The northern boundary was made partly by the citadel, partly by the Khabur. Evidently from the earliest Painted Pottery times down to the Assyrians the town had been enclosed on the three land sides by a wall defended like the citadel wall at regular intervals by towers, with especially strong bastions at the angles, and in parts 6.40 metres thick. This town wall, like the citadel walls, bore traces of having been strengthened and renewed. Outside at its foot a bray or breastwork ran round, before which was a broad and deep ditch. It marks itself clearly in the ground.

In the western half of the southern town wall the existence of a town gate was determined lying opposite the south gate of the citadel, and joined to this gate by a road six metres broad. But the barbican or gate-tower of the town wall had disappeared; its remains were at a later time gradually levelled down through the traffic. Down to the time of our excavations in 1911-13 the caravan road led from the ford above the town, which lies immediately below the Bagdad Railway bridge of to-day, through the west of the town and through the south gate on to the south-east. We have to assume the existence of another gate on the west side and also on the east side of the town wall.

No sculptures were found either at the citadel gate or at the presumed places of the town gates.

The town stands on a low, undulating plateau. The rises in the ground are to be attributed to the old mud-brick houses in collapse; the more marked ones cover buildings of greater size.

The former town walls could in places be recognized through a slight rise like a mound. There were long stretches, however, especially on the west and the east, where nothing was left; here in the course of thousands of years they have been destroyed through floods from the Khabur and the rain-storms that come so often here and with hurricane strength; all this water then streamed outwards from the inner part of the town.

The natural floor of the town lifts gradually from the Khabur southwards. Beyond the depression of the town ditch the land rises sharply to a height that far out-tops the highest point on Tell Halaf. The strategic situation of the town was thus not highly advantageous in itself; and this goes to show how strong were the governments in the time of the painted pottery, the Kapara, and the Guzana town of Tell Halaf. The position of Fekheria-Vashukani within the two arms of the Khabur was much more favourable.

It was beyond our powers to examine the whole wide area of the town at Tell Halaf; we had to restrict ourselves to the excavation of some of the elevations. The Tell Halaf town must have been thickly populated both in Painted Pottery times and in those of Kapara. There was a close net of alley-ways and open places, in some cases ballasted and drained. The dwelling-houses were on the whole primitive, and consisted only of one or more rooms without inside court-yards. This for the old Near East is quite un-usual, and is found otherwise only in Asia Minor and in old Iran. Often there were bathrooms.

While we were seeking to dig a well in the outer court-yard of our expeditionary house, which should make us independent of the Khabur water in case of attack, we came upon two small basalt idols. Later finds of the same kind were made by the west outer wall of this house. They led to the discovery of a room for worship, whose walls still stood to the height of $1\frac{1}{2}$-2 metres. The altar and statues of gods were still in their old places. The design has a great likeness with the archaic Ishtar temple at Assur.

In the north-west of the town, built right into the maze of small houses, we succeeded in laying bare the walls, still about a metre high, of a great temple with fore-court. Setting aside some small differences, it is like one of the three structures of the temple-group of Khorsabad from the end of the eighth century B.C., wrongly known as the 'harem'. Our temple belongs to Assyrian Guzana times. It was built up on older walls, with which we shall have to deal later on.

The diagram of the layers for the town is the same as on the citadel hill. Our deep digging brought up painted pot-tery everywhere under the Kapara buildings. After this oldest period and after that of Kapara, to which latter the houses uncovered belong, only scattered homesteads still stood. At several places in the midst of the ruins of older dwellings we also uncovered Hellenistic burial places.

West and east of the town walls lie the broad belt of its outskirts, in which we found sherds from every period, and among them painted sherds. Here evidently there were gardens, but big buildings also may have stood here which now perhaps lie buried under hillocks of ruins.

In the hilly ground rising towards the south there were no traces of such outskirts. On the other hand, beyond the river as far as Fekheria in the fruitful headwaters district of the Khabur, there were everywhere smallish elevations, in which we probably are to see the remains of dairy-farms and the like.

IV

The Great Statues of the Temple-Palace

BESIDES the painted pottery the stone statues make
up the most important of the finds at Tell Halaf.
With few exceptions they belong to the Subaraic
culture-complex. I do not propose to discuss here in detail
the affinity between all our statues and the finds made at
other Subaraic stations, with which naturally the relations
are very near. I also refrain from making comparisons
with the Assyrian sculptures. The late Babylonian
motives are based on the older South Mesopotamian-
Sumerian patterns, in the same way, indeed, as are the
Old Persian (Achaemenid and Sassanid). The art of the
Assyrians, whose territory belongs to Subartu, is not an
original one; it comes down from the Subaraic and the
Sumerian. In its course it was more and more influenced
and penetrated, owing to the continuous relations with
Lower Mesopotamia, by the art of Babylonia, until from
about the twelfth or the eleventh century B.C. onwards
Assyrian art found its own expression. Nabopalassar (625-
605 B.C.), the king of Chaldaea, still expressly calls the
Assyrians Subaraeans in his inscriptions. Thus in one passage he says: 'The Subaraean I slew and turned his land to
rubbish-heaps and ruins'. In copying astrological texts an
Assyrian scribe adds to an omen referring to the land of
Subartu the remark: 'We are Subartu'. These documents
from so late a time bear witness to the living memory of
very ancient Babylonian division of the then known world
and to the still existing consciousness of how Assyria was
originally part of Subartu geographically and in its culture.

The sculptures from the newly-discovered Subaraic sites
of Tell Halaf and Jebelet-el-Beda, which are also the oldest
belonging to this culture, as compared with those from the

89

other Subaraic sites more to the west and south, occupy an exceptional position in so far as they show particularly evident relations with the oldest Sumerian and with the kindred Old Elamic motives. This may be due above all to the fact that the Khabur headwaters region lies geographically very near both these old centres of culture, and particularly to two temporary centres of Old Sumerian influence: Assur, which about 3000 B.C. was a Sumerian colony, and Mari just below where the Khabur flows into the Euphrates, where a dynasty (the tenth after the Flood) once ruled whose kings bear Sumerian names and which likewise must be dated not much later than 3000 B.C. Many characteristics of the Old Sumerian art did not penetrate any further into the more remote Subaraic regions.

The greatest likeness with Tell Halaf motives is to be found in the oldest Sumerian sites of all, such as Ur and Kish, and we have to bear in mind always the fact that with the Gudea period Babylonian analogies may be said no longer to exist for Tell Halaf. It is significant that the Tell Halaf statues precisely in their most individual forms not found anywhere else at all have analogies with those Sumerian ones which belong to the beginnings of the 3rd millennium.

I have therefore deemed it necessary in what follows to refer to these quite ancient analogies, at least from time to time. For they show us that the Tell Halaf statues come down from the 3rd millennium B.C., which is moreover confirmed by the circumstances in which they were found. Anyhow, as will be seen later in detail, it is quite an impossibility for our statues to have been a product of the Kapara period. This fact again is in full agreement with the historical possibilities which were confirmed by the results of my excavations. Besides our painted pottery period it is only the Mitanni period in the Khabur headwaters district that could in any way come into question for the origin of the Tell Halaf statues. But even this after the

stylistic investigations carried out by Professor Herzfeld
(cp. Appendix I) seems to be an impossibility, since the
Mitanni rulers did not make their appearance in Mesopotamia earlier than 2000 B.C., and Herzfeld —rightly, I am
convinced—makes the Tell Halaf sculptures to be much
older. The results of his investigations, indeed, are in
almost complete agreement with the views of Professor
O. Weber, the former Director of the Hither Asiatic
section of the State Museums in Berlin, who from his many
years' knowledge of sculptures and plaster casts has also
assigned almost all the Tell Halaf sculptures to the 3rd
millennium.

The Gods of the Old People of Tell Halaf

Throughout the old Nearer East we find religious ways
of thought in the representations on stone monuments, seal
cylinders, and even on the earthenware. Gods, half-gods
and demons, acts of worship, scenes of prayer and sacrifice
are depicted. The vessels are always showing mythological
and magical references in the drawings on them.

The life of the Old Eastern peoples has always a strong
religious attitude; this expresses itself too in personal
names, contracts and letters.

On Tell Halaf, especially, this religious attitude is very
clearly to be seen. In the motives on the statues, on the
painted pottery and on the other smaller objects, the religious and mythological thoughts find their reflection.
The finds, therefore, from the Jebelet-el-Beda and Tell
Halaf yield a welcome addition to our knowledge of the
Subaraic religion. Till now we knew but little about it, and
this little was mostly from a later time.

It was only the finds from a time later than the middle
of the 2nd millennium that hitherto could give us any insight from written monuments into the religious beliefs of
the Subaraeans. In this connection there are first of all
two treaties between the Hittite king Shuppiluliuma and
the Mitanni king Mattiuaza to be considered. In them

the chief gods of the two lands are named as strengtheners of the oath and wardens of the treaty. Furthermore it is stated in them that these treaties have been deposited before the chief gods of the Hittite and the Mitanni kingdom: 'One duplicate has been laid before the Sun of Arinna', who thus is given as the most important god of the Hittite kingdom. The other duplicate has been 'laid in the land of Mitanni before Teshup, the Lord of the Kurinnu (temple?) of Kakhat'. According to this the Teshup of Kakhat is a particularly important god of Mitanniland. The two treaties, which were probably exchanged, contain a list of over thirty gods of the Mitanni kingdom. Teshup is found five times, always as lord of another city or of some other conception. He is anyhow the chief god of the Mitanni state, the Lord of Heaven and Earth. Here he is also referred to as Teshup of Vashukani, the Mitanni capital. The goddess appears under the ideogram of Ishtar and as Ishtar-star. Shamash, the Sun god, is in both treaties the third godhead immediately after Sin, the Moon god, who is himself preceded by Teshup. The importance of the Moon god, too, lasted down to the Kapara period. In our temple-palace we found a 25-centimetre copper crescent moon in the form of a standard.

It is also significant for Tell Halaf that after two other Teshups there are named along with gods that as yet can hardly be explained those three Babylonic gods Ea, Anu and Enlil, who according to the first tablet of the Gilgamesh epic come on the scene, like Shamash, as Gilgamesh's particular guardian gods. The Gilgamesh legend plays a great part on the Tell Halaf representations. The occurrence of these Babylonian gods in the religion of the Mitanni is easily to be understood for the lasting relations which had doubtless grown up in the middle of the 2nd millennium between Upper and Lower Mesopotamia. On the list there follow the 'Indian' or rather 'East Indo-Germanic' gods Mitra, Varuna, Indra and the Nasatya, which are undoubtedly the old house-gods of the Mitanni

royal family, which kept to them after coming into Subartu and added them to the Subaraic pantheon it found
there and took over.

In a letter of King Tushratta to Amenophis III, written
in Subaraic-Hurritic, the following gods are invoked:
Teshup, the Subaraic chief god, the Lord of Heaven and
Earth, the God of Rain and Storm, Shaushka-Ishtar (the
goddess of Niniveh), Amon (the chief god of Amenophis
III), Simike (perhaps a Syrian god of the town of Ishipe,
which may have lain within the Egyptian king's sphere of
influence), and Easharri.

In another Tell Amarna letter from Tushratta to Amenophis III the Mitanni king names the Sun god and
Shaushka-Ishrat as being the gods who bring blessings on
Pharaoh. They are probably invoked by him just because
they belong to the Mitanni's own pantheon, and also
because the Sun god as Amon-Re was the chief god of the
eighteenth Egyptian dynasty, while the sick Amenophis III
had begged of Tushratta the holy image of Shaushka of
Niniveh that he might be healed through its magic power.
Niniveh at that time lay within the Mitanni king's sphere of
influence. However the idol came too late: the Pharaoh was
already dead. Already, too, in the lifetime of Tushratta's
father, Shuttarna, Ishtar's image had been sent from
Niniveh to Egypt, where it hád been treated with great
honours 'while it dwelt there'. We do not know whether
this divine image came back again to Vashukani and
Niniveh from Egypt after being sent there the second time.
I believe it to be not altogether impossible that the 18.5
centimetre bronze statuette now in the State museum in
Berlin of a goddess standing on a lion and with a child,
which O. Weber has represented in *Orbis Pictus; Hethi-
thische Kunst* may have been this image of Ishtar. The
statuette was bought in Cairo from an Arab dealer. Its date
is estimated by O. Weber at 1750 B.C.; but perhaps it is
older than that. It is quite Subaraic and shows many links
with Tell Halaf art. The representation of the goddess,

who holds a child to her breast, may have something to do with mother-right, which is an integral element in Subaraic culture as opposed to that of the Indo-Europeans and also that of the Semites, among whom there was father-right, not mother-right.

In another letter, too, of Tushratta's we find the names together of 'Shaushka, ruling Lady among the Ladies of my land' and Amon, 'the God of my brother', that is to say the Sun god.

In these letters we are always finding as the three chief gods of Mitanniland, Teshup, Shaushka-Ishtar and Shamash: the Storm god, the Goddess and the Sun god. It is true that the Goddess does not here appear under the name of Hepet; but we know that Hepet or Hepa from oldest times played a special part in the Subaraic culture-complex. Just as the god Teshup meets us in far-off parts of Asia Minor as the chief god, so the goddess Hepa or Hepet is also found in them, and evidently as wife to Teshup, which once more is a token of old Subaraic culture is Asia Minor. In the treaties of the Hittite king Shuppiluliuma with the Mitanni king Mattiuaza, Hepet as the Goddess, plays the chief part. In three cases she is named along with Teshup as the divine being of the same town, and is called the Lady of Heaven. Among the Subaraic names in treaties of Kassite times from Nippur we meet with many confounded with 'Hepa'. The word shows itself too in the names of two Mitanni princesses, who, as was said above, came as queens to the Egyptian court— Giluhepa, daughter of Shuttarna and wife of Amenophis III, and Tutuhepa, daughter of Tushratta and wife of Amenophis III and IV. In the same period a city ruler of Jerusalem bears a name confounded with 'Hepa'. These grounds seem to me enough in themselves to justify our giving the name of Hepet to the goddess, whom we find Teshup's wife on the Tell Halaf sculptures. There is the further consideration that Shaushka, who is the only other one that could come into question, was probably,

so far as we can determine, an Artemis-like virgin
goddess.

The archaeological finds yield us detailed knowledge of
the religious beliefs of Tell Halaf. We find here as the three
chief godheads Teshup, the Great Goddess and the Sun
god. This trinity of the chief gods is shown in the decorative sculpture of the front façade of our temple-palace—
once in the passage through the façade as gigantic figures
on their sacred beasts, and again along the side walls of this
passage, where altars stand before the relief slabs with the
figures of the godheads. This same trinity of gods is found
for a third time on Tell Halaf in a smaller temple in the
town area.

Teshup is the highest god, the Lord of Heaven and the
Earth. His other title of Rain and Storm god expresses one
of his manifestations, and this again is characteristic of the
land of Subartu, especially the Khabur headwaters district: here man is not, as in south Mesopotamia and Egypt,
dependent on artificial irrigation, but on a natural rainfall. It is with rain that Teshup makes the earth bear fruit.
His wife Hepet is also the goddess of Earth. Their child,
the Sun god, rises daily out of the earth.

It is the same chief gods we meet with on the neighbouring Jebelet-el-Beda on stone stelae from the 4th
millennium B.C. (cp. Chapter VIII). Teshup and the Sun
god have been determined beyond all doubt, and they are
posed in the same way as on other Subaraic sculptures:
Teshup standing on the bull sacred to him, and the Sun
god on two human beings. This same trinity of gods then
clearly maintained itself in the same original Subaraic
nature down to the time just before the birth of Christ, as
the great monument on the Nemrud Dagh shows us (cp.
pp. 250 f. below). Nay more: we find this trinity taken over
from Hither Asia into the Roman world along with Jupiter
Dolichenus down to the fall of heathendom at the end of
the third century A.D.

Besides these chief divinities, however, the Subaraic

pantheon owned a great number of lesser gods and goddesses. Some are also named in the treaties between Shuppiluliuma and Mattiuaza.

The Subaraic culture complex is especially rich in demi-gods and demons of the most differing kinds, such as those we meet with especially on the so-called small orthostats of Tell Halaf and in the form of hybrids of men and beasts and hybrids of beasts.

The Subaraic religion is a nature religion. Chief gods, lesser gods, demi-gods and demons are the symbols of natural forces and phenomena. In them we see the cosmic and personal world of the Subaraeans. When we behold the utterly unbelievable statues of Tell Halaf, we think of the sheer dread that enwrapped the divine in the old East, of the fear felt by the believers of that time before their gods, but also we think of the dark mysticism of the East, which expressed itself in the representation and symboliza-tion of natural phenomena by the images of gods and by the hybrid and fabulous beings. To strengthen the power of the wild beasts, limbs from other beasts are added to them. Demi-gods and demons with human heads have bulls' horns growing out of these, or they wear a headgear of horns. This may originally be connected with the divinity of Teshup, to whom the bull was sacred. The addition of wings to men and quadrupeds seems to stand in relation with the Sun god. The eagle and the winged sun disk belong in Subartu to the Sun god. The love of de-picting hybrid beings, and the shapes given them on Tell Halaf are often taken to mad length.

The Statues

The Tell Halaf statues were lying together in a few places. Most of them are for decorating the temple-palace. The biggest and finest were part of the north front. There were relief slabs and sculptures in the round in the gate-way passage; before it stood a gigantic bird. The second passage, too, to the main hall or room had great relief slabs. The south bastions and recesses in the face of the under-structure carrying the temple-palace were faced below with numerous smallish orthostats. The gateway of the temple-palace was flanked by two huge stone slabs on which were depicted scorpion birdmen.

The second place where a find was made lay just east of the citadel gate under a mass of mud bricks in steps standing out into the town area. Here the two throned goddesses had been set up on graves.

The third such place was a room for worship and with

SOUTH SIDE OF THE TEMPLE-PALACE (RESTORED)

figures of gods, in the town area not far from the south town gate just by our expeditionary house.

Finally there were also many sculptures dug up on Tell Halaf of which we could not determine where they had once stood.

Nearly all the statues are of basalt coming from the volcanic Mount Kbise not far away in the Khabur headwaters district. It was only in the case of the small orthostats on the south outer walls of the temple-palace that there was a mixture of limestone and basalt relief slabs. Limestone could be quarried everywhere in our district.

At the citadel gate and the town gate we found no

G

statues; nor did the great Assyrian temple in the town area yield any figure of a god.

In the third chapter I have described how the visitor reached the upper terrace in front of the temple-palace. Before him here there suddenly spread out the mighty view of the great front façade decorated with sculptures. It faced north and was $21\frac{1}{2}$ metres broad. The gateway passage was flanked at the inner line of the arch (the intrados) of its mud-brick walls by two great winged sphinxes. These were each framed to right and left by three relief slabs (orthostat) set below into the wall of the façade and standing upright.

NORTH SIDE OF THE TEMPLE-PALACE (RESTORED)

Within this gateway passage stood the three mighty statues of gods on colossal animals, and together with the two sphinxes split up the entrance to the temple-palace into four rather narrow and very lofty openings. On the two salients at the side of the façade there were more relief slabs, but of them we found only one undamaged and in its place.

The wall surfaces above the lintel of the passage-gate and above the orthostats on the side walls were covered with a smooth plaster, remains from which were still there. It was bright yellow, but I do not think it impossible that the large surfaces were formerly brightly painted, perhaps with yellow or red ochre, whole lumps of which we found in the Kapara layer. Here we could find no fresco painting whatever with pictures such as often came to be customary in later Assyrian times; it would probably hardly have fitted in with the monumental character and the rhythm of the façade.

The first relief slab on the east corner of the façade, to the left of the onlooker, depicts a wild bull hunt (Pl. 8a). The slab is 1.40 metres high and 2 metres long. As in the other larger orthostats on the façade, the artist has here left at the lower edge of the stone a ledge, on which man and beast are standing. A bull moving to the right is being followed by a hunter standing behind him. The figures are rendered, as in all the reliefs on Tell Halaf, in sharp profile. Thus only one ear and one horn are represented of the bull, the horn being almost on the middle of the head. The right fore-leg is half raised and is playing carelessly, but yet touches the ground with its hoof; it is rather out of drawing. The muscles and hair are denoted by conventional scratches.

What is striking are the double lines diminishing like flames as they go up, which represent the folds in the skin or the muscles of the hind-legs, and one found in just the same way in nearly all the animals on Tell Halaf, as also in Old Sumer. Parallel to the line of the back a stroke is drawn with notches underneath it. The muscles in the thigh of the lifted fore-leg are mostly represented by lines rounded on top. Details such as these are characteristic of almost all the representations in relief both on the older small orthostats and on the large ones of the façade. The eyes both of persons and of beasts are always represented as egg-shaped and seen from in front. In the statues of the façade they are without exception of white limestone with a black stone pupil set in it. We were lucky enough to find many such eyes, some of them still in the eye-sockets.

The hunter has the fleshy, much-bent nose of the Subaraic race. He wears a sailor's beard conventionalized into a kind of zigzag: a full beard, that is to say, with a

shaven upper lip; the curled hair is dishevelled and in
spirals, a band goes round the forehead. The head is remarkably big, just as primitive folk in general are wont to
represent everything very large that particularly strikes
the eye or seems to them the most important. The feet are
carved as seen from above, so that the toes seem to lie one
on top of the other. The breast is represented from in front,
the limbs and head from the side. All this is the mark of
archaic sculptures.

The hunter is wearing a shirt that does not quite reach
the knee, and ends in a fringe; over this a coat or mantle,
trimmed likewise along the edge to the side with a fringe,
and leaving the front leg free. The sleeves are short and
end in a border; round the hips is a broad girdle.

The man is bending a bow, and on his left hand rests the
arrow fitted with a big point. The right hand is under the
ear; the arrow and the string are only drawn from the bow
as far as the bowman's face. The man's and the beast's
body are kept from lying athwart one another; this
principle is kept to with the utmost care in all the sculptures on Tell Halaf.

Just as there are several more such hunting pictures on
Tell Halaf, so too they are found on numerous other Subaraic monuments: their makers were a people that loved
to hunt. The bow and arrow are very old; bowmen are
represented on the oldest finds from Sumer and Elam. On
Tell Halaf we found flint and obsidian arrow-heads in the
oldest Painted Pottery layer.

The fine stone with the wild-bull hunt was undamaged
when dug out, but unfortunately it had been by 1927
almost wholly destroyed. Armenian workmen had broken
it up to use as a mill stone; but luckily a cast had been
taken from it during the first season of excavations, so that
it is saved for science.

The stone next to the bull hunt is the orthostat with
winged sun's disk (1.25 metres high, 1.40 metres broad;
Plate 8b). This is the general emblem of the Sun god in the

Subaraic area. A bird of prey flying forwards fills the whole upper part of the slab with its wings. The bird's tail rests on a stand or stool ornamented with four star-shaped rosettes. Right and left of the stool there hang down from the mighty wings limbs bent like rods, the roughly represented legs with the claws bent in flight into a single curve. For the otherwise usual exaggerated spread talons there was no room here. Instead of the bird's body and head there was a dazzling white, slightly convex limestone disk inset, which we found still in position in its frame between the wings.

Two hybrid beings—human above, a bull below—standing opposite each other are carrying the feet of the stool with one hand, while the other, high-stretched, is holding the bird's wings. A man is between the bull-men in a kneeling position, and is holding up their elbows. His feet, as with the bull-hunter, are carved as seen from above. All three figures again have the sailor's beard. The middle one has thick hair falling down to the shoulders, and it curls outwards in two great ringlets. The bull-men have locks conventionalized almost into twisted strings and ending outwards in ringlets, and conical caps flattened on top and adorned with a zigzag pattern. They have two pairs of horns lying flat on the forehead, whose ends turn up midway between the brows. Two great bull's ears stand up by the roots of the horns. These bull-men remind us of the Devil of the legends in human shape with horns, hoof and tail.

The man in the middle is clothed with a short shirt or coat edged below by a fringe; in front this garment bears a vertical decorative band motive, and is held together over the hips by a broad girdle. The bull-men are wearing a long shirt with sleeves and are likewise begirdled. The archaic principle that the figures are not to encroach on one another can also be noted here: thus the right-hand bull-man is standing with the right hoof on the left foot of the man.

A winged sun's disk like this, borne by one or by two figures, or hovering over a tree of life or in the air, is found in numerous modifications on a great many Subaraic representations, sculptures, and above all seal-cylinders, as in Kerkuk, Assur, Asia Minor, and Syria. On some seal-cylinders the disk with wings is substituted by an actual bird's body.

The sun that has become a god is in Subartu thought of as an eagle, and generally represented with outstretched wings as though flying or hovering in the heavens, but often too it is simply represented as a bird in a perched attitude. On our Tell Halaf all these forms can be seen. The winged sun's disk represents the Sun god. In the Sumerian culture-complex the sun is pictured only as it is seen in the heavens, as a disk, often with beams. In Egypt the winged sun's disk instead of bird's feet has uraeus snakes hanging down from the wings, or else snakes and feet. This calls to mind old Babylonian cylinders on which the eagle holds snakes in both claws.

It has up to now generally been assumed that the use of the winged sun's disk in the Subaraic culture comes from later times and was taken over from Egypt. I believe, however, that this sun motive is of a very high antiquity in Hither Asia. There is no doubt that before 3000 B.C. already there were connections between Egypt and Syria and also Mesopotamia. The patterns could thus anyhow have been brought in oldest times from one land to the other. But in Egypt the winged sun's disk does not make its appearance till relatively late—under the fifth dynasty about 2600 B.C.—and is seen to be at once fully formed and conventionalized, while in the earlier times much simpler motives, like those in Babylonia, were used as emblems of the sun.

Quite apart from the fact that the Tell Halaf stones with the winged sun's disk, taking their style into account, are in some cases to be dated as early as about 3000 B.C., this motive bears on the old Subaraic representations much

more than on the Egyptian ones the stamp of the bird. It
has much more the look of being taken from nature and
much less that of being conventionalized. The convex
sun's disk between the outspread wings, seen from in front,
has indeed a likeness to the representation of a bird's body
with the neck and head stretched forward like an arrow.
But the sun blinds, and hence the bird's body and head
are only represented by a disk. In accordance with that
naïve urge, often noticed by us on Tell Halaf, to express
all that is known of the object, not only are the wings then
inserted on each side of the sun's disk, and of course so far
as possible with all the feathers, but so are also the bird's
tail under the disk and by it the claws. That is how the
emblem of the sun appears here on our orthostat. I myself
have shot eagles on the Euphrates by Jerablus whose
wings spanned over two metres. Birds such as these were
the patterns for our representations.

The kneeling posture of the middle figure finds its counterparts in a great number of very old south Mesopotamian and Elamite delineations, as also upon Tell Halaf
itself and on other very old Subaraic sculptures. The position of the bull-men's arms is precisely the same as in
figures which once were looked upon as Gilgamesh, but
which as the result of an inscription that was found are to
be known as 'Talim', that is, brother or comrade of equal
birth, or perhaps twin. The bull-men themselves have
hitherto been held to be 'Engidu figures'.

Before the sun's disk orthostat there was standing a
small round altar-table of basalt, on which pigeons' bones
were still lying; these were the remains of the sacrifice that
had been made to the Sun god at the last moment when
the town was taken. We found the great stone slab, when
digging, with the carved surface underneath and lying on
the altar, separated by a layer of ashes from it and the
pigeons' bones, which had thus been sheltered and preserved for thousands of years.

The third orthostat is a lion pacing to the right (1.50

metres high and 1.80 metres broad; Pl. 9a) with the jaws
opened threateningly. Besides the small teeth and in spite
of the profile position all four great fangs are represented
in front of the lower and upper jaw in twos next one
another, probably to heighten the impression of dread.
The lion's ear lies back in anger. The mane is depicted by
a small pad treated in wickerwork fashion and tufts coming
to a point like flames. The hairs on the belly, in contrast
with the hoofed animals, which have here lines engraved,
are arranged in wickerwork fashion as far as the hind-legs.
For the muscles on the head and the legs the lines are
drawn in a specific way.

In the feet the three right toes are drawn lying one over
the other, the claws looking out and being seemingly set
underneath so that the paws are almost those of a bear.
This springs again from the primitive feeling that nothing
should be left out that is there. We find the likeness with
bear's paws shown in a still higher degree in other representations of lions at Tell Halaf; and the same thing can
be observed in the oldest lions at Senjirli.

The lines under the back and the flame-like expression
of the muscles or the folds in the skin on the thigh of the
hind-leg are in full correspondence with those in the wild
bull. Here we have to do not with the African lion, which
has a much heavier mane, but with the Mesopotamian,
which is not clothed with such thick hair. It once was a
native of the whole of Syria and Mesopotamia, and in
Lower Mesopotamia lasted on into the nineteenth century.

This orthostat is a magnificent specimen of archaic sculpture, and highly realistic. The dread strength of the roar-
ing lion is wonderfully expressed.

On the other side of the passage another lion (1.28
metres high and 2.20 metres broad; Pl. 10b) stands, which
this time of course paces to the left, towards the entrance.
It corresponds to the one pacing to the right, but is lower
and more slender, and has a relatively smaller head. Its
gait too is different—more crouching, more slinking. It

may be that the artist wished to represent a lioness here.
This suggestion is the more likely in that elsewhere too on
Tell Halaf we see both sexes of this beast of prey depicted.
Thus the lion colossus with the huge goddess in the gate-
way passage is female, the colossus on the other hand to
the east is male.

There now follows as the counterpart of the stone with
the winged sun's disk the representation of Teshup, the
highest god of the Subaraeans (1.33 metres high and 0.80
metres broad; Pl. 9*b*). He is one of the few full-face reliefs
of Tell Halaf. The arms are spread out and stretched upwards. In his right hand the god holds a club, in the left a
weapon which must be held to be a bumerang or a throwing-stick. The bumerang we often find throughout the old
Nearer East; in Egypt it is a sacred emblem of royalty; in
the west of northern Africa it is still much used to-day as a
hunting weapon, especially in Morocco when hunting
hares and other small game. Otherwise Teshup generally
carries an axe in one hand, in the other the lightning-
sheaf, the tokens of storm. The bumerang or the throwing-
stick is here substituted for the lightning. The club consists of a short stout stick, whose upper end goes into a
basalt ball. In southern Mesopotamia and in Elam the
club and the bumerang are also found on the oldest monuments.

On Tell Halaf we found many basalt balls with a hole
through them. The natives still use clubs like these as
weapons. In south Mesopotamia there is still in general
use a club having a ball of pitch instead of basalt.

The countenance of the god has a sailor's beard with
two parallel grooved lines below the under-lip. The hair
falls in two outward-curled bunches on to the shoulders.
On the head is a crest of feathers. The upright feathers are
cut off short, their quills are held by a twofold band
around which is a pair of thick bull's horns, whose tips
meet above the forehead. Bull's horns on a human head
are always a token of divinity. Under the horn-cap the

hair on the forehead can be seen. The god is wearing a long coat-like shirt ending below in a fringe, and which again has the short sleeves ended with a border; the coat is fastened together on the hips by a broad girdle.

Here too the feet are as seen from above, and are set right outwards so as to keep the idea of the full face position.

Before the god once stood a horse-shoe altar of basalt, which was so made that the head of the sacrificial beast could be laid upon it.

The Teshup seen from in front, which we also meet with on another Tell Halaf stone, is quite alone in its kind, for otherwise in Subartu he is always represented in profile. Here, however, the god had to be looking into the sacrificer's face. The wild expression on the face, which can be read in spite of a slight mutilation, and the lifted weapons, are meant to bring the might of the god before the eyes of the sacrificer and worshipper. With his inset eyes he stares into the worshipper's face. As the god of Rain bringing blessings, so as the god of Thunder he awakens dread. Before the Lord of Heaven and Earth, the highest Power, even the King quails. The religions of the old Nearer East know little of a divine love, but stress the fear of the gods.

After the Teshup comes a bigger broad orthostat with the representation of a stag hunt (1.50 metres high and 1.82 metres broad; Pl. 10*b*) as the counterpart of the bull hunt. The left part of this stone after my trial digging in 1899 was smashed by natives. The arrangement and conventions are in essentials the same as in the bull hunt, save only that the stag turns its head backward towards the hunter. The horns, in spite of the beast being seen from the side are, as almost always in the case of stags, represented from front view.

There now follow two narrower and lower basalt slabs without any sculptures, set in so as in a measure to bring the breadth of the western wall decoration into agreement with that of the eastern.

Then in the right hand corner of the façade and against the jutting tower stands a large orthostat (1.55 metres high and 1.90 metres broad; Pl. 10*b*) with a hybrid being on it. It is a combination of man and lion, bird and bull. The body is in profile, the bearded man's head is full face. The mighty wing is half unfolded, and rises above the whole length of the lion's back. The breast has not the flame-like tufts of hair which the lions on the façade have, but shows the downward-directed scale motive which we find again in representations of birds. The head has the sailor's beard, which at its roots has conventionalized ringlets. From the forehead right and left spring two heavy bull's horns, which run along by the head. The hair or a wig falls, as with the bull-men on the orthostat with the sun's disk, on to the shoulders in heavy tresses curled outwards. The head-dress, too, is like the bull-men's, but here there are parallel waved lines, and it ends in a flat knob at the tip, which is only slightly conical. In spite of the bull's horns on the head itself the head-gear has also two pairs of horns. Unfortunately the face when the stone was found in 1899 was already greatly damaged; and in 1911 there were only parts of the slab left. When in 1899 I had uncovered the statues without the district being again stricken with the misfortune which the natives had feared, they tried to break up some of the stones under the delusion that there were treasures or gold in them. When it turned out that this was not the case, Chechens made mill-stones out of the stag-hunt and the winged lion-man and then filled up the holes again. Luckily I was able to reconstruct both these valuable reliefs with the help of the photographs of 1899 and the fragments still left.

The representation of a winged lion with a human head, bull's horns growing on it, and a cap with horns, is unknown to antiquity. In a later Assyrian text a set of fabulous beings is described, one of which fits our sculpture; but the name, unluckily, is broken off in it, so that we are not told what was the meaning of this being.

On the wall of the tower next to the last sculpture there was still room for another relief slab facing the façade; but we could not find anything left of it. As the counterpart to the winged lion with a human head there were on the east tower in the corner made with the façade wall the remains of a big orthostat with the hind feet of a hoofed beast walking to the left. There is, however, too little left for any interpretation to be made.

On all the stones of the side wall of the façade is Kapara's inscription, obviously cut where it had seemed most convenient to the stone-carver.

Among the most important sculptures of Tell Halaf are the two great statues that stand in the archway of the passage to the first room in the temple-palace, that is to say, at the section of the mud-brick wall with the façade reliefs. They are veiled winged sphinxes, parts of which I found as early as 1899. They were so set into the arch of the gateway passage that their fore-part stood out about 0.90 metres in front of the façade into the open, and their flanks made with the mud wall in the gateway arch a continuous surface. The façade wall was, however, thicker than the length of the sphinxes, so that the view of them from behind was hidden by the brickwork. In front the statues are treated in the round, at the sides as reliefs.

The eastern orthostat in the arch (Pl. 11), in spite of some damaged parts, may be looked on as wholly preserved; it is 2.20 metres long. The side is 1.23 metres high; the huge head of the sphinx rises 35 centimetres above the upper edge of the row of orthostats on the façade wall.

A lot of small bits from the upper surface of the relief at the side, especially from the wing, had been splintered off the basalt block when the temple was burned down; but we found them nearly all again. The front part of the sphinx is worked out in a different way to any other of the statues on Tell Halaf. Over the well-chiselled lion's paws—which here again are like bear's paws—the legs rise up like square pillars, and end above directly in the disproportion-

PLATE XI. THE VEILED SPHINX ON THE EAST

Plate XIIa. Huge Lioness in the Façade Passage-way

Plate XIIb. Stand on the Huge Bull in the Façade Passage-way

ately large woman's head, which stands up from the almost flat line of the back between the pillar-like legs.

Here nothing can be seen of any muscles. The look of
the whole reminds us of the later Hermae or of pillar-gods.
On the front of the left leg-pillar Kapara's inscription is
chiselled running downwards.

The head is a masterpiece of old sculptor's art. The flat
chin is strongly retreating. The nose, long and pointed in
profile, forms, when looked at from one side, an unbroken
lightly curved line with the retreating forehead and the
upper part of the head. Involuntarily we are reminded of
the beak-faces of the seal-cylinders and tablets from the
oldest south Mesopotamia, but above all of the huge stele
of Jebelet-el-Beda (cp. Chapter VIII). The hair on the
head is set in curls. Round the forehead clings a band,
which seems to be tied behind the head and ends in two
hanging tassels. On this band there hang alternatively
longer and shorter strips, whose lower ends turn backwards in a spiral, and which beyond the ears cover all the
back of the head. There are the same kind of bands, only
thicker, just before each ear. Round the neck, a hand's
breadth under the chin, strips hang down here. Under the
band on the forehead tufts of hair are chiselled from ear
to ear.

The mouth is marked only by a narrow line; the lips are
barely shown. What is different from all the other Tell
Halaf statues is the eyes. Instead of a big white inset, in
which a small flat round polished centre of black stone is
inlaid as the pupil, we have here an oval black stone centre,
markedly standing out, filling almost the whole eye-socket,
and with a narrow white ring round it. One of these eyes
I found *in situ* when I made the discovery in 1899, and I
was able to save it.

The face has decidedly something mystical about it.
The eyes look far darker than any other inset eyes at Tell
Halaf. From the very first moment I was convinced that I
had a veiled goddess before me. She does not see so well

through the veil, and so her eye is darker, blacker, more piercing. That the artist meant to represent a veil is furthermore shown beyond any questioning by the band on the forehead with the two ends hanging down at the back of the head and emphasized by tassels. The veil makes the effect of a headdress. To-day veils quite like this one are worn on the upper Tigris, in Mosul, for instance. Exactly as on the statue they are kept in place by a band on the forehead. A knot is tied behind the head, and the ends have tassels or silverwork, which are let hang down behind. On the right and left sides these veils are bound with a white ribbon; the veil itself is of black horsehair. It has a slight curve from the forehead to its lower end under the chin and from right to left across the face. As in the statue it reaches up to the ears or covers them. This Mosul veil is the same as the sphinx's, down to the smallest details; only wanting are the small hanging strips on the forehead band and below. Veils like this with all kinds of ornaments hanging down in front are found in many other parts of Islam.

That the mouth, nose, and eyes, as well as the hair under the forehead band, are represented in the veiled goddess is quite in agreement with how the veil is depicted in antiquity. In Egypt, under the garments of veiling, the breast, navel and limbs were drawn so as to be fully visible. But we have only to think too of modern sculptures of veiled persons in Italian graveyards; here also in spite of the veiling we can see the forms, and even the details of the faces.

In this sphinx we have the oldest veiled statue in the world: there is no other of its kind. A face-veil has up to now never been found anywhere in the ancient world before Greece, But the ancient world knew the use of the veil from earliest times. In the Gilgamesh epic the goddess Siduri, who dwells by the Mediterranean and to whom Gilgamesh comes in his search after the herb of life, wears a garment which is read to be a shift, but also to be a veil.

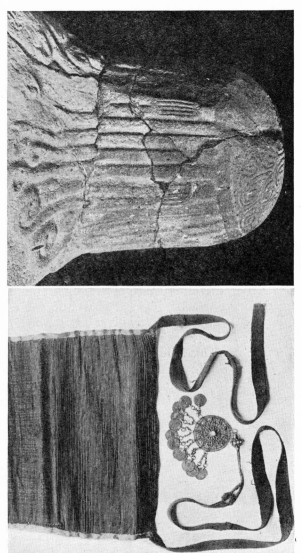

(a) Back of the Veiled Sphinx's Head with the Band of the Veil tied.   (b) Veil from Mosul

In the Subaraic cultural area we have in stone reliefs a set of women represented sitting at a death-meal and wearing a veil thrown back over the head. In the middle Assyrian law book the veil is found as the mark of the reputable woman as contrasted with the unveiled temple harlot. I will not here go further into a discussion of the ancient myths of the veil. I have briefly discussed the subject in my book, *Tell Halaf and the Veiled Goddess* (Old Orient Series, 1902). Professor Alfred Jeremias, however, has given a more detailed account of the subject under the title of *The Veil: from Sumer up to the Present Time* (Old Orient Series, 1931).

The veil also appears in other forms at Tell Halaf. I can see also in the small crouching women's statuettes of the Painted Pottery layer in the painting about the head the representation of a veil. On Syro-Hittite seal-cylinders, too, we often find divinities with a veil or garment they are lifting so as to bare themselves to the eye.

The relief on the side surface of the veiled sphinx shows a winged lion. The artist looks at his statue half sideways from the front, and accordingly gives it both the hind-legs, but from the side view he makes only the side of the left fore-leg appear. This is in contrast to later Assyrian embossed colossi—bull-men and lion-men: they are copied from ours, but in them there are represented on the side-surface four legs in motion, although the front, which is carved as a statue in the round, shows both the beast's fore-feet. Thus on the Assyrian embossed colossi five feet are to be seen. In the Tell Halaf statues everything is more realistic. The beast has only four legs, and so in spite of the combination of sculpture in the round and relief only four are depicted. This is old Subaraic.

Otherwise the relief has the same characteristics as the large orthostats, the same graven lines to depict the muscles, the plaited work to show the hair under the lion's body. Almost the whole flank of the lion's body on the great relief slab coming after the passage is covered by a

mighty wing. It has a scaly-patterned flat length on top of
it of covering feathers, such as the winged lion-man of the
front façade has on its breast. From this wing the rest of the
longer feathers spread out fanwise in two separate rows.

The sphinx's whole body is treated wholly in the flat.
Under the line of the belly the stone goes back sharply at
a right angle. The free surface left underneath between
the fore-leg and the first hind-leg is filled in with a fighting
scene as an independent relief. This picture is a very lively
one, and worked out with the greatest care and delicacy.
Like the other sculptures of Tell Halaf it shows the marks
of an early art.

Two groups are shown. To the left behind the sphinx's
fore-leg a man facing right is fighting against an upraised
winged lion whose head, unluckily, is missing. Perhaps we
have here a griffin and the lion had a bird's head. The
other group shows a man, likewise facing right, with four
wings, who with his left hand is holding up the right
paw of a lion with wide-open jaws, and is about to pierce
it with his short broad sword. In the free space between
this lion and the first hind-leg of the veiled sphinx a
smaller beast is represented springing; its fore-feet are on
the lion's back. Its mouth is shut; the network of lines
under the belly is here wanting. What is depicted is a great
hunting-dog helping the winged man in his fight. We have,
too, on a small orthostat, a hunting-dog represented in
exactly the same way springing upon a wild bull, perhaps,
as here, the object at the same time to fill in a space.

Furthermore not only has Tell Halaf in this statue given
us something new with the veiling, but also representations
below the great body of a beast on the same slab are new;
we find them on Tell Halaf in the case of other stone
colossal beasts also.

The back of the thick stone slab is also worked, although
only slightly and in a cubistic way. The lion's tail falls downward from the straight surface of the back, and is continued
on the great surface of the side, where it lies between the

H

hind-legs. Here it is bent backwards like a hook. But when the stone was set up in the archway of the passage at the time of the Kapara palace there was nothing to be seen of the sculpture behind the stone, as this sculpture was covered by the masonry of the façade wall, which was thicker than the length of the stone. This also is a sign of the sculptures having been used over again afterwards.

The front of the façade wall touched the right shoulder of the veiled sphinx. So far as the right side of the beast's body could be seen, it showed exactly the same sculpture work as was on the large surface of the gateway passage, that is to say, parts of the wing, which here too pointed backwards. The veiled sphinx was met in the east of the façade wall and at right angles by the lion pacing towards the right. Thus the sculpture here became part of the architecture.

The use of carved orthostats for casing the foot of the outside walls of buildings belongs to Subaraic culture. They served to support and preserve the buildings, which in Subartu are made not from baked bricks but only from sun-dried bricks, and protected them from the rain-storms and cloud-bursts, that come so often in the 'upper land', and which the wind so often lashes against the walls for hours together. In Sumer, which has little stone, there were no such orthostats. Here the houses and palaces were built of baked bricks.

The Assyrians took over the use of orthostats from their earlier Subaraic times, and as a result of renewed influences later from the west, although they had not so much practical inducement to do so. Orthostats were for the Subaraeans, who were so original in their artistic fealings and—as is seen from the painted pottery—were fond of playfully altering every motive, the great field for representing in sculpture all that delighted their hearts: their world, their religion, their fights and hunts. Thus did sculpture become part of architecture.

In Subartu was also invented the orthostat which in the

gateway passage leans against the vaulting of the door, and with its fore part stands far out beyond the main wall as sculpture in the round. We meet with it in the Subaraic cultural area as an animal colossus and as a hybrid figure. Tell Halaf, so full of surprises, besides the veiled woman-sphinxes, had also other orthostats in the vaulting such as are found nowhere else. These statues were at the same time gate warders. In Assyria the hybrid beings watching over the gate are called Lamassu; here they always have the divine crown of horns on the human head.

From the treaties already referred to between Shuppilu-liuma and Mattiuaza we know that these Lamassus, there written with the ideogram *KAL*, represented gods. This is highly important in the explanation of our statue and a further proof that the veiled sphinx must have been the representative of Hepet. Later we shall have to come back again to the question how the hybrid nature of the sphinx arose.

In the veiled sphinx the omnipotence of the great goddess is vividly brought home to the onlooker. Even we men of to-day cannot escape the mysterious power in these extraordinary eyes, the mysterious power of the face with its narrow lips, its peculiar expression, and the great veiled head rising directly on the pillars of the legs. To the old Subaraeans the veiling of the 'great goddess' was a much more familiar idea than to ourselves. The legend of the veiled sphinx in Egypt, in possession of all knowledge and with its claws tearing to pieces anyone lifting its veil, has been branded as an invention of the Greek traveller Plutarch. Who can tell whether the neighbouring Hither Asia, whence so much came to the land of the Nile, did not give the Egyptians this legend also from the Subaraic stock? The woman divinity, the Great Goddess, the mother of other gods, the bestower of fruitfulness, is among the Subaraeans worshipped also as a wild goddess of the hunt, and not only as men-loving but also as men-slaying. We do not know whether or not human sacrifices were made to her. In the gate passage of the temple-palace she is standing on a lioness; griffins are here among her beasts. In our sphinx her head is set immediately on the animal body, and under the lion's body demons and lions are fighting one another.

Before the sphinx, too, there stood a horse-shoe sacrificial altar (which we found still in its place), as there was before the Teshup on the west side of the façade. Small statues of squatting women from the Painted Pottery layer and many other finds, however, point to Hepet having been worshipped as the goddess of Love on Tell Halaf also.

The veiled sphinx must be looked at from in front. The altar stands at its feet. The great winged side is only an accessory detail. The statue is one of the most noteworthy and interesting known to us from the Nearer East, and stands alone in its kind.

The western intrados orthostat in the passage of the temple-palace is the counterpart of the veiled sphinx. Its human head had been found by the Chechens when they had been thinking of burying the dead man on Tell Halaf at the time we have already spoken of. They had destroyed the head and thrown it into the Khabur. In 1899 the left cheek had been retrieved out of the water for me, and I was able to take a photograph of this fragment then. In 1911 the right side of the head was found in the river. No more bits could be found, but from these two it can be shown beyond all doubt that the head exactly corresponded with the unharmed one of the eastern veiled sphinx. Of the mighty body a great part was still left; it was just as big as that of the eastern hybrid being. The lower part still left of the fore-legs shows the same square pillar-like shape, with underneath the lion's paws like those of a bear. Here too the horse-shoe altar was standing before it *in situ*.

The side surface turned towards the gateway passage is very much damaged, but we found remains of the wing on the lion's body. The representation under the latter was still quite whole; it shows animals fighting. On the right is a hoofed animal turned leftwards with branching antlers seen from in front, which are smaller than a deer's. It is probably a large steinbock (ibex). Again it has that lazily lifted fore-leg we know from the bull-hunt; at him is springing a winged hybrid being, a lion with a horn on the head and with outstretched paws. Over the back is a great wing. Instead of the hind-legs and the tail of the lion there are a bird's feet and a bird's tail. Here the whole execution is simpler and also not so skilful as in the other veiled sphinx. There is less room for the picture between the sphinx's legs.

On the side of the stone laid against the mud wall of the temple-palace in the vaulting, we found, remarkable to say, another carving. Here we can recognize the two hind-legs and the lower part of the body of a lion, but only roughly carved. The lion was a good deal higher up than it was on the other side of the stone in the gateway passage. The sculptor had not yet finished off his work on the side of the stone hidden in the wall. It is evident that there had once been the intention to carve some other subject out of the block of basalt, which had then been given up.

The passage way, rather over 9 metres wide, between the two veiled sphinxes was broken up by three huge animal colossi of basalt. In the east-to-west direction there stood here a lion, a bull, and lioness (Pl. 12a). The animal colossi are, like the sphinxes, about 3 metres long. On them stood giant figures of gods. The lion and the lioness bore high rectangular bases which were one with the body. In the bull this cube formed a separate intervening part with a pin of its own, which formerly was inserted into the bull's back.

When the temple was burnt down, the statues of the gods fell off the bases, forwards on to the ground, where we found them to some extent in pieces. Two of them had been protected through the burning beams that had fallen earlier and through the surface of the roof covering these, and remained relatively very well preserved in their parts.

Only the third statue, the one that stood in the middle, was quite ruined. The animal colossi, too, have suffered great damage in parts. The pedestal blocks and the upper part of the backs have been split off from one another; the other parts, however, were more or less unharmed. Enough was there for them to be faultlessly reconstructed. It was only in the case of the rectangular blocks that so much was missing that we could not restore every detail. In the case of the lion's head it was found that part of the jaws had already been put together by Kapara. For we found pieces which showed deep squared plug-holes for metal clamps. This again is one of the many proofs that Kapara brought out his statues from an earlier layer and only used them over again.

The animal colossi, standing in detachment, are treated quite archaically; they, too, seen from the front are as sculpture in the round, but seen from the sides they are as reliefs. Perhaps the artist who carved them was a little further advanced than the sculptor of the veiled sphinx. The fore-legs are no longer like angular pilasters, but they are still in the nature of pillars. The breast is strongly arched, the lion's paws are again like a bear's.

Between the fore and the hind-legs the stone is not chiselled away. The belly does not, as in an animal standing upright, hang in the air, but rests on the block of stone thus left. The belly does not pass over at a right-angle into the side surface running back under it but does so in a gentle curve; this side surface as with the sphinxes is adorned with reliefs.

In other respects the details are carried out in the same way as in the great reliefs on the orthostats of the façade: this is so with the hair, the flame-like tufts of the lion's mane, the network of hair under the belly, the folds of the neck in the bull, the notched strips under the back; but the leg muscles are carried out in high relief. The back has a heavy net-like coat of hair; the tails hang straight down behind, where there is not so much work.

Here, too, in principle everything is carried out from the front point of view. Regard is paid to sculpture in the round, so that on the reliefs at the sides only one fore-leg and one hind-leg are shown. Thus once more the Subaraic principle—work strictly true to nature—is followed; the animal that stands clear has only four legs. The bodies rest in front firmly and steadily on the strong legs; the heads are relatively very large.

The head of the lion and of the lioness is very broad. The jaws are opened threateningly; the upper lips, which below are cut straight off, are represented by parallel grooved lines. The tusks are exceptionally strong, the lower ones being rather rounded, the upper ones almost triangular. The tongue hangs down over the lower lip. In the lion the small incisors are represented, but in the lioness they are wanting. The ruff or frill on the neck is shown by a roll or cushion. The lioness is somewhat under-set at the hind-quarters, so that she looks somewhat slenderer, although, strangely enough, the fore-part of the body is perhaps heavier built than the lion's. It is important to note that the lion stretches his fore-legs slightly forward and thus gives more an impression of weight, while the lioness draws them back a little and looks stealthier.

The eyes of the three animal colossi are set in and of a disproportionate size.

The scenes on the reliefs under the belly are the same on both sides for all the beasts. In the lion it is a stag lying on its back seen from the side and with the pluck hanging out. The stag's ten antlers are seen from the front, and the two branches spread evenly right and left. The stag's mouth is open, the tongue is hanging out, and the eyes are shut. The hind-legs are stretched backwards convulsively; one of the fore-legs is stretched forwards, the other backwards. The whole representation is surpassingly realistic.

With the lioness we see a whelp facing her hind-legs and sucking at its mother's udder. In its joy it has lifted a paw and its tail. Behind it hangs a small animal—probably, by its twisting horns, which in spite of the representation in profile stand apart, a steinbock (ibex)—likewise with its bowels hanging out, and probably, like the stag, meant as feed for the great lioness.

The representation under the bull is fitted to it. Behind the fore-feet stands a low, bush-like palm, towards which a fleeing gazelle leaps. Behind the beast stands the pursuer with stretched bow. The muscles in these reliefs are again drawn with grooved lines.

The bull is the mightiest of the animals. The powerful head in every way recalls those we meet in Old Sumer, especially in Ur. Accordingly in putting the statue of the animal together I have added a white blaze of curled hair to a triangular depression in the forehead, as is found in all the bulls' heads in Ur. The blaze on Tell Halaf was, I assume, of white limestone in contrast with the black basalt. The ears, no longer there, were set into square plug-holes.

The front of the plinth in the case of the bull, as also the lower parts of its side reliefs, show the well-known upward turned scale motive, by which from oldest times in the Nearer East, formations of the ground or of mountains are expressed.

All four sides of the cubic pedestal on the lion's back, on which a giant figure of a god once stood, were adorned with figures of musicians, two on each of them. On the front and on the right, on a large piece of the cube still joined to the lion's body, is represented a man in a long robe holding in his uplifted hand a tambourine. The feet are turned out, the head and right side are missing. On his left a second personage must have stood, of whom only a foot is now left. Of the back of the pedestal only a fragment is left, on which the feet of two persons can be made out. On the side surfaces there are still remains of two other musicians. One is holding a five-stringed lyre, the other a tambourine.

The lioness's pedestal shows on its four sides the remains

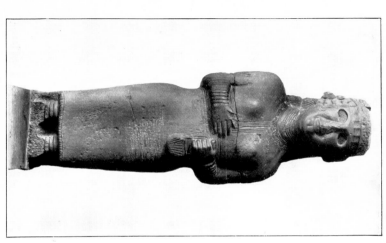

Plate XIII. Gateway Passage in the Temple-Palace Façade

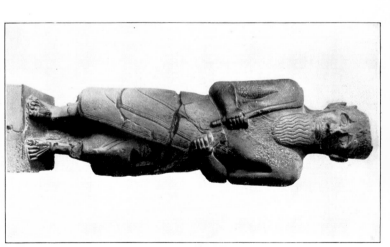

Plate XIV. The Great Sunbird

of griffins. The bull's pedestal we found lying on the ground. The back had split away; on the three other surfaces there were remains of riding scenes. Particularly vigorous is the almost unspoiled relief of a crouching man with a round shield who is reining in a horse. On the side next this a warrior with shield flinging himself backwards is holding in a horse that is trying to get free. The upper parts of this scene are unluckily no longer preserved. On the third side are the remains of a man on horseback.

On the blocks on the three animal colossi stood the three giant statues of gods, ending below in square pedestal slabs with pins or plugs. The surface of the plinths corresponded with that of the blocks on the animals into which they were let.

From the lie of the statues it could be seen that a man's belonged to the lion, and a woman's to the lioness. These two were fairly well preserved. Of the man's statue that had stood on the bull only fragments were left.

Each of the giant statues is carved from a single block of basalt. The mean height from head to plinth is 2.60 metres. The male figures stand bolt upright. With a swell at the shoulders and hips, they have otherwise the look of cylindrical pillars. The top of the heads is flattened and exactly parallel to the pedestal. So as to make this surface horizontal the back of the head was brought high up. On the back of the statues only the heads and hanging hair are carved, but this is done in great detail. The line of the back narrows at the waist.

The feet are slightly apart, the left one a little in front of the right. The axis of the figures was so well calculated that the tall stone bodies were in the right position for equilibrium on their pedestals. In the case of the completely preserved man's figure the greater part of the pedestal was left; in the woman's figure the part in front was missing. Later we found one of the goddess's feet, which was bare.

It is of interest to compare these with a smaller statue of a god which stood in the hall for worship in the area of our town. It corresponded almost exactly to the huge god. It was still standing in its place of old on a stone pedestal, to which it was firmly fastened with a plug and by lead being poured in.

In the same way also our giant gods were probably fastened to the cubes on the animal bases, and the cylindrical tops to the heads of the supporting figures with lead.

The surface on the head of the figures of the gods had a deep squared plug-hole. It was not till 1929 that we found a high round top, slightly tapering conically upwards, and carefully smoothed, whose pin or plug fitted exactly into the plug-hole of the giant god on the lion. It was broken off above, and the height of what was left was 60 centimetres. We also found the remains of like conical cylinders, but tapering upwards more sharply, which at their narrow ends had a smaller plug-hole as though to take a corbel, and probably belonged to the two other giant gods. There can be no doubt that these pieces stood on the heads of the statues, and were the connections between the statues and the timber work of the gate lintel.

The heads of the statues are too big for the bodies. The shoulders are very broad and high, the arms extraordinarily thick and set flat to the body; the arm below the elbow is more or less at right angles to the upper part.

Both figures are wearing ribbon-like diadems. The pattern on the man's diadem is made up of seven-leaved rosettes alternating with conventionalized palm-trees; on the woman's diadem of six- and seven-leaved rosettes alternating with conventionalized palms and *butm*-trees (*Pistacia terebinthus*) lying across one another, which are divided from one another by being coffered in cross-lines.

The head of the man's figure (Pl. 13*b*) shows quite the same type as the carvings in relief. The face is broad, the nose (which is unfortunately somewhat damaged) is hooked, the cheeks are full, the lips are strong and stand out, the line of the mouth does not show much. The ears stand out big and strong from the head and have holes for earrings. The beard has strands hanging in waves that end above and below in curls. The upper lip shows a conventionalized fish-bone moustache.

The hair of the head falls in parallel zigzag lines on to the shoulders and fairly far down the back, where it ends in three heavy rows of curls one over the other. The big inlaid eyes have a small black pupil within a broad white edging.

Above the ears a pair of thick horns, the mark of divinity, comes from the head under the diadem; they must have met in the middle over the forehead like the horn caps; the tips are broken off.

The clothing consists of a shirt with short sleeves. Both shirt and sleeves end in a border with a hanging fringe. Over it is the so-called Cappadocian cloak, which leaves the right shoulder and the left leg free, is rounded off below, and reaches nearly to the feet. It ends off in three slanting flounces, one above the other, whose edge shows a pattern made up of triangles facing one another. Cloak-like garments such as these seem to have been put round the body like a shawl. As the back was only worked smooth the hang of the cloak behind cannot be observed.

The right arm, which lies close to the breast, is holding a bumerang with a loop hanging from below it. The top end lies on the right shoulder. This shouldering of the weapon is a very old Subaraic way; we find it on small orthostats and on other Tell Halaf statues, as also on Jebelet-el-Beda, which, indeed, is closely linked with Tell Halaf, and in south Mesopotamia, too, as in the Digdigi terra-cottas.

The left hand, which is held lower than the right, is grasping the pommel of a long sword, which follows the curve of the body. We find the same great sword on the Subaraic statues, such as the old statues of gods at Senjirli-Sham'al and Jerablus-Karkemish.

On the feet are sandals with toe-thongs. The remains of the second statue of a man, which belonged to the bull, showed that it corresponded almost exactly with the undamaged figure. What distinguished the two was that the border of the shirt had conventionalized palms and rosettes instead of the plain fringe; doubtless this was to mark the figure as being a higher god. Furthermore, the hand holding the bumerang is more skilfully conventionalized and heavier than that of the undamaged god. As a whole this middle figure was carried out somewhat more strongly.

The great statue of a woman (Pl. 13a) was got out almost whole; it had split into only a few pieces.

The face is round, and has the soft lines with dimples and folds in the chin. Part of the nose is missing. The thick hair falls in separate locks down the back. The arrangement of the hair on the forehead and at the sides is quite unique. Parallel horizontal lines under the diadem run across the forehead and then just short of the ears turn sharp down, and finally run together into a plait or curl going over the shoulders and there joining the other hair. The hair, which frames the face above and at the sides, is given a waved look by cross lines.

The goddess's neck is adorned with five rows of beads. The upper three are made up of round beads, while the two lower ones are made up of rather long, flat ones and also smaller beads. Four heavy bracelets round the wrists and three round the ankles make up the rest of the ornaments. The feet have no sandals.

The body is wholly clothed. The style of the garment is hard to determine, mainly because here too the back of the statue is left unworked. It seems to be a long gown leaving in front the ankles free and behind reaching as far as the ground. It was, anyhow from the hips down, divided, the right side being folded over the left. On the shoulders hangs a cape fastened together at the neck: its forepart, which is edged with several rows of trimming, falls down over the breast. It must have been longer behind. Only the lower part of the arms comes out from it. The gown ends at the side in a hatched edging, below it ends in one with a small fringe. It may be that the side edging too should show a hanging fringe. What I am not clear about is an edging that runs right under the lower part of the two arms. It makes the continuation of the hem of the cape, but has no true right to be here. Possibly, however, the garment is really some kind of cloak that was open in front, had a kind of cross slit cut out for the lower part of the two arms, and came down to the ground.

The top hem of the garment is adorned with a neck-ornament made up of half-moons and six- and seven-leaved rosettes. In actual clothing ornaments such as these were undoubtedly made of embossed gold sewn on to the stuff.

The ears are pierced for earrings. In the left hand the woman is carrying something that looks like a small bag. I think, however, that here we have a vessel and handle rendered in the flat, and made of copper or other metal. We found vessels shaped very like this on Tell Halaf, made of copper and also of blue frit, though without any handle. Anyhow the vessel has a meaning for worship.

The likeness of the goddess on the lioness to the Attic over life-size statue of a standing woman from the sixth century in the Old Museum in Berlin is quite astounding. It is only the drapery that is different; also the position of the hands, which otherwise have the same stiff expression, is turned about: here it is the right hand that holds the vessel, and the left that is held stiffly before the body. But the stern bearing, the raised head wearing a low cylindrical diadem that has an almost horizontal top, the remarkable arrangement of the hair—all this is so like our Tell Halaf statue that one cannot but deem the Attic goddess to be of its line.

The two men's statues had the divine bull's horns but the goddess had not. In the same way a god represented on a copper mould on Tell Halaf has bull's horns, while the goddess has none.

The upward tapering cylindrical head-pieces along with the diadem below them make up the head-covering of the giant godheads. This head-covering is like those in the procession of the gods at Yazylykaya; but while there it slopes backwards, with our gods on their animal bases it goes straight upwards in order that the purpose of the figures— to be the carriers of the roof timber-work—may be fulfilled. We know of cylindrical head-coverings elsewhere, too, in the Subaraic culture-complex.

Through the finding of the cylindrical head-pieces the reconstruction of the whole façade (see title page) becomes a matter beyond any doubt. Their being fastened to the roof-beams helped at the same time to hinder the statues falling from the backs of the animals' bodies.

The three statues undoubtedly represent godheads, namely the three highest gods of Tell Halaf. The chief figure, that in the middle, was Teshup. He stood on the beast sacred to him, the bull. To the onlooker's right stood the female godhead, Hepet (or whatever the name was she bore on Tell Halaf) on the lioness sacred to her. To the left of the onlooker stood the Sun god on the lion sacred to him. We find the same order in the arrangement, too, of the godheads in the hall of worship in the town area.

The drawings on the blocks between the animal colossi and the figures of the gods belong to the range of ideas associated with each god: the armed horseman on the bull to Teshup, the griffins to the goddess, the musicians on the lion to the Sun god.

On the great orthostats of the façade also this Tell Halaf trinity of gods is brought before our eyes once more: to the right or west, Teshup in the conventional representation, here with the club and bumerang. On the left the Sun god as the winged sun's disk. The goddess is found twice in the form of the veiled sphinx as an orthostat in the archway. Before these godheads stood the altars on which the offerings were made. It was impossible to make offerings before the statues of the gods on the animal colossi, since to do so would have meant hindering those going through the entrance to the temple-palace.

Everything points to there having been in front of the

façade, resting on wooden columns, a roof, under which the sacrificial acts were carried out. We found on the paved terrace before the façade a good many small drum-shaped bases of columns made of basalt lying about, on which, I think, the wooden columns of the structure in front had stood which were destroyed in the fire. The projecting towers, also adorned with statues, at the ends of the façade shut in the great bay at the sides and gave the place an enclosed character befitting acts of worship, while the wooden roof made it rain-proof.

On the giant gods and on the animal colossi were longish inscriptions with Kapara's name. Even more so than on the great orthostats they had quite clearly been carved here at a later time wherever there happened to be room for it—with the giant goddess this was in front on the drapery, with the giant god, whose garment arranged in folds left nowhere else, it was on the left shoulder, and with the animal colossi it was next the lines of the ribs on the reliefs at the sides.

The standing of gods on beasts is (if I may say so again) a thing of very great antiquity, and one found extremely often in the Subaraic culture-complex. We find this motive already on the huge double stelae of Jebelet-el-Beda. The great figure of Teshup Adad in Senjirli stands on a base with two lions led by a kneeling man; and the Moloch-like seated god of Karkemish is on a base of two lions exactly like it. Both statues are of the same age as our animal colossi, but the lions are smaller in differing degrees than those on Tell Halaf.

Otherwise we find gods standing on beasts as sculpture in the round only in quite small statuettes and on seal-cylinders. On rocky walls, too, there are often found reliefs with gods on their beasts, from Lesser Asia (Asia Minor) as far as Western Persia, but these representations also are much smaller than on Tell Halaf. Such mighty sculptures in the round of this kind are nowhere else to be found in Hither Asia. Further there is the fact of their being used in our case as caryatids, which itself also stands alone.

The impression made by the façade on the onlooker must have been quite overpowering. Even to-day for us civilized men the effect is one of utter surprise. In olden times to the wonder aroused by the mighty monument was further added the dread felt before the gods that showed themselves to the visitor in such huge stature. Here architecture and sculpture unite in a way that fills us, too, with astonishment to make a unified, harmonious whole such as up to now has come to light nowhere else in the Nearer East. It is only the entrance to the rock temple at Abu Simbel in Upper Egypt that may perhaps be compared with this; it belongs to the time of Rameses II (1312-1246 B.C.).

The whole artistic impression of the façade and its passage is so great that from this alone it is at once seen that it was thus and not otherwise that the temple face must have been willed to be, that it was thus that it must have been thought out beforehand. I am convinced that the façade was from the beginning built as we found it. E. Herzfeld puts the date for the making of the animal colossi in the times of the dynasty of Akkad (about 2700 B.C.), the date of the statues of the gods at about 2500 B.C., that is more or less in Gudea's lifetime. Thus the statues of the gods would in my opinion have been made at that time to replace earlier stone figures that have been lost, and which, like the new ones, had stood as caryatids on the animal colossi in the passage through a façade. Several centuries later the old palace disappeared, and just as we to-day, 3000 years after its rebuilding by Kapara, have been able to find again most of the statues in their places, so did Kapara, 1000 or 1200 years after the disappearance of the earlier building, dig the statues and relief-slabs out of the Painted Pottery layer. Many cases of slight damage to the giant statues, I am convinced, were done already in the old times. Our finds showed that Kapara simply

THE GREAT FRONT FAÇADE (RESTORED)

I

used many of the old statues over again with their old fractures. In the great lion the lower jaw, as we said above, had plug-holes, showing that repairs had been made in Kapara's time. We cannot now determine how far the damage to the giant statues went when Kapara used them once more, but it is quite likely that it was by no means slight.

But what is particularly important is that the palace of the Gudea period was evidently not destroyed by fire, which on basalt especially has so destructive an effect, but it must have collapsed for other reasons. This is why Kapara was able to dig the statues out in a much better state than we were.

One proof that the giant gods were meant from the first to be set on the animal colossi is that their plinths, as we saw, exactly fitted the cubes upon the animals, just as the plugs or pins in them exactly fitted into the plug-holes in the bases. In the same way as with other very old statues in the round the draperies of the huge goddess fit along the edge of the plinth in a natural way. The whole aspect of the standing-places also leads us to conclude that from the very beginning they were made in this way.

There was a reason for the height of the bases on which the statues of the gods stood. The god is visible to the visitor who draws near him on the terrace from the steps, and in his full length in spite of the size and massiveness of the animal's head, because the block or cube was correspondingly high. Thus a way was found to prevent the lower part of the god's body being hidden by the heads of the animal colossi, which would have been bound to happen, if the figures of the gods had been put directly on the backs of their beasts. As it is they are lifted above the beasts, and yet stand fast on them, parted from them by beautifully decorated pedestals; and he who draws nearer does not see the block or cube until he stands by the beasts.

From the steps and towards the façade the pavement of the terrace slightly rose, so that he animal colossi and relief slabs seemed through this also to be somewhat raised. I believe it probable, however, that in earlier times, in the 3rd millennium, in their original position before they were used over again by Kapara they stood on stone pedestals, which were at least 30-40 centimetres high. Crosswise under the huge bull lay thick basalt slabs, three of them, one behind the other. At other spots on the hill, too, we found great slabs of this kind, whose use was not clear. It may be that they were remains of former pedestals.

In front of the façade stood a great altar socle of glazed bricks, perhaps for burnt offerings; also a huge eagle of the sun. Of the altar we found a wall about three metres broad of baked enamelled bricks, which had fallen forwards when the temple-palace was destroyed. The bricks were lying on the terrace, with the coloured side underneath, almost in front of the middle of the entry and slightly to the east. The decoration had various strips with geometrical patterns. The parts of the motives were formed from individual pieces of brick correspondingly shaped, which were put together like a mosaic to make up the pattern. At the corners the wall was finished off with pillars of coloured enamel bricks. Numerous other bits of enamelled bricks were found on the terrace and near it. When taken out from the damp ground they showed fairly strong colouring on the enamelled side. Some were yellow or greenish blue only, others were in two colours—white with stripes in one of these two colours. They were at once copied in colours as a precaution; and later they lost their colour more and more. We were able with the bricks to make up strips with nine different designs altogether: rosettes set next to one another, triangles, also stepped pinnacles in which an upright one always alternated with one upside down, and finally the so-called Hittite plaited band in several variations. This last has two lines running in regular waves, that look like a rope twisted from two strings. One of these plaited band motives, where the two wave lines make an oval, had in the middle a nail-like inset of baked clay, like the Assyrian decorative knobs (*ziggatu*), which stood out plastically from the wall surface to give it more life.

Our brick wall shows a great likeness to geometrical decorations in late Assyrian wall-paintings, and also to late Mesopotamian enamelled tiles; but in these latter the patterns are no longer mosaic-like, but are painted on large pieces. The colours of the enamelled Tell Halaf bricks are the same as in similar decorations in the so-called 'Harem' of Khorsabad.

This brick wall, anyhow, was the north wall of a cubical altar or socle about 1.20 metres high. The pieces lying around belonged to the other three walls. The whole thing stood on a low pyramidical base made of four layers of small burnt bricks. Burnt bricks such as these we found only quite exceptionally on Tell Halaf, and never with the stamped names of the builders, contrary to the custom in Babylonia and Assyria. The enamelled bricks, I think, come from the time of the Kapara dynasty. The great brick altar stood outside the wooden projecting roof before the façade.

A little west from this altar we found a sculpture of fantastic appearance (Pl. 14). It was a huge bird of prey, 1.84 metres high, sitting bolt upright on a low, eight-leaved acanthus capital. Its tail and feet were one with the base. The lower, round pillar portion of the capital ended in a stout four-cornered pin or plug, by means of which it probably stood on a basalt column. We found fragments of a fourteen-sided basalt column that presumably belonged to this bird. We are also in possession of one half of a heavy pyramidical stone which had a rounded piece on its top. It is very probable that this was the socle or base for the column and the great bird. It must have stood on four basalt slabs let into the floor, which was paved with irregular white limestone flags, west of the brick altar and at the same distance as it from the façade of the temple-palace.

The representation of the bird on a column corresponds fully with those found especially on boundary-stones (*kudurru*) of the Kassite dynasty in Lower Mesopotamia, being symbols of gods. As already explained, the Kassites before they came to Babylon lived on Subaraic territory, and probably brought this motive with them from there.

But we may here point out also another possible explanation of the great cubical object with its sides of enamelled bricks which we have called an altar. This possible explanation would be that inside the enamelled sides the cube was made up of mud bricks, and that emblems of gods made of wood or some other material and set up on poles were once planted in this cube.

It is, however, not altogether impossible that our gigantic bird in basalt rested on a stand lying within the above described four walls or sides of enamelled bricks, and built up of stones or of great basalt slabs in layers. These walls or sides would naturally then not have belonged to an altar.

For the bird on a rod coming up out of a cubical stand we have also an analogy on a small scale on one of the Kassite *kudurru*. Yet the position on the column seems to me more likely. The bird must anyhow have stood very high up, since its claws were not represented, as if there was no need to see them from below. The lower part of the legs, indeed, were missing, but they must have gone straight into the capital, as is shown by rounded pits in it. The bird when it fell had broken up into several pieces, some of which I had already found in 1899. It was an easy task to put it all together again.

Like the winged sun's disk on the main façade, it undoubtedly symbolizes the Sun god. It is one of the most striking sculptures in Tell Halaf. Straight up it rose on the capital, so that the line of the back and the tail were almost perpendicular. The wings are set close to the body. The head is disproportionately large, the beak is very heavy. What is very remarkable is the way the eyes are represented: they stand out cylindrically like telescopes on each side of the root of the beak. But the artist was driven to this way of representing them, if his aim was that the bird's eyes, which in their natural position lie at the side of the head, should be seen by the beholder or worshipper standing in front of the Sun eagle. The eyeballs were round disks of white limestone; the pupils were of polished black stone. One of these eyes was found by us.

The feathers are represented on the breast by large round scales pointing downwards, and on the wings by the same fish-bone pattern we find in the veiled sphinx. From the middle of the back of the head there fall away towards both sides ribbons with a spiral ending, just like the small ribbons on the sphinx's veil. Two of these ribbons on the two sides of the head are made very wide and at the neck, just under the beak, are joined together by another horizontal ribbon. In the case also of some representations of the griffin we meet with a like ribbon motive on the bird's head. This motive seems to have been often found in the Subaraic area.

The top of the Sun eagle's head shows a flat depression within a pad or tuft of feathers. It may have been there to take some kind of head-ornament in the nature of a comb standing up from it, perhaps made of metal.

The remarkable head of this Sun bird with the eyes standing out like telescopes is not without its analogies. We find this bird as a small terra-cotta in later Assyrian times in one of the Assyrian capitals (Nimrud) and north of this in Asia Minor, that is to say on Subaraic soil again. The sitting eagle without this peculiarity we meet with as a divine symbol in southern Mesopotamia and also on Cappadocian and Syro-Hittite seal-cylinders and further in Subaraic plastic art, in Aleppo for instance. There is, however, nowhere in the Old World where we have such a gigantic eagle monument as on Tell Halaf.

Whoever has ridden through the steppes in Upper Mesopotamia will often have seen a lonely eagle sitting on the

plain on some large stone. These creatures brood un-
stirring and upright on their strong legs, with their tail
against the stone and the heavy beak stretched out horizontally. Here we have the model for our great bird, which
however, has something of the magic or divine added to
it through its great eyes set forward and its huge size. So
as to give stable equilibrium to the tall block of stone,
which is almost a pillar, on the capital, the sculptor has
so shaped and squeezed the bird that in spite of its powerful
effect it strikes us to-day as almost grotesque. In spite of all
its divinity one might at the same time almost look on it as
a caricature—like Jim Crow, the luckless raven.

The great part played in the Subaraic culture by the
Sun god and his embodiment in the Sun bird is confirmed
by Tell Halaf. Besides the winged sun's disk we also find
here on small orthostats an eagle-like bird with outspread
wings, and in one case a sitting bird, represented as the
Sun god, that shall watch over the warrior bowman in the
chariot. On another small orthostat we meet with a Sun
eagle rising above a conical rock and flying upwards.

On our hill a second capital with hanging leaves was
found, which is very like that of the great bird, but somewhat smaller. Here small stumps were still left from the
bird's claws, but of the Sun eagle itself only parts of the
beak and the breast could be recognized. Where this bird
stood cannot be determined. It may have been one of the
statues that belonged to the buildings from the Painted
Pottery time, and which Kapara did not make any use of,
not knowing what to do with fragments.

We found further remains of two other leaved capitals
of the same kind, but no birds can have stood on them.
One of them has a hollow on top, as though a wooden
column or a corbel had stood here. These fragments remind us of the capitals in that so important model of a
house which we were able to dig out (cp. p. 167).

Walking on between the animal colossi with the gods,
the visitor to the temple came into the first broad room.

Its eastern part was covered with wooden ashes coming from the burned roof-beams. Here in the charcoal layer we found the skeleton of a young girl, a temple servant doubtless. Perhaps it was she who had made the last sacrifice, the doves, before the sun's disk orthostat on the façade. There were also lying here many *ziggatu*—decorative knobs —with which the walls of the room were ornamented.

Opposite the passage with the figures of the gods there was in the back wall of the broad room a second passage

THE FIRST AND SECOND PASSAGE OF THE TEMPLE-PALACE (IN SECTION)

with a breadth of nearly four metres. On its sides, too, were fixed orthostats, though not in such numbers as on the great façade. They had suffered particular damage through the burning of the temple-palace.

The statues in the second passage were in equal numbers on each side. Before it, still in the broad room, stood a large orthostat on each side with the figure of a beast stepping up to the vaulting. The western stone was 1.48 metres high and 1.91 metres broad, the other one measured about the same. On the reliefs all we could still make out was the lion's body, which had a long wing above it. The fragments of the slabs with the heads were no longer preserved, but certain signs such as small chains on the breast and the measurements point to our having here a hybrid being with a woman's head that must have been quite like a sphinx on one of our small orthostats. These two reliefs once more bore Kapara's building inscriptions.

Each side of the passage through the wall 2.50 metres thick bounding on the north the inner great main hall (that also ran east and west) of the temple-palace was adorned with a giant griffin and a smaller orthostat standing behind it.

The griffins were mighty colossi still huger than the veiled sphinxes of the great front façade. The griffin on the east (Pl. 15) was 2.40 metres long. Here, too, the fore-part came out far beyond the front face of the wall as sculpture in the round and into the first broad room. The griffins were much damaged especially behind. This must be put down to the fact that to-day the hill falls away southwards right from the front façade, so that the masses of rubbish heaped up in the second entry ended already below the level of what was the upper surface of the griffins in the archway. The back part of the griffins must have been uncovered now, had they not had their upper part knocked away.

The heads of the griffins were lying in fragments in the rubbish from the fire. Practically the whole of the head of the griffin on the west could be put together again from the pieces, even the long crest of feathers running from the bird's head down to the back; this comb is like a mane clipped on top. From the rest of the bodies of the two griffins enough remains, too, were dug out to allow us to reconstruct them perfectly. They are winged lions with a huge eagle's head. This head is almost the same in every way as that belonging to our giant bird with the torpedo-eyes in front of the façade of the temple-palace, only that it is still more massive. It has the same eyes like a telescope, and the head-dress with the spiral band motive falling down on each side is there too; the bands, however, are very much longer and broader.

Under the beak, however, this hybrid being was different. Instead of the band-edging on the neck there were lion's tresses; under these was the scale motive as in the giant bird and in the great male winged sphinx at the salient of the tower of the temple-palace façade. The breast was arched outwards just as strongly—and to our eyes as grotesquely—as in the Sun eagle; but below it the scale motive changed over into the hanging tresses of the lion's mane, which came as far as the start of the mighty legs of the lion. These latter were worked in the same way as those in the animal colossi in the first passage.

At the side of the passage the statue is again treated in relief; here it is a winged lion. The broad wings, however, are not shown rising upwards, as with the veiled sphinx, but lie above the lion's body, and behind they fall away downwards. For this we have an analogy in two griffins on small orthostats. Again the giant griffins had on the slabs at the side only one fore-leg and two hind-legs.

The space between the legs was again filled in with a deeper-lying relief. In the griffin on the east there is represented a fight between a lion and a fabulous being. The lion is leaning in a defensive position against the fore-leg of the giant griffin, and has his right paw lifted; it is only the upper part of its head that is missing, but of its antagonist only the lower parts can be made out. This latter was a quadruped with lion's legs; its tail standing up is a scorpion's. Judging by the space between the two fighting beasts, the head must have been a bird's. Thus here again we have a griffin before us, which is attacking and over-coming a frightened lion.

The picture under the body of the griffin to the west shows a fight between a lion and a bull; the lion's paws are worked particularly like a bear's.

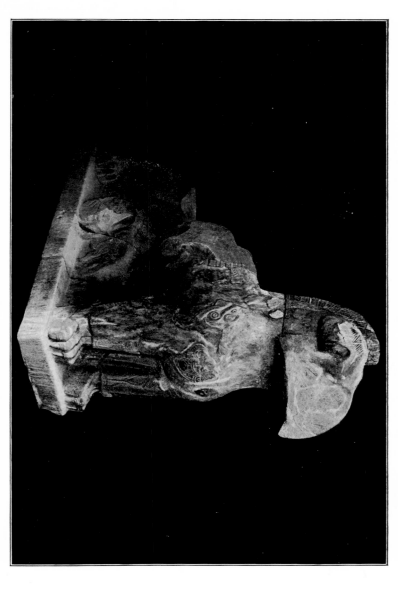

PLATE XVI. PARTS OF THE BASTIONED WALL WITH THE SMALL ORTHOSTATS

The western giant griffin put together by us is, in spite of its partial destruction, one of the most striking of the Tell Halaf statues. What perhaps gives it its particularly strong effect is that the fabulous being has the look of a crouching bird-headed lion standing on its mighty fore-legs.

Behind the giant griffins at the walls of the archway stood rather narrow relief slabs, of which only the lowest part of all could be found again. On each side there is only a human figure with pointed shoes.

The pointed-shoe men were striding along behind the giant griffins. The width of the eastern stone is 55 centimetres, what is left of the height 60 centimetres; the width of the western stone is 55 centimetres, the height left 98 centimetres. The latter in contrast with the former has a strikingly high plinth for the figure to stand on. Already when they were being dug out I got the idea that before us Kapara had only found the lower half of these two statues, and had used them then to fill in the surface of the wall behind the griffins. We were not able to find the slightest fragment more of these two stones.

In reconstructing the two stones with the winged pointed-shoe men I had to have recourse to analogies such as we meet with on small orthostats. For the eastern stone, in which the feet are standing almost on the floor of the passage, I made use of an orthostat on which is repre-sented a woman standing upright with six wings and the crown of horns; for the western stone, on the other hand, I took a much lower orthostat with a four-winged male genius with uplifted hands. These narrow sculptures are the only ones where we had to grope in the dark in re-storing them.

However great the difficulties were in reproducing the second passage in the temple-palace with its statues, the reproduction of the first great façade was proportionately easy. Here it was only the figures on the cubes or blocks of the animal colossi that were no longer wholly preserved, and also the representation on the orthostat found as a fragment on the eastern tower salient could no longer be made out, this orthostat being the counterpart of the winged lion on the western tower with a man's head. Otherwise, however, the statues here were all undamaged, or so little damaged that they could be set up again in perfect order.

The decoration of the second passage, especially with the mighty griffins looking out from the wall, is again something wholly new. It seems to me more than likely that these statues in their original use stood at some outer gate of a building, and not, as here, on the inside of a place which is also so cribbed.

V

The Small Orthostats

WHEN the outer walls of the foundations of the Kapara palace were laid bare there was a fresh surprise. The 57-metre long south wall was found to have five rectangular bastions jutting out, each one of which supported a corner. Starting north of the south-western bastion, the foot of the walls was faced with one row of sculptured relief slabs (Pl. 16). Originally they had followed each of the walls of the reserves in the great wall and of the bastion-like salients without a break and had run on a little further to the north beyond the south-east bastion on the east outer wall of the mud-brick sub-structure. So far as they could be seen from outside we numbered them from west to east, beginning with the northernmost stone on the west front.

The south front of the substructure of the temple-palace presented an overpowering sight after it had been dug out and in spite of the destruction of the walls above it. It was impossible for the eye to take it all in at once with its mass of relief slabs.

This set of reliefs is hardly of less interest than the more monumental front façade with the great statues. It tells us much about the life, thought, and beliefs of the Tell Halaf people and their oldest art.

The use of such relief slabs is Subaraic. But no other excavations, not even at Senjirli and Karkemish, have yielded so much as Tell Halaf. Up to now they have only been known as decoration on *hilani* entrances and within guard-houses of gates and palaces; their use on outer walls is alone in its kind. They are in general 60-80 centimetres high and 45-55 centimetres broad; in four cases only were they twice as broad or still larger. In general they are 20 centimetres thick, and so very much smaller than the relief slabs on the front façade and in the second gateway passage of the temple-palace. Thus we have always called them the small orthostats.

The architect had so arranged the stones that their upper edges made a straight line. On this was laid a wooden frame-work hidden in the masonry. The wall above the stones was faced with plaster. The orthostats rested below on small stones that were laid on a plastered socle of mud bricks and about 45 centimetres high, jutting generally 25 centimetres beyond the wall. Above the orthostats the wall must have been extraordinarily high, as high, that is, as the mass of mud bricks serving as substructure to the temple-palace, including, too, the height of the south outer walls of the palace itself. When the temple-palace collapsed, the outer walls crashed into the depths below towards the citadel walls.

Altogether we found 187 small orthostats, 182 of which were *in situ*, fitted into the wall where Kapara had put them. They had not been damaged at the burning of the temple-palace. In some places later settlers had driven grain-holders into the ground in the rubbish above the walls where the orthostats were—funnel-like silos that widened as they went downwards, and like those that are still in general use to-day in the Nearer East. This has led to the loss of some 50 orthostats; five we found again at other places on the hill.

The orthostats were made alternately of black basalt and of limestone tinted red with ochre.[1] This red ochre was repeatedly found by us when digging in lumps up to the size of the fist.

The only other series, though very much smaller, of basalt and limestone orthostats in an alternate arrangement is to be found in the Processional Way of Karkemish, while in Senjirli there are alternately carved and uncarved basalt orthostats standing side by side.

[1] B following the numbers of the orthostats means basalt, L means limestone.

Our small orthostats were not made by Kapara, but were likewise brought out by him from the Painted Pottery layer. They were then evidently set side by side by his architects so as to fill the walls. To make them fit properly several had a little chipped off along the thickness without any heed being given to the picture represented on them. In one case, indeed, a broad stone, but only 22 centimetres high, was put upside down (143 B). Two beasts, one behind the other, are now running perpendicularly upwards. As there were not enough orthostats, use was made of some uncarved slabs of one size to fill in at the ends of the row. All this in itself shows that the orthostats were not new-made, but were used over again; and there are further facts pointing in the same direction. Some of the stones were much damaged on the carved side, and in a way which shows that this was already the case when they came to be used to decorate the wall. Thus in the limestone orthostats the ochre coating is found both on the undamaged and on the damaged places. In some of the orthostats hardly anything can be made out of the old sculpture; others seem to have been cut in half from top to bottom. Many have carvings also on one thickness, and so were doubtless once corner-stones. Kapara, however, fitted them into the row as ordinary stones. Only two stones with a subject both on the broad surface and on the edge (170 B) were used by Kapara properly as corner-stones. A stone that was too big (63 L, with an elephant represented), and was moreover much damaged, was partly covered by the other row of orthostats at right angles to it. In several stones there was chiselled lengthwise on the back a deep groove; either they had been used for a time as a gutter, or formerly a pole stood behind them for a flag or a religious emblem. In one corner-stone one of the top corners had been chiselled away (100 L). The other stones in the row this orthostat belonged to were higher, and the next row began with a particularly small stone; the knocking away of the corner was meant to make the change easier.

In the case of one very small stone (113 B) there was another orthostat (with a Gilgamesh subject) put underneath it, so that its top should lie in line with the others.

The stones were not grouped according to subject. The various carvings were put alongside one another at random; often we find several trees, beasts, or warriors next one another, and the beasts often have their backs turned to one another for no reason.

It is highly probable that originally the stones, anyhow to some extent, stood in relation to one another, so that, for instance, a palm together with two animals turned towards one another would have made a group of three stones. This is indeed a very old motive, and one which we find united on one Tell Halaf orthostat. So, too, orthostats with warriors may once have stood next each other, so that taken together they represented a battle scene.

But each orthostat bears a picture complete in itself, and to represent one beast the old sculptors have not used more than one stone.

Of the small orthostats 123 have the same inscription of Kapara's as the great stone reliefs of the front façade: 'Palace of Kapara, son of Hadianu'. Here too it is carved on any place that happens to be free, and no heed is given to the effect on the picture—one more proof that old stones have been used over again in Kapara's time. In many of them even a part of the surface, that had been roughened by time and weather, is knocked away to make a better place for the inscription. Often much more was chiselled away than was needed for this; in one case even part of the high relief is got rid of for the inscription.

It is an interesting fact, too, that the orthostats found by us elsewhere than on the bastion walls, as also the Gilgamesh orthostat under the stone with the fisherman, are all without Kapara's inscription.

Of one small orthostat, representing horsemen, we found only the upper part, which was embedded in the pavement of the terrace before the façade of the temple-palace with the carved side downwards. The fragment is undoubtedly one of the orthostats which Kapara took out of the Painted Pottery layer but could not put into his great row of orthostats as being too far destroyed. The stone happened to be handy for the pavement and so was used there.

All this shows clearly that Kapara found the small orthostats and used them over again, they are not his own work.

The pictures shown on the individual stones are of very many kinds. Gods and warriors, animals and fights between animals, scenes of worship and every-day life—and above all, hybrid beings of unbelievable kinds are found on them.

Beyond all doubt many more carvings were made originally for the palaces of the Painted Pottery period, but they had already been lost before Kapara's time.

When Kapara was seated on the throne it may be that only chosen persons had the right to come into the inner part of the temple through the Scorpions' Gate. Other dwellers in the town probably only had leave on special occasions to approach the magical representations of gods and demons and other figures on the small orthostats on the outer walls of the temple, and to worship here. Anyhow the carvings on the walls of the bastions must have made an extraordinarily strong impression on the people of old, and taken hold of their imagination. We who were digging could not hold ourselves in for joy as more and more orthostats from the endless series came to light; and even afterwards we and the few visitors who saw the stones still on Tell Halaf in their places remained under the spell of the mighty spectacle.

On grounds of style Professor E. Herzfeld holds the small orthostats to be the oldest sculptures at Tell Halaf. Their date is estimated by him at 3000 B.C., or in some cases at 2900 B.C. In his view they are older than any other

K

statues of the Subaraic culture that were known before my excavations. He believes the limestone carvings for the greater part and some of the basalt to be the oldest. With his view I find myself fully in agreement.

In spite of slight differences in style the orthostats all show substantially the same features, so that they make up one whole. They are archaic and primitive, and in part are wonderfully faithful to nature. Here also, as in the cave drawings of the Old Stone age, beasts are understood and rendered much better than human beings. Perspective there is none. Beasts and men are put in space simply over or beside one another. In the result some figures are often found unnaturally small in comparison with others. Overlapping is as far as possible avoided; it is only definitely found in the case of fights between animals, a characteristic shared again by the Tell Halaf sculptures with the oldest Sumerian.

An important thing is the treatment of animals in space. While in the great orthostats all four legs always stand on the plinth, the animals on the small orthostats as a rule are rearing up, and are set along the diagonal of the narrow stone. The picture is in this way made livelier. This particular characteristic is very seldom found in other Subaraic statues. Often the beasts are standing right on their hind-legs, almost upright like men; the fore-legs then generally hang down. The lion always holds one paw up, as though ready to strike.

There are many human beings represented on the small orthostats: human beings alone, battle scenes, scenes from daily life, some pictures of worship; then there are hybrid beings of men and beasts, and gods in human shape. Thus we now know fairly well what the dwellers at Tell Halaf in those old days looked like, especially if we take in the few statues in the round. The people generally have a serious, almost surly, expression. It is the same type as meets us also in other Subaraic sites. The head is short, the face is round with a large, fleshy nose.

Almost all the figures are shown in profile. It is only in

PLATE XVIIA. WARRIOR IN LONG GOWN WITH SPEAR

PLATE XVIIB. WARRIOR WITH THROWING-STICK (BUMERANG)

Plate XVIIIb. Horseman (22 B)

Plate XVIIIa. Bowman (187 K)

three cases that we have human heads seen from in front, which are then correspondingly worked out more plastically; once we have a lion seen from above. When human beings are represented the heads often take up to a third of the whole figure. Nose and eyes are particularly large. In animals and human beings the eyes are drawn quite oval, and are not sunken. In the same way as with the profile figures of the great orthostats, the breast and shoulders of human beings as opposed to their head and limbs are shown from in front. The arms are often shortened and wide outstretched, the five toes lie on one another. In one case only—the Teshup on stone 106 L—are the feet wearing pointed shoes.

The manner of wearing the hair and the beard is not uniform. As a rule men's and women's hair is held together above the forehead by a narrow band. It is represented by a network of scratched lines, and falls on to the shoulders and back in heavy locks, which in men are not very long. Most of the men wear a sailor's beard with a clean-shaven upper lip. Only in one case (Pl. 35a) is a moustache to be seen (it may be seen, too, on some of the stones of the great front façade). The beard is usually kept fairly short and cut away below with a sharp edge. The hair of the beard is conventionalized quite archaically into waved lines, parallel straight ones, and zigzags. Some of the men are beardless.

We find two different kinds of clothing for the men. In the case of a few there is a long gown ending below in a fringe and held together at the waist with a girdle. The sleeves are edged on the upper arm by a ribbon. Only in one case, on a rather weathered limestone, is the long gown all divided up into small squares by cut lines, either for ornamentation or to show a quilted stuff armour. The latter is pointed to by the greater width of the gown and the lack of the girdle which elsewhere holds the gown together at the waist. It almost looks as if this man, too, is wearing pointed shoes.

This long gown seems to be worn only by gods, demons and kings. Originally, in contrast to Subartu, it is not found in old South Mesopotamia; it first makes its appearance there in the Kassite period, in the 2nd millennium B.C. This dress is probably one of the Subaraic elements introduced into Babylonia.

What we find far oftener is a short loin-apron, which is held on the waist by a girdle and leaves the upper body free, reaching down short of the knee. On the side it has either a fringe or a design. This short apron is already known to us from the oldest monuments. In Ur it is worn by servants or foreign slaves, in Egypt by people who are shown as Asiats by their cast of countenance and type of beard.

Head-coverings are seldom seen. We find once a pointed cap, and several times a pointed helmet.

Representations of single armed men, that is, warriors, play a great part on the small orthostats. As to weapons, the long lance with broad blade, which is held downwards in both hands (Pl. 17a), meets us only on two carvings. Twice we find a warrior with a shorter lance or a throwing spear in one hand, and the shield in the other. On one carving he is seen kneeling; his gown here is particularly richly ornamented.

Most often the man is fighting with bow and arrow, either standing up or kneeling (Pl. 18a) or in a chariot (Pl. 19a, b). The bow in most cases is stretched, and about half the warrior's height. The string is pulled back as far as the ears, or behind them. The arrow and bow-string, as on the reliefs of the main façade, are not represented over the face so as to avoid the signs of overlapping.

Often, too, we find the bent throwing-stick, the bumerang (Pl. 17b), either as the warrior's only weapon, or together with a throwing-ball.

The club is found only three times—twice in Teshup representations, and once in the case of a man holding a sling in his left hand. It is quite possible that this latter statue also must be looked on as an embodiment of Teshup, as with ordinary warriors the club is never found otherwise; and the sling, like the bumerang and the true lightning-sheaf could very well be taken as the symbols of Storm. The sling is found again a second time; here a warrior is hurling it with both hands over his head. Slings of a like kind are still used to-day in this district. We found quite a lot of smallish sling-bullets, and also large throwing balls as we went down even to the deep layers.

In two reliefs a warrior is carrying a stout long wooden staff as a weapon.

On the small orthostats we do not find a sword of any length, such as we find in the case of the giant gods of the front façade; on the other hand there are short, straight or sickle-like swords and heavy daggers.

The shield is small and round with a boss and bound rim. We find it only once in the case of a warrior on foot, namely in the case of the already mentioned man kneeling with a spear; but in the case of horsemen we often find it (Pl. 18b).

Thus, setting aside the axe and the hatchet, all weapons known in olden times seem to be represented. The hatchet we find on Jebelet-el-Beda on the double stele (cp. below, p. 237), while several axes or hatchets of bronze were dug up on Tell Halaf.

The representation of horsemen and chariots is especially interesting. On three orthostats we see mounted warriors with helmets. All three are carrying the round shield and, as I believe, a sword, and are wearing the short gown or smock. The horses' headgear is in one case a halter wound round the lower jaw, in another (stone 22 B, Pl. 18b) a true bit with a cord or leather strap over the upper jaw and a halter-strap round the neck. The third riding picture has only its upper part preserved. It is the only orthostat that is edged with a Hittite woven band.

Besides these there were three other carvings of riders on the rectangular basalt socle which made the base for the

Teshup on the giant ox in the passage through the great façade (cp. above, p. 121). Best preserved was the side with a kneeling warrior in a loin-apron and with a shield, holding a horse by the bridle. Here, too, the horse is not saddled. Even to-day the Beduins usually ride, on their plundering and war forays also, without a saddle, guiding the horse with only a quite simple halter and nothing more than a long cord—that is to say, exactly as in the days of Tell Halaf.

The hunting and war chariot of Tell Halaf had two wheels; it is always manned by two men, the driver and the warrior proper. The Egyptians took over the chariot from the Mitanni; with them, too, it is, as in Ur, meant for two. The same is true for older Assyrian representations of chariots. Among the Hittites, however, and the later Assyrians three men go to a chariot. The charioteer on Tell Halaf is holding the reins in both hands. Only once is he seen with a whip-like stick in his right, but perhaps this is again a sword. The fighting-man, so far as can be seen, is armed always with bow and arrow. Only once does he seem to be holding in his left hand a club or hatchet(?) sloped horizontally backwards.

On the carving always one horse only is to be seen. But the chariot undoubtedly had two horses in it; it is only that here, too, the artist, stubbornly carrying out the profile principle for pairs, always represents one member only, but shows it, on the other hand, as a complete whole. Thus, too, the two fore-legs cover one another. Moreover the way the reins are managed also points to there being two horses. While on Tell Halaf and in Senjirli only two horses are represented, the finds at Ur and in Cappadocia show four-horsed chariots.

On stone 17 B (Pl. 19a), which is twice as wide as the other orthostats, we see a lion under the horse. What it is sought to express is probably 'next to' or 'in front of' the horse, but archaic art has no other way of expressing this. The primitive custom of rendering the feet as seen from

PLATE XIXA. LION-HUNTING FROM A CHARIOT WITH SUN-EAGLE (17 B)

PLATE XIXB. BULL-HUNTING FROM A CHARIOT (45 K)

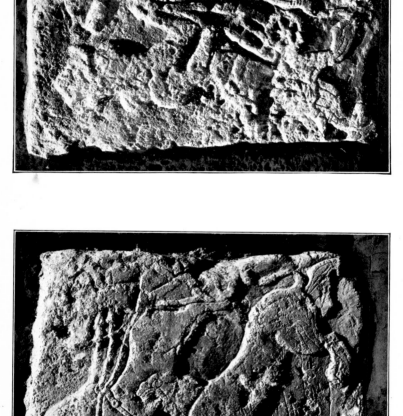

PLATE XXB. LION-MAN FORCING THE CHARIOT ON A HORSE

(110 K)

PLATE XXA. LION-HUNTING FROM A CHARIOT

(27 K)

above, so that the five toes can be represented, is here also followed for the hands. On the hands of the chariot driver and the bowman all the five fingers are drawn side by side. Between the horse's head and the men in the chariot there is an eagle flying towards them; it is the Sun eagle, that is watching over the hunter.

Stone 146 B is quite like the last. Here the chariot is driving over a naked fallen foe lying under the horse. Where the Sun eagle was we now find Kapara's inscription; the eagle has been chiselled away and made a smooth place for the inscription, the rest of the stone being porous. The representing the fallen foe naked is in agreement with the oldest sentiment of the Nearer East; we find the same thing in the land of the Nile and in Sumer.

On a third orthostat (45 L, Pl. 19b) with a chariot scene the hunter is following a wild bull, which for want of room is represented running away over the horse in the reverse direction. This particular detail is found also on a highly archaic painted pot from Tell Halaf; here the horses in front of the chariot are drawn facing the opposite way. On our orthostat with the bull-hunt the Sun eagle is sitting above the head of the bowman, who wears a long cloak and a helmet.

The bird in conjunction with chariot subjects we find otherwise only on the Cappadocian seals, that is, within the Subaraic culture also, and it has other divine emblems with it. One seal shows in much the same way a bird sitting before a horse. Here also we have the Sun god, who is watching over the fighting king. In the representation of a hunt on a small Cyprian ivory box in the British Museum a bird is flying exactly as on our Stone 17 B towards the hunter. In my opinion it, too, is the guardian Sun bird.

On stone 27 L (Pl. 20a) we have another hunting piece; a bit has been struck off this stone on the right and left sides. The lion, shown in an exaggerated size under the chariot and horse, this time is the conqueror. Springing up from the side, it has fastened its teeth in the horse's belly. The fine picture, full of dramatic action, is somewhat blurred above.

But the most important chariot scene for cultural history is shown on the limestone slab 110 L (Pl. 20b): a hybrid being is here making the horse take the chariot. The upper part of his body is a bearded man with a horned crown, whereby he is characterized as a half-god; he has the body and feet of a lion. In his left hand he is holding a chariot which is very small compared with himself and the horse, in his right what looks like a bridle. The horse rears up before him with its back turned; the chariot is going to be harnessed to the as yet untamed beast. The picture on this stone is unique. The chariot has a square body of the simplest kind divided up by rods, which is very like the back part of the chariot on the standard of Ur and on Cappadocian seal impressions. In the other Tell Halaf carvings the chariot bodies widen out upwards like a funnel. These bodies correspond almost exactly with the two-wheeled chariot on the limestone relief of Ur, which is seen in the burial procession without a driver and heavily laden with skins and other things. It may have been the war chariot of a dead king.

In other ways the Tell Halaf chariots are exactly like the fighting chariots that came to Egypt from Hither Asia in the times of the eighteenth dynasty. There is an undamaged specimen now in the museum at Florence. The same form was developed as a two-wheeled war chariot into the Roman *quadriga*. It seems to me that the chariot, too, on the standard of Ur was only two-wheeled. The artist wanted to represent both wheels, and put them next one another. The great erection on the front wheel is, I believe, a high shield-like barrier to shelter the men in the chariot; the reins are led over it. The same is true of the Cappadocian chariots.

Out of five chariots two (stones 17 B and 146 B) have the rounded end of the shaft ornamented with a griffin's head; the reins run through it. This corresponds to the rein-holders of Ur and Kish, which bear the effigy of an animal in metal. The head ornament of the chariot horses is like that in other Subaraic reliefs.

On Tell Halaf the chariot wheels have spokes—six always, except in the case of the bull-hunt from a chariot (stone 45 L, Pl. 19b), where the wheel has eight spokes. From oldest times in south Mesopotamia we know the full or solid wheel; spokes appear in Babylonia for the first time in Hammurabi's reign. In Old Elam on the other hand the wheel with 12-15 spokes is found, and on Cappadocian seal-cylinder impressions that with four. In small models of chariots at Tell Halaf from the Painted Pottery period models, which have a great likeness with those from the archaic Ishtar temples of Assur, spokes painted on to the wheels can be made out.

It is important to note that the south Mesopotamian solid wheels had a broad tyre coming out beyond the rim, this tyre being of bronze. The solid wheel to me seems not to be more primitive than the spoked wheel, but the latter rather to be more natural and certainly stronger. Perhaps in Ur there were no spokes because strong and straight boughs of trees, which are needful for them, were wanting there.

The chariot horse and the riding horse are of the same type. The mane is clipped short as with horses on painted potsherds from Tell Halaf.

The small orthostats with chariot scenes are the most eloquent witnesses for the continued life of Subaraic ways of thought in Assyrian art. They have the effect almost of originals for the Assyrian works. With Herzfeld I am of the opinion that our pictures of horsemen and chariots are still older than those at Senjirli. They have more life in them because all the animals are represented with raised fore-legs.

With the representations of horses on Tell Halaf is bound up an important question for cultural history. It has often been disputed which came first, driving or riding, the taming of the horse as a beast of burden or as one of draught. In my opinion, in the East—as in all lands where every-day life means that man and the domestic animals live in close contact with one another—riding is the older of the two. This will be understood at once when we see how even children there clamber up on to horses, cattle and buffaloes to ride them to their drinking-water. In the dim past camels were undoubtedly used just as little for draught as they are to-day, and were used only for riding and as pack-animals. In the time of the Assyrian trading colonies in Cappadocia (3rd millennium) almost the whole of the traffic in goods was carried on by pack-animals; it is only in a few cases that we hear anything of vehicles.

Riding is an obvious and natural activity, especially on unsaddled horses as they are shown by our old sculptures. On a very old cylinder of the 4th millennium there is already to be seen a rider on a beast that is undoubtedly meant for a horse. The harnessing of the vehicle to the horse, on the other hand, is something out of the ordinary, a gift from the gods, and this was meant to be brought before mortal men on Tell Halaf by stone 110 L (Pl. 20*b*) also.

The question, again, as to when horses are first found in Mesopotamia has long been much debated. It was once thought that they were still unknown in Hammurabi's time (after 2000 B.C.). Through the finds at Ur, however, it is shown by archaeology that about 3000 B.C. mules and perhaps horses were already brought there. In Elam we find horses represented on painted pottery and on very old seals from the 4th millennium. In western Asia Minor, whose soil was very like that of Elam, they are, indeed, not found earlier than the end of the 3rd millennium on Cappadocian seals, but this does not necessarily mean they were not already there before this.

For Upper Mesopotamia horses are indicated through our painted pottery, and on the oldest specimens, that is at least as early as 3000 B.C. This is a clear proof that there were horses at this time on Tell Halaf. It is therefore quite natural to find them represented on the statues of the 3rd millennium, on the cubical block on the giant bull of the temple-palace façade, and about 3000 B.C. on the small orthostats.

Together with the 'ass of the east' or the 'ass of the mountains', which we may probably quite rightly assume to have come from Elam, the old south Mesopotamian inscriptions also speak of an 'ass of the west', which would according to the old Babylonian picture of the world be really from Amurru, or speaking more particularly, from the desert steppes of the mid-Euphrates area and Arabia. But here, I believe, and in the whole of Upper Mesopotamia, the original home of a specific kind of horse is to be sought for, one of another kind than the mountain horse of the east. To-day also there are still two kinds of horses in the west of Asia: the smaller one of Asia Minor, and the bigger, slender, noble Arab horse. The Arab horse has undoubtedly in course of time through repeated crossing given much of its blood to the horse of Asia Minor.

The steppes of Upper Mesopotamia and of Arabia exhibit a fauna differing in many ways from that of south Mesopotamia or other alluvial areas, such as, for instance, Lower Egypt. To the steppe-lands belong the horse, the camel and the ox; to the soft lowlands belong the ass and the buffalo. The camel and also the horse can be shown to have been brought from the steppes of Arabia and Syria to the Nile land. Both of them degenerate in the Nile delta even to-day after only a few generations, and fresh ones always have to be brought in. In Babylonia horses and camels have become native, but the buffalo has made its home only in the south of Mesopotamia; in the north it is hardly found even to-day.

From the Indo-Germanic names for 'horse', which names we find at a very early date in Lower Mesopotamia and in the 2nd millennium B.C. in Upper Mesopotamia, too, it has been concluded that the horse was brought in in very ancient times from Indo-Germanic lands in the north to Elam, and that later it was brought also into Mitanniland, that is to Upper Mesopotamia, by the Aryan immigration. It is quite possible that the Aryans who made their way about 2000 B.C. into Upper Mesopotamia, Mitanniland, brought with them a new stock of horses for this area, and that thenceforward in the Subaraic-Mitanni speech the Indo-Germanic name for horse may have been adopted here. We know that the Mitanni rulers in the 2nd millennium were particularly fond of horses. Their rules for horse-breeding, for managing horses, and for chariot-racing were adopted at the Hittite royal court of Khattushash. This, however, cannot in any way upset the view, which for me is incontrovertible, that the horse was domiciled in Upper Mesopotamia from earliest times. The fact of its having been wild here in earlier times is confirmed by the relief slab of the demi-god, who is taming a horse and forcing the chariot on it. Long before the Indo-Germanic wanderers of the 2nd millennium B.C. came in from the east and the west horses were used in Subartu by armed riders and chariot-warriors. The fighting-chariots in Ur, harnessed to horses or mules, come from about 3000 B.C., and the representations of horses on the painted pottery of Tell Halaf are still older.

On our small orthostats there are, moreover, quite a number of riding beasts which recall sometimes a wild ass, sometimes a wild horse. The Tell Halaf sculptors of the Painted Pottery period probably meant to represent both kinds. The wild primitive horses and asses—found still to-day—are as a matter of fact more like each other than are the tame horses and asses. From the type of head I am inclined to look on the animal on Stone 70 as a wild ass, and those on Stones 157 and 126 as wild horses.

Wild asses, indeed, there were in the very neighbourhood of Tell Halaf, round about Jebel Abd el Aziz, down to 1911. It was only in the dreadfully cold winter of 1910-

11 that they died out. During my two and a half years'
work on Tell Halaf, 1911-13, and later in 1927 and 1929,
I took the utmost pains, but in vain, to get a wild ass alive
or dead. The beasts shown alone on the small orthostats
were all wild or to be hunted. We know of wild asses being
hunted from Assyrian times. The horse may have still been
found wild in 3000 B.C., when the small orthostats were
made; later it was undoubtedly only found tame.

The occurrence of the horse on the painted pottery and
on the Tell Halaf statues seems to me a further proof that
the much debated question whether the beasts before the
chariots in Ur are asses or mules (or horses) must be
answered in favour of the latter suggestion. I should be
astonished at the courage of the warrior who should dare
to let his chariot be drawn into the fight by asses. The
amusing mishaps of sporting English officers driving asses
in the gymkhanas in Cairo show that asses cannot be properly driven.

My theory that the horse was already existing in the
steppes of Upper Mesopotamia and Arabia and also in
Asia Minor in Painted Pottery times of Tell Halaf and
long before is confirmed by discoveries which have been
made by Prof. Barnum Brown of the American Museum
of Natural History in New York on one of the Aegean
islands, where he found parts of the skeleton of a horse
structurally resembling the Magdalenian horse.

At the time when this horse was living, Greece and the
islands were not yet separated from the Asiatic continent
by the sea. In North Africa, too, a horse, *equus lybicus*, was
in existence many thousands of years before our era.

But his discoveries in the Aegean Sea have led Professor
Brown to the belief that the horse was indigenous in
Upper Mesopotamia long before the 3rd or 4th millennium
B.C. He thinks that the *equus Przcwalsky*, the wild horse
still living to-day in Central Asia, wandered at some time
to this area from the Near East.

The horse probably originates from North America,

where it became extinct not later than 2000 B.C. From America it wandered in the remotest times through Alaska into Asia and Europe.

The original horse, we may remark, was a small animal, no bigger than a whippet. This primary horse had four toes and a rudimentary fifth on the front feet, with three toes and a rudimentary first and fifth on the hind feet.

The camel is only once represented on Tell Halaf. Stone 102 L (Pl. 21a), one of the most realistic and valuable orthostats, shows a man riding a camel. He is beardless, and has drawn up his long gown while sitting. Under the bunch of his hair the neck of the gown can be seen; we have probably therefore a man of rank. In the right hand he holds a staff to guide the camel; the left is represented as if it held a bridle. He is sitting on a square box saddle fastened by crosswise girths on the camel. Three of the beast's legs seem to be planted fast on the ground, the right foreleg being lifted. This representation gives an interesting illustration of the Bible tale of Jacob's flight with his two wives, the fair Rachel and the cross-eyed, red-haired Leah, from the camp of his father-in-law Laban in Harran (1st Moses, xxxi, 19-54). The picture reminds us of how Laban in vain searches through Jacob's caravan for his house-idols, the Teraphim, stolen from him. He comes to his favourite daughter Rachel, seated on the camel, who in spite of her father's bidding does not get down but excuses herself as ailing. The house-idols are not found, for Rachel has hidden them in her camel's saddle. Thus Jacob, under the agreement made with the angry father-in-law, can go on unhindered to the Promised Land with his wives and children and the herds he has earned. Rachel's saddle must have looked like our camel-rider's. (Cp. with this the small house-idols on Pl. 46.) As E. A. Speiser in his excellent book, *Mesopotamian Origins*, p. 162, rightly insists, the great store set by Laban on getting back his lost Teraphim and by Rachel on keeping them is explained by the fact that the son-in-law was looked on as the lawful heir to the

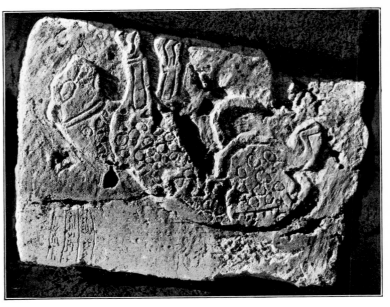

PLATE XVIIb SPOTTED PANTHER (124 K)

PLATE XVIIa LION AND SMALL BOWMAN (72 R)

belongings of his wife's father if he was in possession of the father's house-idols.

Five small orthostats show hunters on foot. On stone 147 (Pl. 21*b*) a man is plunging his sword deep into the body of the lion standing straight up before him, and biting into the man's other arm. In the second fight with a lion (stone 73 B, Pl. 22*a*) the hunter (shown disproportionately small in the upper right-hand corner of the stone slab) is shooting an arrow at the lion, who is already wounded, a second arrow being already planted above in his neck. Here we have an example of how the artist is at pains to fill in an empty space. The motive of the hunter shooting again on a lion already wounded by arrows is found in just the same way again on very old Elamite seal-cylinders.

On the other three hunting pictures men are fighting a winning fight against an upstanding griffin or other bird of prey, a great hoofed beast, and a giant wild goose.

The many representations of warriors and hunts on Tell Halaf and on the reliefs of Senjirli, Karkemish and other places, bear witness to the warlike bent and love of hunting among the Subaraic people. In old south Mesopotamia pictures of war are often found, but hunting pictures only seldom. In Elam, on the other hand, hunting scenes are by no means rare.

Tell Halaf art is very fond of representing the wild beast —alone or fighting with his kind. The lion is found alone eleven times on the orthostats; in some cases we see that it is a lioness that is represented. He is always set along one of the stone's diagonals, and always one paw is uplifted. The tail is always curled a little as he lashes it, and either stands up or is held between the legs. On two carvings he is turning the head backwards. The hair, muscles and paws are treated quite like those in the beasts of the great façade. The jaws are always opened. Here again two canine teeth in the upper and two in the lower jaw are shown next one another in exaggerated size, while the other teeth are left out. The head is often separated from the neck by a roll of flesh as in the old lions of Senjirli. The characteristic parallel lines, too, on the upper lip of the mouth opened threateningly correspond with the representation of these lions in Senjirli and on the façade of our temple-palace. In spite of the general uniformity each of the carvings has its peculiarities.

Besides the lion we find the spotted panther once (stone 134, Pl. 22*b*). He is squatting on his hindquarters with his tail tucked in and is stretching his two fore-paws forwards. At Ur there are several representations of spotted panthers.

The bear—which is not now found in the Khabur area, but is still at home to-day in the mountains of Asia Minor and Syria—is represented on two orthostats by itself. These two are both of limestone and not well preserved. On stone 98 L the bear has a long tail, which he holds up. We shall meet with this peculiarity again on the animal band (p. 180). On the above mentioned small stone, 143 B, standing upside down, a hunting-dog is bounding along at a gallop after a wild cat. This stone had probably before that been put to quite another use. The carved surface is 40 cm. long and 10 cm. high, while on the other hand the stone is 20-25 cm. thick or deep. From this we may conclude that the stone before this served as a base for some object, perhaps a god's statue, unless Kapara's architect carved a much thicker stone with a picture of which this hunting scene was a part, to fill in the empty space between stones 142 and 144 on the bastioned wall.

Next to the lion it is the wild bull that is oftenest shown. He, too, stands along the diagonal or is upright. On stone 133 B (Pl. 23*a*), perhaps to fill out space, a great hunting-dog, recognizable as such from the collar, is jumping up at the top of the slab over the wild bull. We are here reminded of the stone of Beisan in Palestine, which appears to be much later. On this stone, a large dog, chasing away a lion, is represented. Palestine also belonged to the Subaraic culture-complex.

PLATE XXIIIA. WILD BULL (133 B)

PLATE XXIIIB. DEER WITH BUTM-TREE (69 B)

PLATE XXIVB. PALM BETWEEN TWO GAZELLES (79 B)

PLATE XXIVA. GAZELLE (181 K)

The bulls on the limestone slabs, and the one followed in a chariot by the hunter, all have two horns represented parallel to one another, while with the bulls on the basalt slabs, in accordance with the profile principle, it is one horn only that is represented. This is bent almost into an S, and is set far forward on the forehead. The tail is generally hanging down, but sometimes also it is raised above the back. The muscles are drawn in the same way as with the lions; the hairs on the belly are hardly ever drawn. In other respects the drawing of the details here is on the whole like the drawing of the wild bull hunt on the great façade of the temple-palace. In spite, however, of such agreement the representations on the small orthostats are far more primitive.

Two types of the wild bull can be distinguished: one is slender with a narrow, long head; the other is thick-set with a broader and smaller skull. The thicker-set wild bull perhaps is meant to represent the bison, the one with finer lines to represent the aurochs. There are still bisons in the Caucasus to-day. The aurochs has died out in Europe. We find both kinds on the old seal-cylinders of south Mesopotamia and also in Elam.

The deer, sometimes characterized as a forest or mountain beast by the addition of a *butm*-tree (wild pistachio), has been already seen by us on the great façade. In general it is treated in the same way as the wild bull, but the horns are always represented from in front. The number of the antlers varies; usually it is six or eight. On the deer carvings, too, there is often another animal as well to fill in space; in one case this is a beaver, such as is still found to-day on the Khabur, in another case a desert hare with large ears. The Tell Halaf deer seems to have been a buck; it is no longer found there to-day, but I once dug up half a head of horns. Very powerful bucks with few mottles are, however, still to be found in Anatolia to-day.

One of the most primitive of our Tell Halaf stones is that numbered 69 B (Pl. 23*b*). The deer there shown strikes one

L

as quite flat and stiff, and altogether archaic, I would almost say 'Gothic'.

In the case of many of the horned beasts it is not easy to determine their species. The gazelles can be clearly recognized, so also the more powerful, thick-set ibex, which on both the stones that show it is marked by the *butm*-tree as being a mountain beast. The gazelle is a favourite subject from the time of the oldest monuments of south Mesopotamia and Elam. For every attitude of our gazelles' analogies can be shown on the oldest seal-cylinders. The plastic characteristics of the horns of the gazelles and ibexes are shown very realistically, while the horns of the wild bull are treated quite smoothly, just as they should be.

One of the finest gazelle pieces, a splendid carving of great artistic worth, is stone 181 L (Pl. 24*a*). Here the animal is turning its head backwards.

On stone 79 B (Pl. 24*b*) a palm is standing between two bolt-upright gazelles, surrounded as it were by guards. This is a scene often found throughout the old East. Instead of the gazelle there are often other animals or divine hybrid beings, and especially the so-called Gilgamesh and Engidu figures standing opposite one another, with or without some object between them. This stone is also of particular importance in that it combines on one stone a scene which was often, I am convinced, represented by three separate stones set alongside one another before Kapara made use of the orthostats a second time.

On some of the other limestone carvings there are hoofed beasts without horns. These stones are badly preserved, and it may be that the horns have broken off. The slender shape of the heads, however, points to a hind or a she-antelope.

The wild pig, too, has its place in the zoological garden of Tell Halaf. We find several vigorously drawn wild boars with heavy tusks. The domestic pig is also found once, but, it is worthy of note—for it is not game—in a carved scene and not on a single stone.

PLATE XXVa. OSTRICH AND FALCON (114 K)

PLATE XXVb. WILD GOOSE (15 B)

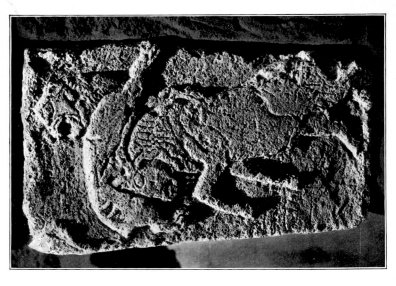

Plate XXVIb. Wild Bull overcoming a Lion (47 K)

Plate XXVIa. Lion Fighting with a Bull (172 B)

On the already-mentioned stone 63 L is an elephant. This orthostat is much larger than the others, and was evidently put in place when it was already partly destroyed—the lower right-hand corner, for instance, was missing. Another orthostat put at right angles before this carving had covered the whole of the front part, and with it the head as well. As a result of damage arising perhaps from the pressure of this stone next to it, the trunk is very hard to make out. The rest of the body, however, unmistakably belongs to an elephant. The ear, as in other old carvings of elephants, is small; the neck shows very thick rolls. The four remarkably heavy legs stand on the ground at the same height—this is exceptional; and the beast is not set along the diagonal. The elephant was hunted by the Mitanni and the Assyrians in Upper Mesopotamia. To-day it has died out in the Nearer East.

The representations of birds yield much information. One of the most impressive carvings is stone 114 L (Pl. 25*a*). Here an ostrich stalks majestically along, the right leg lifted. To fill in space a small bird—a falcon it looks like— is put in above on the left. On a second stone (121 B) the ostrich is on heavier lines. The ostrich, too, was undoubtedly domiciled in earlier times in Mesopotamia; we find it on a good many seal-cylinders. Down into the Middle Ages ostriches were plentiful in Arabia. At the present time this bird is only seldom found, and that in the southern parts of Arabia.

The bustard, which to-day also is found in great numbers and several kinds in Syria and Mesopotamia, is represented on two orthostats. On two stones a heavy wild goose is carved. The carving on stone 15 B (Pl. 25*b*) is even for the taste of to-day an example of splendid realism. On another stone a goose is being killed by a hunter. A wild duck in flight (stone 13 B) and with very big feet makes a picture uncommonly full of life.

The very old subject of fighting animals is often found, and always in most extraordinarily powerful carvings. On four stones great hoofed beasts are being slain by a lion; two of these stones also show the animals' bodies over-lapping one another in the way we find on so many old carvings from south Mesopotamia and Elam belonging to the 3rd millennium, but which we do not find so pronoun-cedly as this in later times.

On stone 172 B (Pl. 26a) the lion represented behind the bull is leaping at it; one of the lion's hind-paws is still on the ground. With the upper part of its body turned back-wards it is biting into its victim's neck, while with the right fore-paw it clasps the throat; the left one is plunged above the lion's jaws into the back of the bull's head.

On another limestone slab the overlapping takes place right at the hind end of the hoofed animal. This stone is badly damaged along its upper edge. The lion is striking its right fore-paw into the top of the bull's left leg and biting into its back behind. In both cases the animals fight-ing are rearing up against one another and set along the diagonal of the stone.

On two other carvings the bull is the winner. On the limestone slab 47 (Pl. 26b) it has spitted the lion on its horns and is carrying it horizontally above its head and strong neck. The helpless lion throws its head back as it roars. The bull's horns have penetrated the lions fleshy parts from below, the tips come out from the top of the lion's right leg. This makes a treatment such as I have not seen elsewhere in the old East.

On stone 159 L (Pl. 27a) the bull has spitted the lion in the fleshy part between the hind-legs, and holds it high up in the air, so that the body hangs perpendicularly down. The lion has its head turned towards the bull, and tries uselessly to bite it in the fore-legs.

This very same motive of the vanquished beast of prey hanging down is found on two engraved mother-of-pearl plaques underneath a harp from Ur. Here there is a Gil-gamesh and an Engidu figure lifting on high two spotted panthers by the tail or the hind-leg.

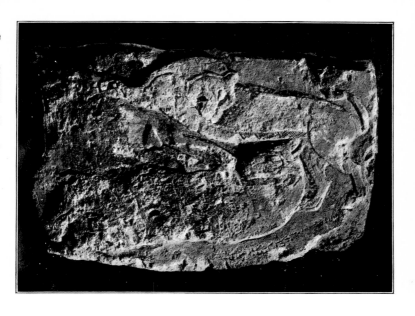

PLATE XXVIIA. WILD BULL SPITING A LION (159 K)

PLATE XXVIIB. LION SPRINGING ON A HIND (84 K)

Plate XXVIIb. Lion carrying a Lamb (131 b)

Plate XXVIIIa. Lion Strangling a Deer (80 k)

On stone 84 L (Pl. 27*b*) the lion has leapt from behind on to a hind (?). The left hind-paw is already lying on the victim's back, the right one is still in the air. The left fore-paw is driven into the hind's left shoulder, the right is round the hind's neck and can be seen just above this latter's left fore-paw. The lion's head makes a great turn on the neck, drawn over-long, and with its mouth turned upwards it is biting through the hind's throat.

Perhaps the most striking of these animal fights is that between a lion and a deer (stone 80 L, Pl. 28*a*). Each stands reared against the other. The lion is holding the deer fastened between its paws. The right paw lies under the deer's left fore-leg; the left is seen on the victim's back, thrust well forward under its uplifted right fore-leg. With visible delight here, too, the winner bites through the throat of the deer, whose legs are stretched in the struggle for life or death, and its eye growing dim. A modern artist could hardly make a better or more dramatic picture of it. This composition, too, we have on one of the harp plaques found not long ago at Ur, but the fight as shown there is not nearly so striking.

The plaques from Ur are certainly no older than the small orthostats at Tell Halaf; rather I believe that they are not so old. Such a likeness between subjects cannot be thought of without the idea of influence being brought in. Either there was a still earlier pattern for both or one artist learned from the other. But here it seems to me more likely that the smaller art objects, the plaques and also the seal-cylinders, found their originals in the larger stone carvings.

Stone 131 B (Pl. 28*b*) stands artistically quite apart from the others. The lion is holding a sheep in its mouth between its fore-paws. But this lion is now not shown in profile, but drawn from above with fore-paws and hind-paws stretched wide apart, while the sheep or lamb is in profile. For this we have no analogy in old south Mesopotamia or in Elam. All that we can bring in here for comparison are the Subaraic magic slabs of Hama.

All the animal fights are master-works of ancient freshness and naturalness, and show an unbelievably keen ob-
servation of nature and powerful execution. They bear
witness to artistic gifts in spite of all the *naïveté* of the out-
look. Carvings such as these have not till now been known
to us from olden times.

Only two kinds of trees are represented on the small
orthostats: the palm (Pl. 24*b*) and the wild pistachio, the
butm-tree (Pl. 23*b*). We find them on many of the stones.
The former is always much conventionalized, the latter
is fairly naturalistically rendered. The conventionalized
palm of Tell Halaf and other Subaraic archaeological
sites came to be the prototype of the almost uniform treatment of the palm in Assyrian art. Of Upper Mesopotamia,
Syria, Asia Minor—of the land of Subartu—the date-palm
was not a native. In Babylonia the date is an important
part of the people's food; but in the higher-lying terri-
tories of the north it does not ripen. This palm is here only
occasionally found or is only for ornament. In south Mesopotamia what touched the imagination was rather its importance as a food, in Subartu it was rather the striking
aspect of the tree itself and its well-known length of life. In
olden Babylonia the palm is represented but seldom, and
then more naturalistically; in Subartu, on the other hand
—although here the sculptor's art follows nature so
straitly—the unusual tree often appears, but conventionalized. On the stem, which is often represented quite slender,
but often, too, almost cubistically thick, the crown of palm-
leaves is in principle only shown by a fan-shaped top.
Under this at the sides scrolls are then added in a motive
that winds on itself in a spiral from top to bottom, these
scrolls usually repeating themselves below at the foot of
the stem. This is the rendering of the grape-like cluster of
fruit, which over and above this is also often represented
especially above or else below the scroll, either going upwards or hanging downwards. From our motive of the
scrolls up at the top of the palm comes the Ionic capital.

Very often we find on the representations of palms from Tell Halaf rings round the stem, but only in the case of the very slender palms.

The Tell Halaf palm hardly gives the impression any longer of a tree, but rather that of a symbol, of an emblem. For the Subaraeans it is the Tree of Life that bodies forth the Eternal. As such it had a magical meaning and betokened immortality, or was at any rate the emblem of long life. This is the explanation of the palm motive on the diadem of the three giant godheads in the gateway passage of the temple-palace façade, and on the gown of the Teshup on the giant bull; something of the divine is recognized in the palm. Thus, too, we can understand the frequent occurrence of the palm-tree on the small orthostats. In the Subaraic culture the tree from the beginning has an importance for the cult and a symbolical meaning. The idea of the Tree of Life comes not from Sumer, but from the Subaraic culture-complex; and it is from here, not from the Sumerian culture, that it came into Assyria, and thence into New Babylonia.

We find the palm motive also on a basalt model of a house on Tell Halaf. Here the palm appears on the corner-pillars of the outside walls. Perhaps the wish was thus to be expressed for long life for this house and its dwellers. In Subartu, the land where the pillar has played a leading part in the *hilani* building, the pillar-like character of the date-palm was naturally recognized from very early times. It is in this particular regard that a special weight may attach to the palm motive on the corner-pillars of this so important model of a house.

The date-palm in Babylonia is artificially fertilized. In the Tell Halaf sculpture we find fertilization scenes, both conventionalized with demons and naturalistically represented; they may go back to the relations in the dim past with south Mesopotamia. In Assyria these fertilization scenes are very often found.

The conventionalization of the palm on Tell Halaf

makes an even more striking effect on us when we compare it with the representation, likewise frequently found, of the second holy tree, with the *butm*-tree, which has its home in the very neighbourhood of Tell Halaf and is found particularly on Jebel Abd el Aziz, on Jebelet-el-Beda and in the Tektek mountains. It is the only tree that forms a kind of grove here. Among the Beduins it is still looked on as holy to this day, this being in connection with Abd el Aziz, the son of one of the greatest Islamic 'saints', the famous founder of an order Abd el Kader el Gilani, who founded the brotherhood of the Kaderiye, spread in great numbers throughout the Mohammedan world. He gave the mountains, on which he dwelt, their name. The mosque which is his grave is in Gharra on the northern slope of these mountains. He is said to have called the *butm*-tree holy, and to have laid a curse on anyone needlessly felling it. In this way the *butm*-tree has been saved from extirpation.

The rendering of the *butm*-tree on the Tell Halaf orthostats is exactly taken from nature. On them it is often used to give a background for forest and mountain animals. This combination of animal and plant is of great antiquity and is to be seen on numerous south Mesopotamian seal-cylinders. The *butm*-tree is also shown on a deep Painted Pottery bowl from Tell Halaf (which may be a sacrificial vessel), and in the same way as on the stone slabs: out of a twisted stem branches underneath and above come out in different directions. The *butm*-tree is also found with two stems on the orthostats as in nature.

Sumerian art knows of no holy tree. In it all trees are only elements in the landscape. On the other hand sacred water plays a great part in Sumerian culture, which again is natural, since in Babylonia the watering is artificial.

Pictures from every-day life are seldom found on Tell Halaf. On stone 173 L a man is climbing a twelve-runged ladder up a date-palm. In one hand he is holding a vessel and with the other he is grasping the umbel of the palm. We seem to have here a realistically shown fertilization or

Plate XXXʙ. Priestess with Knife and Bowl (75 B)

Plate XXXᴀ. Act of Worship or of Investiture (86 K)

harvest scene. In the Subaraic Iyik near Boghaz Keui we meet with the ladder again, this time by a house in building. On stone 138 L a man is climbing a *butm*-tree; below him stands an animal that is perhaps meant for a dog; in the tree above a bird is perched.

On a low stone carving (113 B, Pl. 29*a*) an angler is shown squatting on one leg. From the short rod he is holding a line hangs down.

Stone 35 L (Pl. 29*b*) has a scene with a ship. The ship is flat-bottomed and has a stem and stern-post that stand up almost straight. They are nearly the same height and flat-topped. In the left of the boat a steersman stands on a raised place; his head unfortunately is almost all missing, as the left top corner of the stone is broken off. The seaman is holding a great curved steering-oar that widens downwards like a scoop and rests on a support. In the boat are also seated two persons facing one another, of whom only the enlarged heads stand up above the boat's side and are seen. Under the boat three disproportionately great fish are seen swimming.

On stone 86 L two men are standing opposite one another; one is handing the other some object. Perhaps it is a buying contract (Pl. 30*a*).

On several stones evidently acts of worship are shown. Stone 75 B (Pl. 30*b*) has the only woman on the small orthostats that is rendered quite as a human being without any admixture of animal forms; she is probably a priestess. She is bowing, and in her right hand holds a knife, in her left a bowl, perhaps to catch up the blood of the sacrificial beast. She is wearing a long gown with a fringe below and has a girdle round her waist. The only part of her arm showing outside her garment is the hand. This priestess, like the giant goddess in the façade passage, has three thick rings on each foot.

Animal hybrids are found of the most diverse kinds. The simplest combination is between winged wild bulls and winged lions. The griffins are more complicated. By griffins we understand fabulous beings with a lion's body and wings. Often they have a lion's legs, often those of a bird of prey. When they have a bird's head they are called bird-griffins, when they have a lion's head lion-griffins.

We have already met with a lion-griffin under the body of the western veiled sphinx on the temple-palace façade. Fully corresponding to it is the beast on stone 148 B (Pl. 31*a*); the hybrid being has the winged body of a lion. The hind-feet and the tail are a bird's claws and tail, while on the lion's head there is a bull's horn.

The two orthostats in the archway of the second *hilani* passage are bird-griffins; under the eastern one was also represented a second and smaller bird-griffin, evidently fighting a winning fight against a lion. Bird-griffins are also represented on the cubic base of Hepet standing on the lioness which is in the passage-way of the large façade. The griffins must have had some connection with the 'Great goddess'. We find bird-griffins on four small orthostats. All have a winged lion's body and the bird's head, three of them also have a scorpion's tail (Pl. 31*b*) instead of a lion's. The bird's beak is generally a huge one. The transition from lion's breast to bird's head is shown in various ways. Twice a motive with bands or ribbons hanging down from the bird's head is used in just the same way as with the giant bird and the giant griffins of the façade and with the veil of the sphinx in the archway of the front façade of the temple-palace. Always the bird-griffin has a heavy mane-like comb of short feathers that reaches from the beak to the top of the wings. All the bird-griffins are full of movement; in two cases the wings are half-opened. Only once is the animal standing with its four legs on the ground; here a heron-like bird is standing on one of the wings of the griffin.

Besides the wholly animal hybrids we find on the small orthostats a good many hybrids made up of human beings and beasts. Most frequent of all is the combination of man and bull, which we have already met with on the great

PLATE XXXIa. HORNED LION-GRIFFIN (148 B)

PLATE XXXIb. BIRD-GRIFFIN WITH SCORPION'S TAIL (119 B)

Plate XXXIIB. Goddess (seraph) with Six Wings (184 B)

Plate XXXIIA. Winged God (99 B)

sun's disk orthostat of the front façade of the temple-palace. Several of the small orthostats show bull-men carrying a stool with the winged sun's disk. Another hybrid being is a winged man with bird's feet, while another, instead of the human head, has a bird's. The two are shown together on one stone with a date-palm between them. The man with the bird's head is carrying a vessel with a handle to it, and seems to be fertilizing the palm. The stone was already much mutilated in Kapara's time. On another stone, which earlier was probably twice the size, a two-winged man with bird's feet is holding a bar bent in an angle, which probably belonged to a stool for some emblem of the gods.

The hybrid being adorned with the divine crown of horns, which is a man above and a lion below, we have already met with on stone 110 K (Pl. 20b). Owing to the damaged state of the carving it cannot be certainly determined whether this hydrid had wings. If, however, we may judge by small remains, it would seem to have had two.

A highly fantastic being meets us on a basalt stone that was dug up outside the walls with the orthostats, but undoubtedly belonged there. It is a man with two wings that stand out backwards, one pointing up the other down. He is wearing the Cappadocian gown, has a human arm and a lion's paw, and one human and one bird's foot. He holds in the hand and the lion's paw a large staff. This staff has a special importance. On the small orthostats we find a great many men marked off by the long gown as being of high rank or kings, but also demons or godlings adorned with the divine crown of horns and holding in one or both hands a stick of greater or less size. This stick is—as we learn from a great many old south Mesopotamian words denoting the staff—the token of power, a kind of royal emblem.

Very important is stone 99 B (Pl. 32a). It shows a god-ling or genius. He is wearing a crown of feathers and two

upstanding horns, one on the forehead, the other on the
back of the head. The arms are raised, the hands opened;
the left foot is lifted as if to dance. In the Subaraic culture-
complex we often meet with uplifted hands, as on Tell
Halaf in the case of two Teshup figures—on a copper
matrix and on an old seal (cp. vii, pp. 216 and 224). Our
god or demi-god on stone 99 B has four wings. Otherwise
winged men (not women), who are represented as altogether human, but also as hybrid beings, have on Tell
Halaf regularly only two wings. Bearing in mind, however,
the principle of the sharp profile position of our reliefs this
means two pairs of wings.

Three orthostats (stones 19 B, 167 L and 184 B, Pl. 32*b*)
show winged women's figures. Two have three single
wings; that on stone 184 B has three pairs of wings. The
first of these pairs grows upwards out of her shoulders, the
second grows out of the hips, the third grows towards the
feet. The winged women of Tell Halaf as opposed to the
men have usually three pairs of wings, but in this case, too,
according to the principle of representation in profile, only
three single wings are generally shown. Actually the
woman godling or genius was always six-winged. It is
hence that the Bible took over the motive of the Seraphim,
of whom the prophet Isaiah says (vi, 2): 'Seraphim hovered
above Him, each with six wings. With two he covered his
face, with two he covered his feet, and with two he flew'.
We often meet with this figure down to to-day in the arts
and crafts of the Nearer East. Angels are here mostly
drawn as children's heads with six wings.

The winged women godlings are highly interesting. In
two, long feathers come out of the feather crown like ribbons, which reminds us of the very ancient Sumerian
Dame aux plumes. In one flames shoot out from the hip.
They are all clothed with the girdled Cappadocian gown.
All have a single bull's horn rising out of the forehead and
independently drawn, this betokening their divinity, and
they all have thick staffs in their hand, one also carrying

PLATE XXXIIIa. Demon with Two Lion's Heads (60 B)

PLATE XXXIIIb. Winged Scorpion-man (141 B)

PLATE XXXIVb. WINGED SPHINX WITH CROWN OF HORNS

PLATE XXXIVa. WINGED LION WITH LION'S AND

a bow. The woman with the six wings is carrying two large staffs in her outstretched hands; here, too, the staffs must undoubtedly be a symbol of power.

A very remarkable fabulous being is the winged demon with two lions' heads (stone 60 B, Pl. 33*a*). On a human body, which is rendered in full front view and clothed in a long girdled gown, are set two lions' heads in profile turned away from one another. From the shoulders two wings stand out towards the sides. The feet are turned outwards; all five toes and fingers are drawn. In the outstretched hands the demon holds bars pointing downwards and twice broken into an angle, but it almost looks as if he was to be represented as an emblem carried on these bars.

Near akin to this stone are combinations of birds with outstretched wings and lions' heads, and also birds with two birds' heads on long necks, such as we find in other places. They play a great part in the oldest times, partly as animals on coats of arms or as banners. The motive lasted down to the time of the Persians and later. In Ikonium (Konia) we find the double eagle as the arms of the sultans of Rum; and then, having been brought by the Crusaders to Europe, it became the arms also of the Austro-Hungarian and of the Russian monarchy.

This demon on stone 60 B reminds us of the staff with two lions' heads which we often come across in Old Sumer and on Kassite *kudurrus* (boundary stones). In south Mesopotamia it is the emblem of the god Nergal and Ninurta; and as the sign of the Twins (Gemini) it passed into the zodiac.

Stone 141 B (Pl. 33*b*) shows us a scorpion-bird-man. On massive bird's legs with disproportionately big claws the bird's body stands straight up with wings pointing upwards. A bearded man's head is planted on the body without any neck between and is wearing the crown of feathers with bull's horns pointing forward. The effect is like 'Chanteclair' in Rostand's play. We shall come across the same fantastic being again on two of the orthostats on the archway of the temple-palace gate.

The scorpion and scorpion-men we meet with from oldest times in south Mesopotamia and in Elam. We find it on the animal orchestra of Ur with a man's feet and a heavy scorpion's tail. The scorpion is a symbol of the goddess Ishchara (Ishtar). As a constellation the scorpion-man is also the Archer, Sagittarius. Of the twelve constellations of the zodiac ten can be seen on our small orthostats.

The next set of hybrid beings are women sphinxes. This symbolical figure developed, I believe, in the following way: The goddess at first stood upright on the back of the winged lion, sacred to her, as for instance on old Babylonian seal-cylinders from the beginning of the 3rd millennium. Some mythological idea or an artist's whim then set instead of the goddess's whole body only her head on the lion, though at the same time the lion's head was also kept. This is what we find on sculptures in Senjirli and Karkemish, where the woman's head rests on the sphinx's shoulders, and on Tell Halaf, where it is put on the lion's head itself. Finally the lion's head was wholly left out, and only the human head was left. Thus the sphinx came into being. On Tell Halaf we have the whole course of development. First of all there is the great goddess sculptured in the round on the lioness in the passage in the front façade; here on the cubic base or socle between the lion's back and the goddess griffins (winged lions with birds' heads) are cut. Of the small orthostats some show the lion, others the winged lion, and others still this latter with the lion's head along with the woman's head decorated with horns and therefore divine (stone 43 L, Pl. 34a). Lastly appears the completed form of the sphinx—the winged lion with the woman's head—on Tell Halaf on several orthostats and as sculpture in the round in the veiled sphinxes of the front façade of the temple-palace as representing the great goddess Hepet. Always on the small orthostats the sphinx is turned to the right. The limestone lion with the woman's head on it wears a particularly ancient look. It is not set, as always in other cases, along the diagonal of the stone;

all the feet, on the contrary, except the right fore-paw, which is, as always, lifted threateningly, are standing on the ground, as though the winged lion were hereby to be shown as the beast of burden for the goddess standing on it.

As in the case of the winged sun's disk, the question arises out of the sphinxes, whether they came to Hither Asia from Egypt, or to Egypt from Hither Asia. I believe that the sphinx, too, is older in Hither Asia, and of course in the Subaraic culture area, than in Egypt. Its process of change from the simple lion to the winged sphinx points in itself to this.

A male sphinx is found only once on the small orthostats. On stone 81 B (Pl. 35*a*) there is a man's head resting on a lion's body with wings lifted straight up. The head is represented full face, a thing found only twice elsewhere. The full beard is in zig-zag lines; above the lips a moustache can be seen. The locks of hair fall like a wig on to the two shoulders and are heavily coiled outwards on both sides. On the head is the horned cap with stout bull's horns wide apart. The cap itself goes up to a point and shows parallel waved lines. The motive is the same as on the great stone that lies perpendicular to the western wall of the temple-palace façade, with the exception only that in the small orthostat the hybrid being is again represented from the side standing up along the diagonal. In the great relief slab also of the front façade the winged lion, as we saw, stands in profile; the head in all its details agrees almost exactly with the small orthostat, and it, too, is rendered from in front.

Of great interest is stone 77 B (Pl. 35*b*) with a fish-man. We meet him in the same form on a seal-cylinder of Gudea along with the ibex-fish hybrid on both sides of the god Enki-ea, who plays jets of water down on them. The fish-man there symbolizes Oannes, the being through whom, according to Berosus, the revelation of all knowledge was granted in oldest times unto the men of Babylonia. In our relief the human upper part of the body grows up in front

at right angles from the fish-body, whose head is wanting. The man is bearded and, like all the fabulous beings of Tell Halaf, is wearing a coat or gown with short sleeves. He is the only hybrid being in which the divine emblem of the bull's horns is not found. In his hands he is holding a ribbon with sharp windings, which old examples show to mean water. The fish-man, too, belongs to the sign of the zodiac. The first idea for the carving came undoubtedly from the huge fish (one of the carp family, *Cyprinidae*) which in the summer often swims up to Tell Halaf. Professor Friedrich Hommel especially busied himself with these hybrids.

The pictures on several of the reliefs seem to me to be connected with the Gilgamesh legend. We saw that the subject-matter of this saga appears also among the Subaraeans, and more than this, that the origin of the Gilgamesh saga is not yet certainly known, whether Sumerian or old Subaraic (cp. above, p. 51). A part of the splendid epic was found in the Hurritic-Subaraic tongue, and with the significant title 'Khuvava Epic'. The Khumbaba of the Babylonians (that is, the Khuvava of the Subaraeans) is also represented outwardly as a monster with a broad face which we find made up of entrails. As a dwarfish, hideous god with an over-sized head always represented from in front, he evidently was taken over into Egyptian mythology as the god Bes.

On stone 180 B (Pl. 36*a*) we have this Khuvava being killed by Gilgamesh and his friend and comrade Engidu. The surly Khuvava, drawn with a broad face, a full beard and long hair, is between two young beardless persons, who are holding his legs fast in a hooked position and trussing his arms crosswise on his body. This position reminds us of ju-jitsu grips. Khuvava is fronting us, his two opponents are in profile. They are plunging two short knives from above into his head; a third knife is already sticking in the top of his skull, and has almost the effect of a horn. In the Gilgamesh epic we are told that the heroes wrought the daggers themselves with which they slew the monster. It is in the same way that Khuvava is killed on an orthostat in the Subaraic Karkemish also. D. Opitz has described a Babylonian terra-cotta relief in the Berlin museum on which also Gilgamesh and Engidu are plunging a short sword or knife from above into the head or neck of Khuvava, who is lying stretched on the ground. Khuvava's head is here seen full face again, while his vanquishers are shown in profile. The face is here likewise broad and ugly. Gilgamesh, the demi-god, two-thirds god one-third man, is on this and other Tell Halaf orthostats represented as wholly human.

Another orthostat, stone 182 B (Pl. 36b), shows a duel, perhaps that between Gilgamesh and Engidu, who was later his friend. According to the epic the strong Engidu had appeared before the town of Uruk, where he lived with the animals and sheltered the weak ones against beasts of prey. All in Uruk were afraid of him, but a temple harlot sent out by Gilgamesh had succeeded in bringing him before Gilgamesh in Uruk. When the two met, they fell on one another. Gilgamesh overcame the stranger, but spared him, whereupon the two became inseparable friends. Here we are reminded of Castor and Pollux. This fight, I believe, is represented on stone 182 B. One of the fighters is smaller and with a shaggy beard, perhaps to mark the wild Engidu before he was civilized. The other is taller and slimmer, like on stone 180 B. Both are in the same fighting position: one hand is laid on the opponent's forehead to keep him back, the other hand points the sword against the foe. But Gilgamesh's sword is already thrust into Engidu's body.

To a fight between two opponents shown exactly the same in figure and position we find various counterparts on seals from the first half of the 3rd millennium, and also on Subaraic seal-cylinders. Up till now such scenes were generally called Gilgamesh figures facing one another, or Gilgamesh triumphing over himself.

M

The broad orthostat 170 B (Pl. 37*a*) also probably deals with the Gilgamesh legend. It is a corner block that stood at the south-eastern corner bastion of the temple-palace just by the slope up to the Scorpions' Gate. It is 110 centimetres long, and 59 centimetres high on the left, 70 centimetres high on the right. The broad side and the right-hand narrow space are carved.

On the main carving there sits on the left a bearded man with the face turned rightwards on a low four-legged chair without a back. He has a full beard and shaven upper lip, and the stereotyped band round his hair. He is wearing the long gown that on Tell Halaf always marks people of rank. The right hand shows outside the cloak and is lying on the knees; in his left hand he is holding a herb with three separate flowers and bringing it to his nose or mouth. On his right two bull-men facing one another are carrying on a low stool-like stand the winged sun's disk, as in the carving shown on the great sun orthostat at the front façade of the temple-palace. I think it not impossible that in the seated man it is Gilgamesh growing old that was meant to be shown with the Herb of Life for which he yearns that he may escape death. Before him stands the emblem of the Sun god. The Sun god is named in the Gilgamesh epic as the hero's helper in his fight with Khuvava. That Gilgamesh is not standing, but sitting, before his god, may mean that he is sick or dying. On later grave stelae, for instance in Senjirli, women are represented sitting at a table with different kinds of food, and holding in the hand a like herb, though here it is less simple and more Egyptian-looking, and above it the sun emblem can be seen. Here again we have the thought of death. The figure on the narrow side (Pl. 37*b*) of corner-stone 170 I think to be Gilgamesh beyond all doubt. It is turned to the left, and this time has no beard; in the uplifted right hand it is holding a club. The left hand is hanging down and looks to be mutilated, but is not. The man is wearing a half-length shirt with a belt. Over this he has a lion's skin, of which only two paws, below to right and left, can be seen. The skin is worked below into bow-shape. The man's left hand, badly carved in its fore-shortening, is holding the lion's skin.

A picture of the same kind, on which the remarkable lion's skin can be made out still better, is shown on another stone that was found outside the series on the bastion walls. The man, who here, too, is turned to the left, has a short beard. He is carrying, and in the same position, instead of the club a weapon bent upwards—a bumerang or a crescent-sword. With his left hand he is holding the lion's skin, which can be much better seen. In the same way, with the paws shown below standing asunder in bow-shape, a panther's skin is represented in Egypt, a skin worn in the Old Kingdom by all persons of importance.

Among the most remarkable sculptures of Tell Halaf are two limestone slabs with dancing and music-playing animals. One (stone 57 L, Pl. 38), 117 centimetres broad and 78 centimetres high, is more than twice as great as the other small orthostats; the other one (stone 92 L) is of the usual size.

The drawing of the animals is very full of life, and they are put in space free without overlapping one another. On the larger stone (57 L) by the left edge a lion is sitting like a human being on a high rocky block, which, tapering conically upwards, is like the representations of mountains on Tell Halaf and in Sumer-Akkad. The lion is playing with its right hand on a harp seen from in front and widening upwards. This is the usual form in the oldest Nearer East, though the Tell Halaf harp is somewhat higher, and the bull's head usually found in south Mesopotamia or the effigy of an animal on the sounding-board are wanting. The number of strings cannot be exactly made out, but seems to be five. On the cubical stand with the musicians between the lion and the Sun god at the great front façade we find five strings on a harp.

Towards the lion a giant ass is striding on its hind-legs, it and the lion being the main figures in the picture. The ears, one of which points forward, the other sideways, are the mark of the grey beast; the mouth is half open as he brays.

The other animals, too, are running on their hind-legs or leaping. All but one are facing left towards the lion. The donkey is followed above by a bear, which here again has a long tail; it is holding a great cymbal in its paws. Behind it a gazelle or antelope is carrying a bowl.

In a lower row there walk behind the ass a dog, that seems to be holding the ass's tail, then a pig with a cymbal or a drum, and behind them another bear holding a stick on its shoulder on which it is carrying two vessels slung on its back. To the right by the edge there stands above this bear a smallish beast that cannot now be made out, and above it in the top right corner an ape sitting like a human being is carved. Before it is a four-legged angular stand with a rounded vessel running to a point upwards and downwards. The ape is making what must be an intoxi-cating drink flow into a bowl by means of a suction-tube.

Between the lion and the donkey there are four beasts arranged over one another. The three upper ones are facing left and turning towards the lion. Right at the top is a leaping dog, under it a cat, under this a dog or wolf, and lastly, right below, clearly to be recognized by its bushy tail, a fox walking to the right towards the ass. All the beasts have cymbals or rattling instruments in their fore-paws and seem to be dancing and also drunk; the lion, the king of beasts, is also playing to them. The ass in its great excitement lets fall seven droppings.

The smaller animal orchestra is unfortunately much weathered; evidently it was painted over by Kapara in the badly preserved state as he found it, so as to be used again. The ochre coating, when we dug out the stone, was lying also on the damaged places. This was also the case with several other limestone slabs—a proof once more that Kapara had used them over again.

In the second animal orchestra we have once more a

lion sitting at the left-hand edge on a block of rock with
the same harp seen from in front; and again from the
middle an ass strides towards him, and leaves his droppings. Under the lion's feet a fox is springing at the ass.
Above these two main figures is shown a dog leaping to the
left with cymbals in the fore-paws. Under the lion a cat
jumps to the left; it has its head turned backwards and is
fleeing from a dog to which it stretches out one of its fore-
paws. In the paw it is holding a tambourine. Behind the
dog goes a pig, holding perhaps a rattle. This is held downwards and reminds us of a bunch of three rods such as we
find on archaic Susa seal impressions. Behind the ass is a
bear standing right up. Above on the right another ape is
squatting; before it there is here, too, a square open stand
with feet, in which is a vessel, and from it the ape is again
running wine into a bowl out of the bent suction-tube.
But here the stand has something on top behind, that is
to the left, which we cannot very well make out. Evidently there was some object shown, perhaps some part of
an animal, as in the orchestra at Ur, destined for the lion's
feast. In this animal orchestra, too, the beasts seem to be
dancing and to be filled with wine.

The whole treatment, as seen in the animal orchestras, is
highly original, and they are of the utmost importance for
the Old East. At the same time we know of certain parallels from the oldest times of all to some of the details. Thus
on a seal from Fara in Lower Mesopotamia a seated hybrid
being is striking the harp, while animals dance below.
Animals dancing and playing on musical instruments
treated humorously, some in human attitudes, we also
find on many old seal impressions from Susa, but without
any animal orchestra. On an old Egyptian rouge-pallet
from Hierakonpolis there is a jackal walking upright and
playing the flute with other animals represented around it.
The animal orchestras, however, have for the first time
found a real and striking analogy through the finds at Ur.
On one of the finest of these, a harp, a mother-of-pearl

plaque is fixed under a bull's head of gold and lapis lazuli ornamenting the instrument. On this plaque there are three rows of music-playing and dancing animals represented. Here, too, the chief performers are the lion and the ass, but their parts are exchanged. The lion is carrying a wine-jar and a bowl, the ass is playing the harp. The attitude and the gait of the seated and the standing beasts are in part amazingly like the others, only that the animal orchestra from Tell Halaf seems still older, more natural, freer and with more movement than the one from Ur. Finally the distribution of the several animals in the space available reminds us of the oldest carvings from Susa. All these examples are either prehistoric, like the Egyptian, or, like the Babylonian and Susa examples, belong to the very earliest historical times. In all of them the subject is treated very summarily, while on Tell Halaf it is set forth in greater detail and on far more primitive artistic principles. The animal orchestra from Ur in particular has come to be 'classical' when compared with those from Tell Halaf. From this we have to conclude that the peculiar form of the motive on Tell Halaf is the model for the other examples mentioned, and therefore older than these. The animal orchestras on Tell Halaf are the work of the Painted Pottery period, when there were still close connexions between the Subaraeans of Upper Mesopotamia and the dwellers in Elam-Susa, and probably also between the former and the Lower Mesopotamian folk of the pre-Sumerian Painted Pottery layer, whose remnants had become subject to the Sumerians, who had penetrated into Lower Mesopotamia. It is from this subject people that the conquerors may then have inherited the theme for the animal orchestra at Ur.

In recent times the thesis has been advanced that the Sumerians did not immigrate into Upper Mesopotamia at all, but that they had been settled there from farthest times ago. On this view, the similarity between the finds at Tell Halaf and Jebelet-el-Beda, particularly the motives on the small orthostats (such as the animal orchestra and animal fights), and those of oldest times from Ur, Kish, etc., and also from Elam, becomes more easily explained. The same is true for the likeness in cultural thought, as well as that between some deities and symbols (the bull's horn, for instance, a token of godship) and in the epic figures of Gilgamesh, Khumbaba (Khuvava), etc.

Sumerian art and culture, as they become clear to us in the latter half of the 4th millennium, would then be a natural further growth of the oldest Painted Pottery periods of Neolithic times. When the Sumerians emerged into history they had already attained to a certain individuality in this art and culture. This was shown in the beautiful finds of Ur and Kish. Thence this culture went along its own ways. In north-west Subartuland where the painted pottery was much longer preserved, the ancient traditions lived on for a greater length of time, in some respects even down to Hellenistic times, as we may see from Nimrud Dagh. But even in this case the Sumerian art and culture, as well as the Subaraic culture (or Hurritic, or pre-Hittite, or however it may be called), would still both have had their roots in the great Near Eastern culture. That this culture (at least from time to time) reached even further to the east than we had previously believed, may be seen from the newest finds of Prof. Aurel Stein in Beluchistan, and from the finds of Muhendjo Daro and Harappa in north-western India.

We find also in Egypt, on the so-called satirical papyrus of Turin, which belongs to a time later than the eighteenth dynasty, humorous representations of dancing or playing animals. This document is an unusual one for Egypt. The motive of animals moving and behaving like human beings may well have reached the Nile land in the Mitanni period from Hither Asia. Musicians are often found in the Subaraic culture area, and repeatedly along with beasts, to whom they are playing. This is the Orpheus conception that then went on to Greece. But it is worthy of remark that music-playing beasts are not to be found either in later Babylonian or in Assyrian art.

The train of thought behind our animal orchestras takes its rise undoubtedly in animal fables still unknown to us, and belonging to the primitive Subaraic culture. Furthermore we have to bear in mind that music stands in a close relation with the Sun god. It may be that our animal orchestra was meant to depict the celebration of a solstitial festival.

Gods

The carvings on the small orthostats have undoubtedly much that refers to the religious life of the oldest dwellers on Tell Halaf. We do not yet know, however, what was the meaning in the religion of the old times of most of the demons and godlings or genii, and most of the human and purely animal hybrids. But one thing I hold to be certain —that the chief gods of Tell Halaf and of the Subaraic complex are often shown on the small orthostats. Teshup, the highest god, the Lord of Heaven and Earth, the Rain and Thunder god, is found on many of the carvings, and always as a man with the bull's horn, and once (on stone 89 B) full face with bumerang and club, as on the great front façade. We would call particular attention to the very old stone (106 L, Pl. 39a), where he is represented in profile with club and lightning-sheaf. In both pictures he is wearing the long gown, on stone 106 perhaps pointed shoes.

The emblem of the Sun god, the winged sun's disk, is often found. Where the chariot is depicted the Sun god met us in bird's shape. Among the most effective carvings of Tell Halaf is stone 87 B (Pl. 39b), where a sun eagle in flight soars over a conical mountain—the rising sun.

I think the women sphinxes—the winged lion with woman's and lion's heads, or with the woman's head only —must be looked on as representing the great goddess

PLATE XL. DIGGING OUT THE SCORPION'S GATE

Hepet; so also the woman godlings or genii with three pairs of wings. All the heads have bulls' horns on the forehead.

Thus the trinity of the Tell Halaf gods is fully represented on the small orthostats also. But while the representatives of the great gods at the front façade of the temple-palace were set up in an outstanding position with altars before them, their carvings on the small orthostats upon the bastions and wall recesses of the back façade of the palace are arranged quite at random. And here ordinary mortals were allowed to visit them.

Space forbids me to describe any more of the reliefs on the small orthostats. We can imagine what impressions rushed in in olden times on the beholder to whom the meaning of the sculptures was fully known, when he approached the rows of orthostats.

VI

The Other Stone Carvings

I

THE entry into the hallowed *hilani* area was guarded by two statues of wardens. They belong to the gate building over against the gate of the citadel wall.

These wardens of the gate are two scorpion-birdmen (Pl. 40, 41, and 42*a*). They are again archway orthostats, carved in front as sculptures in the round and at the sides as relief slabs. On the back and on the broad side of the eastern stone leaning against the wall of the gateway traces can still be made out of earlier work done on it, the tail and hind-legs of a lion. We had already observed in the case of the west veiled sphinx of the temple-palace the same occurrence of a second partial carving, but only in the raw block, on the second broad side of an archway orthostat. In the scorpion-birdman the lion's tail, which had been left no longer visible when the sculpture was set up at the extension of the gateway, runs round the hind-quarters to the side of the figure now seen. It is evident that the block of stone was originally meant to be used for quite a different representation. This east scorpion-birdman is older than that on the west; it is shorter and more squat. I believe that it was carved not much later than the small orthostats. The socle slab of the older one is 1.85 metres long and 0.58 broad; that of the newer one is 2.06 metres long and 0.47 broad.

Both sculptures were lying in the middle of the gateway passage with the carved side to the ground. The heads and the upper narrow sides of the stone slabs were turned to one another. To our exceeding joy we found when they were set up again that they were wholly undamaged.

The human head, the breast and the bird's legs are

PLATE XI.A. YOUNGER SCORPION-MAN (p.)

PLATE XLIIa. OLDER SCORPION BIRD-MAN

PLATE XLIIb. THE TWO THRONED GODDESSES IN THE MUD-BRICK MASSIF

treated as sculpture in the round; the bird's body and scorpion's tail as a relief slab. Both these hybrid beings have long seamen's beards with shaven upper and lower lip. On the older statue the beard is simply waved and ends in spirals; on the newer statue, on the other hand, the beard has two rows of spirals below and a third one above, under the upper lip. The side whiskers are in both shown by spirals; the same thing holds for the thick hair on the head, which comes down in four rows on to the nape of the neck. In both the head is covered by a low crown of feathers or cap with three ribbons and two pairs of bull's horns. Under these the hair is drawn in net-work on the older statue, and on the later in spirals.

The facial expression of the older stone shows the archaic smile; in the later one it is grimly severe. Worthy of particular note are the thick, very projecting lips of the older stone; they greatly remind us of the beak-nosed faces on the double stela of Jebelet-el-Beda. The breast of the two gate colossi is broad, strongly arched, and worked like a net; the work is softer on the older statue, and harder on the later one. The bird's feet and claws are powerful, the bird's body is stretched out to an extraordinary length, probably to fill up the broad space on the wall. The feathers on the body are depicted flame-wise. The bird's body ends in feathers in a cylinder-like clump, out of which comes the scorpion's tail bending upwards. Over the whole body is spread a wing with a threefold division: the uppermost part shows rows of balls, the two others are made up by the well-known fish-bone feather pattern; in the case of the later stone there is furthermore on the breast in front the scale motive which we already know. On the sides turned towards the wall the two carvings have in the front part the attachments of a wing. Here in the case of the older stone the three rows on the wing are represented by simple stripes, going deeper and deeper; in the later stone the top row of feathers is rendered by the balls. This treatment on the side turned towards the wall is in the case of both carried out for about a metre's length from the head. It is clear that the sculptures originally were meant as orthostats in the archway to stand with the front part left free, in the same way as the veiled sphinxes and the giant griffins of the two passages in the temple-palace. Instead of this they were put all their length along the wall by Kapara, so that nothing of the carvings on the sides, and not even the side of the bird's feet turned towards the wall were visible—once more a proof that the two archway orthostats also were found by Kapara and were used over again to set up at the gate of his palace. In the older of the two scorpion-birdmen on the side turned towards the mud-brick wall, on top behind, a bit of the stone was missing. I am convinced that Kapara found the statue with this damage beyond any doubt already done long before.

It is easy to read the meaning of the scorpion-birdmen. They were put as archway orthostats before the gate as wardens to refuse the entry to any but those summoned. They keep off foes and evil-minded men with their sting. They are the same fabulous beings that Gilgamesh comes to when he makes the journey to Utnapishti to win the Herb of Immortality. They watch over the gate through which the sun daily goes out and comes in. Above them the slopes of Heaven rise up; their breast below reaches the Underworld. 'Scorpion-folk watch over the gate, whose awesomeness is dreadful, the sight of whom is death', is what we read in the Gilgamesh epic. The only difference is that here these watchers are not both men, but the scorpion-man and his wife.

We find on old seal-cylinders, likewise, scorpion-men, which have wings as in our case, and which stand opposite one another and are therefore probably gate wardens, the idea being remembered from the Gilgamesh epic. But nowhere do we find that sculptured scorpion-men are actually set as wardens before a gate, as in our case on Tell Halaf. And with it all they are here of such a huge size.

PLATE XLIII. GREAT THRONED GODDESS

PLATE XLIVB. SMALL THRONED GODDESS

PLATE XLIVA, GREAT THRONED GODDESS

Perhaps the most impressive statue on Tell Halaf is the great throned goddess (1.80 metres high, 0.82 broad, 0.95 deep; Pl. 42b, 43 and 44a), which we found walled in in a huge mass of mud bricks, and over a grave shaft driven into the living rock not far east of the south citadel gate.

The statue, weighing almost four tons, is of basalt, like all the large pieces of Tell Halaf sculpture in the round. It represents a woman seated upright on a high chair without back or arms. The stiff, calm and stately bearing at once marks her out as a goddess on a throne. Her feet are resting on a low stool. Seen from the side the chair shows cross-pieces below and has a net-like ornamentation on the edge of the seat.

The statue is, as it were, put together from three cubes or rectangles climbing like a pyramid. From the foot-stool rises the lower part of the woman's body which is shaped like a cube. Its rigid lines show hardly any bodily form, and it almost gives the impression as if the goddess were holding a broad board on her knees and the clothing were hanging down from it. On the upper surface of the squared block rests the outstretched forearm with the hand laid flat on it, while the right hand is holding a beaker well forward on the lap. Perpendicular to this cube, set far back, a fresh cubic block then rises to the woman's shoulder. From this the head stands up on a high neck. In spite of its highly primitive lines the expression on the face is remarkably impressive. The chin is retreating and runs downwards to a point; the cheek-bones and cheeks are strongly marked. The eyes (they are not inlaid) are on the small side. In the somewhat low-set ears there are holes for some metal ornament that seems once to have been there. The hair on the forehead is depicted in the usual way on Tell Halaf by curled ringlets and hangs low down on the shoulders. From the forehead there falls on each side of the face and in front of the ears a heavy lock on to the breast; it is independently carved and grooved in a slant. The lower part of the face is flat; the lips of the small mouth are delicately and beautifully curved. The wings of the nose are broad, and somewhat damaged below on the left. The line of the nose runs up over the forehead and head in a single bold curve. Particularly striking is the retreating forehead, like that which we find on the oldest Hither Asiatic statues. Seen in profile the head reminds us of the beaked-nose faces on the very early Sumerian cylinders and the double stela of Jebelet-el-Beda.

The feet are small and carved with great care. Although the forearms are shown too short, this is more especially true of the upper arms and the whole of the upper part of the body. This is too low in relation to the immense breadth of the shoulders. The stunting of the arms, too, is shared by this figure with the god on the double stela of Jebelet-el-Beda.

The woman is wearing a gown. Its sleeves reach just short of the elbow and have a broad edging. This edging bears a zigzag motive and runs on at right angles down to the lap; another strip made up of ribbons or bands with an angular motive follows the lines of the upper arms and shoulders up to the neck. The gown ends below in a zigzag ribbon motive, which, however, at the bottom is not finished off, as though a hanging fringe were to be represented reaching almost to the bare feet.

The upper part of the body leans slightly backwards.

The throned figure in its great calm has something majestic about it. The countenance shows in a very high degree the mystical archaic smile. In spite of the over-great head and the cubical shape, of the wholly lacking indication of the breast and the too broad shoulders and equally broad lap, the effect is extraordinarily impressive. The goddess's smile has a fascination that grows on the onlooker. It is a work of the greatest artistic perfection. Anything like this so to speak 'Cubist' goddess is not to be found anywhere else in the world. In some ways the well-known beautiful old Greek seated goddess in white marble of the Berlin Museum might be compared with her; this, too, has the mysterious smile. But in strength, originality and dignified character the goddess of Tell Halaf stands above the Greek goddess, who is a descendant of ours, coming 2000 years later.

It was one of the great events of my excavations and one of my greatest joys as a discoverer, to see this statue literally rising out of the ground. After the greatly denuded mass of mud bricks had been laid bare—the part, that is, projecting into the town—its surface was cleared. In doing this we first of all came on the top of the head. It looked like a great dark iron pan, but soon the outlines of the head showed themselves. Now one layer of mud bricks after the other was carefully lifted away. It was just here that the work of digging was difficult, as the old brickwork was very strong and progress was slow. The work, however, had to be carried on most carefully so that the pickaxes should not do any hurt to the statue. It was hours and, indeed, days, before the great throned goddess at last stood before us in all her greatness. What was our joy when we found that the statue was wholly unhurt! Our Beduin workmen came to call this goddess my bride, because I kept on going to her and could not be out of sight of her.

As a result of finding this statue I decided to keep on digging northwards in the front structure. I was convinced that we should find another statue of the same kind, likewise embedded in the brick mass. Slowly the work went on in the hard mud-brickwork, and my hopes were not in vain. We came upon a second and smaller throned goddess (Pl. 42b, 44b).

That the statue was found over a grave and held a bowl in the hand was almost ground enough for believing that we had to do with a deified queen who was buried here. That the queen should be making the drink-offering seated is, however, an impossibility; those praying are always depicted as standing with a vessel lowered, from which water is offered to the godhead. Beyond all question what we have here is the great Subaraic goddess—Hepet.

The motive of the throned goddess with the bowl in her hand is not unknown to the old Nearer East. Thus we find it on a pre-Sargonic limestone votive tablet at Nippur. Here the goddess is seated on an almost ostrich-like goose, the holy beast of Ba'u or Gula, one of the chief goddesses of the Sumerians in the 3rd millennium, though it may be that also her worship goes back to Old Subaraic tradition.

The second goddess, whom we found $5\frac{1}{2}$ metres north of the great goddess, is of basalt also, but somewhat smaller. The treatment seems to be akin to that of the great figure, but yet it is different. The figure is stouter-built. The sculpture is 1.42 metres high, 0.55 broad, and 0.72 deep. This goddess, too, sits on a stool-like chair with cross-pieces, but without any ornament at the sides. Her feet are on a low stool of the same workmanship. The shoulders are sloping, more womanly, and the breasts are more marked. The left hand hangs down a little from the lap; the right is again holding a bowl. Round the arms are three thick rings. The locks of hair hanging down in front of the ears of the larger statue are here wanting; the hair is set still further back in independently twisted braids. On the head is a low crown of feathers. There are no holes for the ear-drops.

The face has a quite different expression. It is more fleshy; the chin shows three folds across it; the nose far more curved, not so pointed and thicker. The forehead does not 'retreat', but rises higher above the nose. This goddess has not inset eyes either. The lips are thick and broad; the expression is that of an old person and serious. The face is far nearer akin to that of the gigantic goddess standing on the lioness at the main entrance to the temple-palace, although in this latter, contrasting with the morose expression of the seated old woman, an archaic smile can be seen. This smaller statue, too, represents the great goddess of the old Tell Halaf town, and it watches over a grave likewise.

The sculptor of the larger goddess was perhaps the same

who carved the veiled sphinx. There is undoubtedly a certain likeness in facial expression between the two. The great goddess is undoubtedly older than the small one. E. Herzfeld believes that the former must be dated about 2800, the latter about 2400.

Both goddesses were wardens of graves. With the small one the shaft lay a little to the side of the ground slabs she stood on. No skeletons were found in the shafts, but only traces of remains from fire. The dead had undoubtedly been burnt and their ashes buried. The grave gifts came from the most various times. In one grave was found a very old limestone bowl with three feet (Pl. 48a), whose edge shows men in long gowns fighting with beasts and fabulous beings. The pottery, on the other hand, was from the Kapara period. The use at burials of grave gifts coming from a much earlier time than the grave itself is repeatedly found by us in the Old East. Our graves hold, I believe, the remains of more ancient members of the Kapara dynasty, these being, to judge by the gold ornaments laid with them (cp. below, p. 222) the remains of women. The shafts and statues were lying within small, cell-like grave buildings, of whose walls only remains were still left. It is in this state that Kapara may have found the whole. He then made fresh use of the grave shafts and built a great mud-brick mass over the half-destroyed cells, the graves, and the basalt goddesses, without leaving any hollow space. That he was responsible for the brick mass may be concluded from the shape of the bricks. In this way the graves and stone figures were saved from any meddling till we could dig them out.

Besides the temple-palace on the citadel of Tell Halaf we dug out in the town area another temple building of the Kapara period: a small shrine near the town wall, east of the road that led from the south gate of the town to the citadel gate (Pl. 45a). We called it the 'cult room.' It lay partly under our expeditionary house. In the holy of holies we were able to dig out two extraordinarily inter-

N

esting fair-sized statues. The plan of the cult room has a certain likeness with the old Ishtar temple of Assur (about 3000 B.C.), which because of its non-Babylonian form has been brought by W. Andrae to a certain extent into connection with the temples of Boghaz Keui from the middle of the 2nd millennium. The architecture of the Ishtar temple follows old Subaraic traditions, which as in Boghaz Keui so, too, on Tell Halaf had lasted down into Kapara's day. Our room for worship was built by Kapara. We found it quite untouched. On the floor before the statues of the gods lay offerings: household idols (Teraphim), necklaces of stone and frit and much besides. These objects were evidently dedicated to the gods in the last moment before the town was destroyed.

On a plastered mud-brick shelf 40 centimetres high at the rear narrow side of the temple was standing a double statue (Pl. 45b). A little in front of the shelf stood a single statue on a base of its own. Before the gods was a rectangular socle 75 centimetres high, of plastered bricks, and before it lay a rectangular basalt trough on the floor, with an ornamented partition with a hole in it. The socle made an altar for the slain offerings, whose blood ran off first of all down into the first compartment of the trough and then flowed through an opening in the partition into the second and slightly lower part.

The double statue (0.80 metres high, 0.88 broad, 0.43 deep) is worked from one stone and represents a man's and a woman's figure. They are sitting on a bench, their bare feet resting on the base-slab. The figures have a great likeness to the small throned goddess. As in this latter, the left hands rest on the lap, while the lower joints of the fingers hang over it. The right hands are clenched; they may once have held the handle or the foot of some kind of beaker that was afterwards knocked off. The man and the woman are slightly damaged on the nose only, but the woman also on the chin; it is almost certain that Kapara found them like that. The lap and the gowns, that fall to the feet, are once

Plate XLVa. The Cult Room after being dug out

Plate XLVb. Double Statue from the Cult Room

PLATE XLVI. BASALT IDOLS

1. Head of an idol (12 cm. high). 2. Figure of woman with hands pressed to the breast (20 cm. high). 3. Figure of woman (19 cm. high). 4. Figure of man with long pointed beard (10 cm. high). 5. Figure of woman standing with vessel (16 cm. high). 6. Figure of seated woman (20 cm. high). 7. Figure of seated man (25·5 cm. high).

more almost cubistically treated, just as they are in the small throned goddess.

The man has no head covering. The hair is drawn in thick rings of curls and falls heavily behind the ears on to the shoulders; we are almost reminded of a wig. The sailor's beard is divided up into slightly waved zigzag lines ending in natural curls, in the same way as in the older scorpion-birdman. The cheek-bones are very prominent; the eyes, as in the other two figures in the cult room, were inset. We found them in part still in the sockets; they are as usual made of limestone with a polished black centre. The man is wearing a long gown with sleeves, the gown we already know from the great Teshup and the small orthostats; around the breast and shoulders runs a broad belt or band.

The woman gives a younger effect than the small throned goddess. The expression on the face is milder than in the man, who has an extraordinarily serious and severe gaze. On the head she wears a low crown of feathers. Her hair hangs in plaits behind the ear over the shoulder. The breasts are slightly moulded. Round the neck are two rows of beads.

In both figures the gown is cut wide open above, and at the neck and sleeves it is edged with a heavy band; otherwise the clothing shows no ornamentation.

The second statue of the cult room is a man 100 centimetres high standing straight up on a base (Pl. 45a). While the double statue rested on a mud-brick socle, the single statue was fixed on to a large and heavy basalt slab by a strong plug and made fast in the plug-hole with lead poured in. The double and the single statue stood at the same height above the ground. The man has the same beard and the same cast of countenance as the man in the double statue. He is wearing a low crown of feathers, under which the hair falls in heavy curls on to the shoulder. His garb, however, is like that of the giant gods on the great façade. He wears first of all a shirt, which can still be seen on the left thigh (stretched slightly forward), and which here, as on the loose sleeve, ends in a hem. The gown or overall is open in front like the Cappadocian cloaks and leaves the left leg free. But it is more simply draped below than it is on the giant god; the slanting flounces are wanting. In the right hand we see a shouldered bumerang, while the left fist clenches the handle of a long sword. His expression is stern and harsh.

E. Herzfeld dates the double statue about 2500 and the small standing god about 2400. The man in the double statue has a decided likeness with the bronze seated statuette of a god from Boghaz Keui in the Berlin museum, which O. Weber has dated about 3000 B.C. The head of this bronze statuette, however, is more like that of our older scorpion-birdman.

The double statue is one of the most impressive and noteworthy sculptures on Tell Halaf. It has no analogies in the Nearer East, but shows certain likenesses with the well-known Egyptian representations of divine and human married couples which are found as early as in the oldest dynasties in the Nile land.

The statues of the cult room are likewise without inscriptions.

The meaning of the three figures is not hard to read. Again we have the Tell Halaf triad of gods before us: Teshup with his wife Hepet in the double statue and the Sun god. They are set up in the same order in the cult room as at the front façade: to the right of the onlooker Hepet, in the middle Teshup and to the left again their son, the Sun god. While, however, in front of the temple-palace façade offerings were made to them individually on separate altars, in the cult room we have one great altar only.

Furthermore we found—in the great east part of the temple, that appointed for the laity—a round shallow basalt bowl with a diameter of about 40 centimetres.

On the floor of the holy of holies there were lying a great

many basalt idols (Pl. 46), beads, seal-cylinders, some bronze statuettes (Pl. 57), and remains of bronze bowls. Several of the idols were leaning against the double statue. We evidently have here objects that had been deposited in the cult room before the chief gods in the last moment before the town was taken. A block of basalt that was lying next to the double statue on the socle did not belong to the cult room. Under it we found broken beads and other small objects, so that it must have been thrown down from above anyhow during or after the destruction of the shrine.

It will be one of the tasks of our next expedition to make a further examination of the surroundings of the cult room, over which the remains of the old expeditionary house are still standing to-day, and in particular to investigate the deeper layers here too.

Besides the great finds our excavations also yielded a great many smaller statues. First of all there were two seated basalt figures of women, one of which is complete but for the head. Up to the shoulder it is 55 centimetres high. We have here a woman with a long upper body and clearly recognizable breasts. The elbows are sharp, the arms bent almost at a right angle and rendered with no rounding in the outward outlines. In the right hand the figure is holding a bowl, while the left hand rests on the lap. The woman is sitting on a low stool; under the drapery the bare feet are seen on the floor between two projecting parts of the stool. The second figure is worse damaged in the upper part, but it must have been very like the first.

We found further the basalt torso, 27 centimetres high, of a very slender woman, with the head and legs missing. It is about 20 centimetres broad at the shoulders. The forearms are laid against the front of the body at a sharp angle; the hands are grasping or covering the breasts. The figure was undoubtedly unclothed. It is very old and recalls the well-known terra-cotta naked statues found in the

Subaraic and in the old Babylonian culture. These three smaller statues certainly represented goddesses.

The basalt idols are figurines of women standing (Pl. 46), highly archaic, with no head-covering, some with hands laid over the breasts, some with only the right hand on the breast and in the left a vessel with a cross-handle like the one carried by the Hepet of the great façade. Most of these statuettes do not have inlaid eyes; the body is rounded; the hair falls far down the back. Only one seems to have worn a feather crown. Many have bead necklaces. Their height is 14 to 21 centimetres.

When we were digging a well in our expeditionary house we came upon two statuettes, a man and a woman, each seated (Pl. 46, Nos. 6, 7); the former was 26 centimetres high and 11 broad, the latter 20 centimetres high and 8 broad. Both wore a low feather crown, the arms were again laid on the lap, and the right hand held a small bowl. They, too, have a Cubist touch about them; the man's figure has a heavy beard and inlaid eyes.

Specially important is a very small statuette found on the citadel hill—a roughly worked man with a narrow beard hanging down almost to the navel (Pl. 46, No. 4). The forearms are stretched out horizontally before him, his hands are clenched and held close to the body on each side, the legs and feet are only suggested. There is no sign of a neck, so that the upper part of the body is only slightly tapering. The nose can no longer be made out, but we seem to see where the eye sockets were. The top of the head is squared, and indeed the whole statuette is quite on Cubist lines. Its height is 10 centimetres.

I came across an object among the Syrian art dealers that had certain points of likeness with it. It is cylindrical, and broadens upwards; the arms are made like handles, the eyes project, the nose can barely be made out, and under it there is again a pointed beard hanging very low down. The clothing is shown below the arms by parallel stripes running diagonally downwards. Right below, where the feet would be looked for, a phallus is represented on the low socle.

I would also call attention to a very archaic head on an idol (Pl. 46, No. 1). All these idols are of basalt. In limestone there is a statuette 25 centimetres high and painted with red ochre, which we found in front of the temple palace in the Kapara layer. It is the figure of a cloaked woman with one hand on her breast the other uplifted; on the grotesque head is a high cap.

The idols were undoubtedly used for the house. Household gods like these were worshipped, we may be sure, just as the larger statues of the chief gods, throughout many centuries. As a result of their long use they are often so worn that their original shape cannot always be quite made out. In Qatna, the Mishrifeh of to-day, not far from Homs in Syria, a small basalt statuette of a seated man has been found which has analogies with our idols. I am convinced that it, too, comes from a much older layer than the one where it was dug out. In Qatna Subaraic names surviving from olden times have been noted.

Among our most interesting finds are two sphinx socles, or rather their remains. On a horseshoe plinth stood five couched sphinxes facing away from one another. We found only fragments of the two socles, but the material was more than enough for them to be put together again with absolute certainty (Pl. 47a). Judging by the remains it even looks as if there was a third socle as well. They were evidently meant to be put up against a wall with the side that was cut away The sphinxes are winged lions with men's heads. The fore-paws are stretched out in front and reach to the edge of the base. The pairs of wings, that pointed upwards, touched one another. The heads have sailors' beards; this beard falls in waved lines from two rows of curls under the lip. The breast is covered with scale-like feathers as in the giant bird and the giant griffins. The scales here, however, point upwards. A crown of feathers with two pairs of horns ornaments the head,

from which hang locks ending below in a spiral. Only one
head was fully preserved; it is very fine. The face wears
very distinctly that archaic smile which we know from
many other statues on Tell Halaf.

The socles had a diameter of 90 centimetres and were
about 62 centimetres high. Within them there was a deep
hole, which may have been meant to take a statue. We are
here reminded of round socles from the Gudea period with
small crouching figures. However, we found no statues or
their parts that would fit our socles.

Of interest, too, is the bust of a bearded man with high
shoulders, whose arms, pressed in tight to the sides of his
body, are seen as broad bands in high relief. The head is
flattened on top; the hair is parted in the middle between
the forehead and the back of the head. The strands of hair
hang down over the top of the head, which is almost as
flat as a board, on to the forehead, temples, and nape of
the neck. Unfortunately this piece, which is about 28 centimetres high and 28 broad, is so damaged that the face can
no longer be made out. It is undoubtedly very old.

Much later is another bearded bust, almost life-size and
comparatively well preserved; this one is from Assyrian
times (Pl. 47b). The facial expression, the way the hair is
worn, the net-like representation of the beard, and the
sloping shoulders—all these give a thoroughly Assyrian
impression. This head comes from Kapara's time. It is
among the few Assyrian sculptures that have been found
on Tell Halaf. Had the statues of the great palace façade
and the reliefs of Tell Halaf been made by Kapara's architect then they would have been bound to have this appearance and no other.

Very remarkable, indeed I believe it stands alone, is a
limestone holder (15 centimetres high, 8 broad at the
opening above), which was evidently meant for taking a
bundle of plant fibres as a fly whisk. One of the flat sides
is worked like the box altars known to us from the Ishtar
temple in Assur (3000 B.C.). On the bowed narrow sides

PLATE XLVIIA. SPHINX SOCLE (RESTORED)

PLATE XLVIIB. BUST OF A BEARDED MAN FROM ASSYRIAN TIMES

PLATE XLVIIIa. OLD LIMESTONE TRIPOD BOWL

PLATE XLVIIIb. FLINT, OBSIDIAN AND COPPER IMPLEMENTS

FLINT: 1 and 4. Knives.   3. Arrow-head.
OBSIDIAN: 2 and 6. Knives.
COPPER: 5. Arrowhead.   7. Spear-head.   8. Hatchet.

the holder has holes, so that we might almost suppose that it served as the socle of a bronze seated figure. On the other three sides, however, figures are cut whose heads are turned up to the wide opening above. The engravings on the broad side show a chariot scene. The chariot body is square, the wheel has six spokes. On one of the narrow sides a wild bull stands straight up before a hunter. On the other narrow side there is an upstanding deer behind the chariot.

Many of the statues were found only in fragments, though these were of some size. First there was the 67 centimetres broad lower part of a fairly large relief slab showing a resting hoofed animal, whose legs are tucked in under the body in just the way we find on our painted pottery. This parallel, too, is important for fixing the age of the statues.

Then there was the torso of a winged man or godling carrying a vessel with a handle in his left hand, while the right is uplifted. He is wearing a gown. The torso is about 90 centimetres broad and 50 high; only the middle is left.

Of smaller sculptures we may finally mention a lion about 12 centimetres long with the head missing.

Further we found in the Kapara layer a great many smaller or larger fragments of stone carvings—statues and reliefs—above all numerous bits off the upper surface of carvings that did not fit the great works of the temple-palace. Evidently what Kapara had done was, apart from the stone carvings he used over again, to fetch out of the Painted Pottery layer any larger pieces of basalt he could find, and then have them worked up into bowls, fighting-balls and the like. What was left over was thrown away. From the remains we gather beyond any doubt that before his time there were in existence a great number also of other very large sculptures in stone which have not survived. Many of the fragments, great and small, show fresh details in the ornament and parts of figures represented. All these, from their style, belong to the old period.

On the ruined site of Fekheria we found in 1927 the
torso of the body of a lion in the round bearing on its back
Kapara's inscription. The head and limbs were missing.
It belongs to a piece of sculpture very much smaller than
the animal colossi of the façade. No one knew how it had
come to Fekheria. Perhaps it was brought up by spoilers
looking for building stone here for the rising village of Ras
el Ain, and they left the sculptured object lying where it
was as being useless. But it may also be that it was
brought here from Tell Halaf by Chechens only quite
lately.

This lion, in spite of the likeness in the way the hair is
shown, seems to me to be later than the statues of Tell Halaf.
In our old carvings of animals in the round the piece between the belly and the plinth has always been left. This
is even so in the small statuette of the lion (cp. above, p. 201).
In the Fekheria torso, however, the belly is carved quite
round underneath, so that the body must have rested clear
on the legs.

VII

Small Objects

I

THE excavator has not only to recover works of sculpture and smaller objects of beauty, but he must also collect everything that has been made at different periods for the household, for worship, and in the building art.

Stone Implements

In the Painted Pottery layer we found great quantities of flint and obsidian tools (Pl. 48*b*). They mark this layer as being Neolithic (Pl. 48*b*, Nos. 1, 4). Besides tools we found a great number of throwing balls of flint. The most interesting piece is a small very finely worked arrow-head (Pl. 48*b*, No. 3).

Especially numerous were the objects in obsidian, particularly knives, with smaller ones down to only a few millimetres breadth and barely longer than 2-3 centimetres; they were every kind of shape (Pl. 48*b*, Nos. 2, 6). They were undoubtedly used for the most various purposes of daily life, including shaving. They range through all colours from an opaque black and brown to a quite transparent grey-green. We also found unworked lumps of obsidian. Evidently in the volcanic district about Tell Halaf there was an obsidian deposit that to-day is forgotten.

Hammers, hatchets and axes, both as weapons and for working basalt, were found, made of all kinds of stone, as for instance nephrite. Many were undoubtedly imported. Particularly numerous were throwing-balls of basalt, many of a great size and weight and meant probably for catapults; those made of limestone were very few. Club-heads, too, of basalt came to light in quantities, exactly the same as they are shown as weapons on the scupltures: round or flattened balls with a large hole through which was put a wooden shaft. Finely worked club-heads of porphyry and serpentine were undoubtedly brought to Tell Halaf from outside.

Architectual stones are not easy to determine in time, the most important we found are door pivot-stones. So long as doors and gates turned round a post fitted below with a metal rod, pivot-stones of basalt were used, which we found in quantity. Sometimes a horseshoe cap served to prevent the pivot coming out of the pan of the pivot-stone. For wooden door-posts, hinge-pans of limestone were used. These door pivot-stones may have been used over and over again through thousands of years.

Of the utmost importance for the history of architecture are the remains of pillars found by us. On Tell Halaf there were wooden pillars and stone pillars. Wooden pillars, for instance, carried the shelter-roof in front of the great façade of the temple-palace. For wooden pillars such as these we found stone bases with a pan on top; many are cylinder-shaped, others have turban-like ornamentation. Round stone pillars were probably used later to roll the layer of earth and mud hard on the flat roofs, just as the people of the country still do after every heavy rainfall.

We also came upon pieces of a fourteen-sided pillar. I do not believe, indeed, that it was meant for a building, but rather it bore the great sun eagle. We also found several capitals with decorations of falling leaves of exactly the same kind as in the case of the giant bird. As to the way these capitals were used we had information from the basalt model of a house already mentioned. It shows exactly the same pillars in passages and window-openings. The pillar till now has been looked upon as a 'Hittite' invention, but it is an Old Subaraic culture element. From an architectural point of view the animal colossi, too, with the giant gods are nothing else than pillars.

Among stone objects used in religious worship mention

may be made above all of the most various kinds of altar stones. The finest are found in great numbers; they are 10-40 centimetres across, rectangular, and with four basalt feet (Pl. 49*a*, No. 4); on the narrow side they are decorated with one or with two bulls' heads. They belong undoubtedly to the cult of Teshup, to whom, of course, the bull was sacred. The bull, holy to Teshup, undoubtedly played an important part in the old Near East. It is beyond all doubt in connection with the worship of Teshup that the bull's head is so often found in the painted pottery and further on stone altars etc. at Tell Halaf, as also on numberless art objects at many other places in the Near East. It is quite possible that the addition of bull's horns to human representations (which we find as the symbol of divinity in the Subaraic, the Sumerian and later in the Assyrian culture complex) is to be derived from Teshup's bull, and further that the Golden Calf of the Jews, too, may be connected with it.

Other altars consist of rectangular basalt stones exactly like mud bricks in size and shape. They have an almost semicircular depression like a bowl in one of the upper corners. This same depression is seen in the model of the house, here surrounded by a Hittite plaited band. These stone altar objects were probably used at the dedication of building-foundations.

Bowls with three feet and small round ones, on a high finely-worked foot (Pl. 49*a*, No. 1), may be looked on as burnt-offering or incense vessels. Among the former is the old limestone bowl in the grave shaft under the great throned goddess.

On *kudurru* (boundary stones) of basalt and limestone, as also on a very small rectangular limestone altar 10 or 12 centimetres high, the lightning-bunch is found as Teshup's emblem. A small stela broken short shows a set of various chiselled symbols of gods.

Our excavations likewise brought to light great numbers of stones for household use and for the needs of daily life.

In the Painted Pottery layer these were found only in fragments; in the Kapara layer and the Guzana layer they
were particularly numerous and undamaged. There are
bowls (Pl. 49a, No. 5), dishes and plates, mortars and
grinding-stones with pounders (Pl. 49a, No. 3) of all sizes
and kinds, rounded tools of various stones, evidently for
polishing earthenware or carved stones, stone weights—
among them also the duck-shaped stones well known from
later Assyria (Pl. 49, No. 6), in which the head and neck
are represented on a squared stone rounded towards the
top—other stone weights in hemisphere shape with ornamentation, and lastly some pierced stones that were used
as weights for looms.

Very numerous are the mill-stones, especially the loaf-
shaped ones. Mostly they have a deep furrow lengthwise,
into which a wooden stick fitted by means of which the
upper stone was rubbed on a flat nether stone. Also there
were round mill-stones. These have a prong at the middle
fitting into the other stone; this has a hole in its side into
which a wooden stick was thrust by which the stone was
turned on the mill-stone.

There was a third form of mill-stone which we dug out in
great quantities in the upper layers and which is perhaps
the most interesting of all (Pl. 49b). A fairly large, only
slightly concave stone is furrowed in various ways. On it
is laid a heavy squared stone about 10-12 centimetres high
and with corresponding furrows underneath it. On top in
the middle it has a slit into which the corn is poured. In the
narrow sides there are holes for strong wooden handles, by
which it is pushed to and fro, perhaps by two persons on
the nether stone. I do not know of such mill-stones from
any other Mesopotamian sites.

A good many limestone slabs with squared grooves or
regularly arranged holes were also found. These are boards
for games, like those from Ur and later from Assyria. Perhaps the many bones of sheep's trotters which we kept
coming upon as we dug belong to them.

PLATE XLIXA. BASALT BOWLS AND OBJECTS (scale about ⅕)
1. Censer. 2. Tripod bowl. 3. Grinding-stone. 4. Sacrificial bowl, with bulls'
heads. 5. Underside of a bowl. 6. Stone duck-shaped weight.

PLATE XLIXB and c. MILLS WITH SLITS OR GROOVES (scale about 1/17)

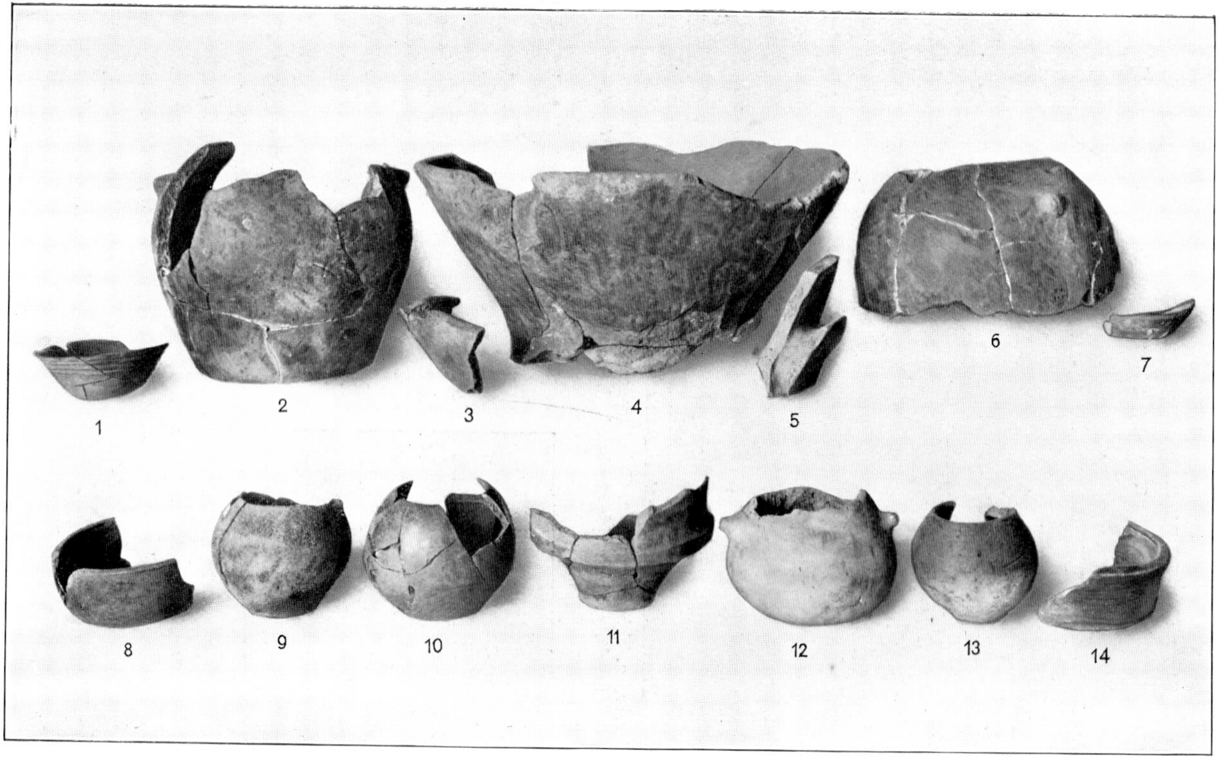

PLATE L. SELF-COLOURED PREHISTORIC POTTERY

Certain larger stone slabs without any carving, or with only a little, in the rooms of dwelling-houses must have had bathing uses.

Some rare objects of alabaster—small pots for cosmetics, bowls, plates and small bottles with lids—are probably imported wares.

The door-hinge stones, balls for slings, knobs for clubs, and household stones, may be more or less looked on as timeless. Many are certainly contemporary with the stone carvings of the Painted Pottery period and were then kept in use afterwards, just as the people of the land still use them to-day if they find them.

Pottery

Earthenware makes up the most important part of the smaller objects found at Tell Halaf. In every layer we found pots and sherds in many thousands. This must undoubtedly be put down to the fact that the ground yielded exceptionally good raw material for earthenware. Even on the surface sherds of all kinds were lying in great quantities. The explanation of this is as follows: In our neighbourhood there is a species of jerboa (jumping mouse) that builds its nest in sloping burrows driven deep into the ground, often down to the living rock. In so doing these animals bring up sherds, obsidian, flints and other small objects from the deepest layers on to the surface. Thus from the objects lying on the surface of a hill a conclusion can almost always be drawn as to what old settlements it holds in the layers below. On the other hand the jerboas often mislead the excavator until he has made a more thorough examination of his ground, for they also take small objects down below along their burrows, so that the impression is given of later objects occurring in older layers as well.

From the very first time I discovered Tell Halaf I was struck by the fact that in contrast with all the other hills of ruins for far around there were a particularly great many coloured sherds lying about. Setting aside the excavations for uncovering the buildings, at many spots on the citadel hill and in the town area we drove round shafts several metres across—we called them 'maiden wells'—down to the bed-rock, so as to examine what the different layers held. The results were aways the same. The lowest layer yielded a hand-made ware, black, red or grey, and mostly polished, often with simple handles in the form of bosses or knobs, round underneath or standing flat. The vessels are also found unpolished and often show marks of smoke from a fire. This is one kind of prehistoric pottery (Pl. 50), which comes down also far into the second, the true Painted Pottery layer. I also found some pieces belonging to it on Jebelet-el-Beda. The second and very old kind of earthenware is also prehistoric, partly hand-made, partly made on a potter's wheel. It is made, however, from quite a different clay, mostly bright yellow or reddish, and is burned harder than the former; it is mostly thin, seldom self-coloured, and generally beautifully painted (Pl. 51-54; Coloured Pl. I, II).

For the present we must leave the question open whether the makers of the prehistoric self-coloured pottery at Tell Halaf belonged to the same race as those who made the painted pottery. On the one hand it seems possible that the painted pottery was invented on Tell Halaf itself or by others belonging to the same race and resulted from the development of the self-coloured pottery. On the other hand the view is possible that the Self-Coloured Pottery folk belonged to some other race settled here before the Painted Pottery folk. In this case the origin of the painted pottery would have to be set down to an element of immigrant conquerors, whose coming heralded a new period on Tell Halaf, in which the self-coloured pottery was at first preserved along with the painted, but afterwards wholly given up in its favour.

Only my future excavations can shed light on this point for Tell Halaf, as I hope they will. I think, however, that it is important for this question to be followed up also at

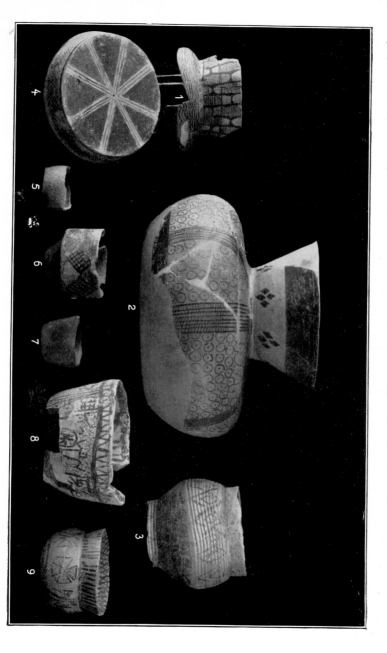

PLATE LI. PAINTED VESSELS OF THE OLDEST PERIOD (scale ⅕)

1. Upper part of a necked bowl. 2. Large vessel with geometrical designs. 3. Relief-surfaced vessel, imitation of basketry. 4. Cover

PLATE LII. PAINTED VESSELS OF THE OLDEST PERIOD (scale about ⅕)

other excavation sites in Mesopotamia and thereabouts where prehistoric painted pottery has already been found, and that it should be determined whether there is not here, too, the same kind of self-coloured pottery as on Tell Halaf under the painted pottery, and in what relation it stands to the oldest painted pottery here.

For the time being I am led to the belief that the self-coloured thick prehistoric earthenware was made by the people of the same autochthonic race as afterwards invented the refined and mostly otherwise shaped painted pottery.

Professor Hubert Schmidt, probably the leading specialist, and who is at work on the Tell Halaf pottery, has come to the conclusion that in the whole of the Ancient East it is only on Tell Halaf that all the various stages of the development of the painted pottery are found. The oldest kinds show a rich glazed or varnished painting. The bottom of the vessel is almost always flat or round; feet set round it are remarkably rare. The Painted Pottery artists were very skilled at engraving and making rows of lines with the finger-nail or a graver of stone or wood. Indeed, we find perfect imitations of wickerwork (Pl. 51, No. 3), and also applied bosses and looped handles. Applied figures are rarer, such as a naked woman's figure outside the rim of a vessel.

The shapes and ornamentation of the vessels are of infinite variety. All sizes are there, from tiny bowls and pots to the hugest vessels. Occasionally they have spouts. Several of the round vessels had two or three necks.

In the painting geometrical designs prevail (Coloured Pl. I, II; Pl. 51-54). But animals, too, are often found (Pl. 53). Four-footed ones, especially bulls or gazelles, are mainly represented, lying or half lying, with the legs under the body. It is of importance in determining the age of the stone carvings to note that this subject occurs on a relief slab as well. The head is very simply depicted, often in profile and looking backwards, while the horns are seen

o

from in front; the animals are often arranged in rows behind one another, and between them are all kinds of dotted or line patterns to fill in the space.

We find flying birds with wide-outstretched wings, birds flying towards us or away, pasturing herds, snakes, poisonous centipedes, locusts and so on. It is probably only mere chance that so far no scorpion has been found. I have already mentioned that horses, too, are shown on the painted pottery. The bull's head is often found, being the symbol of the chief god of Tell Halaf, Teshup. It is found in all imaginable forms alongside or over one another in rows. These Teshup bowls were probably for religious purposes.

Human beings are represented in a much more primitive way. We find long rows grasping one another with the hands, dancing or squatting down. On one pot (Pl. 51, No. 8) we see persons with hands uplifted, just as they have been found in south Mesopotamia under the Sumerian layer, in Susa and in western Persia. On this pot is pictured a chariot with two men inside it. The great wheel has eight spokes. The horses are drawn one above the other in front of the chariot, and are shown extraordinarily small, just as we can see them also on Cappadocian seal impressions of the 3rd millennium. On our pot they are, moreover, drawn in the opposite way to that of the chariot. For this, too, we have an analogy on a small orthostat (45 L, Pl. 19*b*) from Tell Halaf itself, where the bull which is being hunted is likewise represented above the chariot, going in the opposite direction. Here, too, the reason was evidently want of room on the picture.

One bowl shows the *butm*-tree in the same way as the small orthostats. Very noteworthy is a spherical vessel from the period of decay (Pl. 54, 1), on which creatures—flying-fish or swallows—are shown in a free space within semicircles and with arrows between them.

The first group in our painted pottery corresponds in time with the first layer at Susa; the second group has

PLATE LIII. PAINTED SHERDS OF THE OLD PERIOD WITH NATURALISTIC FIGURES (scale about ⅓)

PLATE LIV. PAINTED VESSELS OF THE LATER PERIOD (scale about ½)

much in common with the second layer at Susa, where, too, the vessels found are not self-coloured only, but are also painted in several colours. The third group, belonging to the period of decay, no longer uses glazed painting; the colours are lustreless or dull; new shapes emerge.

The painted pottery of Tell Halaf is a pure joy. It is amazing to see with what artistic skill modifications were always being made anew in the shapes of the vessels and in the patterns. The pots often are thick in make, often, in spite of their size, as fine as cardboard. No one down to our day has succeeded in imitating the technique of the painting.

Often as the result of uneven firing the varnished painting has taken on a varied coloration. Thus it happens that often the same vessel looks on one side to be painted dark brown or black and on the other red.

Unfortunately just in the Painted Pottery layer up to now comparatively few whole vessels have been brought to light; this must be put down not only to their having lain thousands of years in the ground, but also to the fact that the new Aramean masters threw the soil of the tell about and raked it up in all directions, when they were levelling the surface to build their new palaces. When I find, as I hope to do, graveyards from the oldest times, more painted vessels are bound to come to light, and well-preserved.

The next group in our pottery is called by Professor Hubert Schmidt the pottery of the Kapara period in the Babylonian-Assyrian style (Pl. 55). It is characterized by uneven bottoms, cone shapes and studded bottoms, and has a great wealth of forms: we have clay plates, bowls, cups, flasks, beakers and rings for stands. Now and again it is also painted with simple geometrical designs (Pl. 55, Nos. 1, 9), mostly in a reddish colour inclining to violet. It is often very thin and delicate. We found delightful small beakers most beautifully shaped and pitted in rows either for ornament or to give a better grip (Pl. 55, No. 5).

Belonging to this pottery are also objects polished red, such as strong bowls with three feet.

To the Kapara period must also be assigned the great altar with enamelled designs before the temple-palace. As already pointed out, it is remarkable that the bands with geometrical designs are made up like mosaic from separate pieces and not as yet from large slabs with designs drawn on them. Burnt bricks, indeed, are otherwise remarkably seldom found in our case.

In the first broad room of the temple-palace a number of *zigattu* were found, that is decorative knobs for the walls, some glazed, some unglazed, just like the well-known Assyrian ones. In other ways, too, the Kapara pottery shows many likenesses with the pottery from the end of the 2nd millennium that has been found in Assur.

The Hellenistic layer also was rich in pottery. In a wine cellar above Kapara's dwelling-palace we found a great many wine amphorae from Rhodes with stamps that include the name of the Byzantine eponym, so that they are really a kind of label giving the vintage year. Wine was therefore brought as far as this from the Greek islands.

Among the pottery, too, of earlier times we found pieces that can be proved to have been imported. In the case of the painted pottery they came from Samarrá; in the Kapara layer they are glazed vessels from Assur—a proof that there were extensive trade relations in earlier times. The great distances travelled even in olden times by objects from one land to another can be gathered from the fact that in the amber region of East Prussia a 'Hittite' bronze idol was found. I myself became possessed in Cologne of a large Babylonian ornamental boss (*zigattu*) with cuneiform characters from the newly opened grave of a Roman legionary, which the dead man had brought from the land of the Two Streams to my Rhineland home, probably as an amulet.

We came upon a regular Hellenistic earthenware deposit above Kapara's palace. This shows that in these

PLATE LV. POTTERY OF THE KAPARA PERIOD IN THE BABYLONIAN-ASSYRIAN STYLE (scale about ⅓)

1. Painted with simple geometrical designs. 2. Tripod bowl from the grave tower. 3. Large rounded vessel with flat bottom.
4, 5, 6. Vessels with pointed bottom. 7. Beaker with high foot. 8. Cylindrical beaker. 9. Thin-walled vessel with simple stripes.
10. Ring-footed plate with knobbed bottom. 11. Clover-shaped lamp. 12. Bowl. 13. Lamp with spout. 14. Bowl with foot from

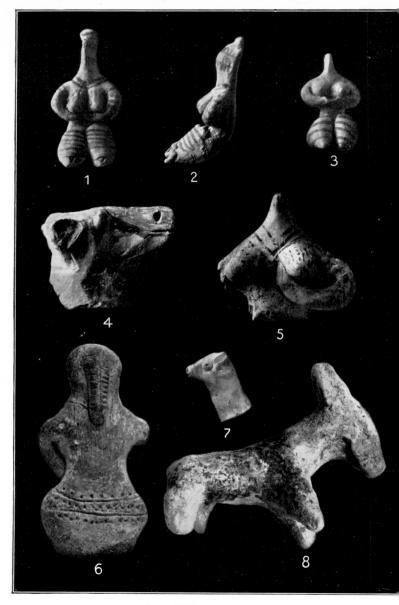

PLATE LVI. TERRA-COTTAS

1, 2. Painted squatting woman with tuft of hair, face veil and garment (83 mm. high).
3. Painted squatting woman with hair-tuft (60 mm. high).   4. Painted bull's hea
(73 mm. high).   5. Upper part of the painted statuette of a woman with arm lai
round the breast, the arm showing wart-like erections (73 mm. high). 6. Woma
seen from behind with hair-plait (106 mm. high). 7. Animal's head (40 mm. high
8. Bull (88 mm. long).

latter times, too, thanks to the goodness of the raw material, the potter's craft was a flourishing one.

A special group in our Tell Halaf pottery is formed by lamps in various forms. In the oldest times they were bowl-shaped and with a swelling in one side, probably to take the wick. In the Kapara and in the Assyrian layer lamps with a spout predominate (Pl. 55, No. 13).

Pottery of great size is represented by various store vessels from the Kapara period, but above all from the latest Guzana period. In the Painted Pottery layer, too, huge painted vessels occur. We were able, for instance, to put together a pot 45 centimetres high and 50 centimetres broad. Late sarcophagi for crouched bodies, quite in the Assyrian way, have been already mentioned.

Our excavations also brought to light terra-cottas from every period (Pl. 56). Of very great interest are small statuettes 5-8 centimetres high from the Painted Pottery layer—squatting women with knees drawn in (Pl. 56, Nos. 1-3). The waist is slender, the pelvis and shoulders are broad, the breasts in some cases well shaped, but much too developed. The arms lie generally under the breasts; hands and feet are barely sketched. For the head the pro-longation of the neck is simply squeezed together with the fingers. The resulting flat figure reminds us of the old beaked-nose faces of our Jebelet-el-Beda and Old Su-merian seal-cylinders. An extension of the 'head' is meant as a tuft of hair, whose locks fall separately down to the back of the figures. Some of the statuettes are decorated with parallel brown stripes that follow the lines of the body and on the breast are led forward. Professor Hubert Schmidt rightly sees in this painted work the indication of a garment. Dots and lines on the face are meant to repre-sent the eyes and veil. The drawing-in of the waist and the great width of the pelvis are typical. We find the same thing in very old Egyptian figures made of Nile mud, in a statuette 16 centimetres high from Sesklo in Thessaly, in the figure on the painted stucco frieze of an archaic Ishtar temple in Assur and in an asphalt statuette from Susa, of which only the upper part of the body with breasts, waist and hips are left. Our terra-cottas are most akin of all to the standing statuettes in the nude from that layer at Ur which has likewise a mixture of painted pottery and lies below the Sumerian layers. These unclothed statuettes have decided bird's-beak faces and wear a wig; one has the squeezed head; here also the breasts are heavily stressed and the figures in some cases painted. Even the same wart-like erections on the upper arms as in Ur are to be seen in a figurine from Tell Halaf (Pl. 56, No. 5).

Besides the squatting figures of women we also found a few nude standing or lying women. They occur throughout the Nearer East. The hands lie on the breast, the waist is small; often they are deliberately made without head, hands or feet. In some the eyes and nipples of the breasts are put on by means of little clay balls.

Once only there occurred in the Painted Pottery layer a very stout woman of black stone about 5 centimetres high in a squatting position with knees drawn high up, reminding us greatly of the Palaeolithic Venus figures.

Lastly on Tell Halaf there were also found a few terra-cotta statuettes of men, and many animal representations in baked clay (Pl. 56, Nos. 4, 7, 8), such as snakes' and birds' heads, often on a very long neck. Among the animals the bull is the most often represented, sometimes painted, sometimes not, like Old Sumerian and Elamic figures. Bulls' heads of baked clay are often found as handles to vessels.

Important for cultural history in our Painted Pottery layer are model chariots of baked clay. They have wheels with spokes painted on them, and fixed to the front of the floor high shielding walls with two openings pierced in them. They are very like the chariots from the temple of Ishtar in Assur.

In the Kapara layer we found playthings of baked clay ending in a long slender neck with a small bird's head.

PLATE I. PAINTED SHERDS WITH GEOMETRICAL DESIGNS
(scale about ⅔)

The round part was hollow and held a small stone for a rattle.

Of great interest is a clay vessel like a horn of plenty. Its closed end has a lion's head with angular lips exactly like those of the giant lions in the entry to the temple-palace. The Greek rhyton had its origin in the Subaraic culture. From the Guzana period we have some small figures of horsemen of the rudest kind—the legs being simple rods— such as we know from Assyrian and above all New Babylonian sites.[1]

Copper, Bronze and Iron

Tell Halaf was comparatively rich in copper and bronze implements. Near Diarbekir, in the Kurdish mountains and not far away, there are, as already mentioned, the copper mines of Arghana-Maden. According to inscriptions found there they were already being worked in Assyrian times, but this was undoubtedly also the case far earlier than that. To-day they are still among the richest in the world, and before long they are to be exploited by modern methods.

In the Painted Pottery layer there are only small remains of copper objects and their nature is beyond recognition. The metal objects, too, were recovered by Kapara's men and used over again. Only just a few bronze statuettes of the old period could be found in the Kapara layer, and these especially in the cult room (Pl. 57, Nos. 1, 3, 4, 6, 9). They had been deposited in this room at the foot of the chief gods, like the basalt idols and rows of beads, just before the catastrophe. By the people of the Kapara period they were, we may well believe, looked on as something especially holy and venerable and were held in high honour. In this case also we again meet with standing and seated gods and goddesses. They remind us of our stone idols, but also have certain analogies with Old Sumerian

[1] Further we refer the reader to Appendix IV ('On the Smaller Finds'), where Professor Hubert Schmidt deals in systematic detail especially with the pottery.

bronze statuettes. Some of them have a prong for fixing in a wooden or stone socle.

We also found copper bowls and implements of the most varied kinds, such as punches and spatulae for spreading paint or salves, surgical probes, and also copper ornaments such as arm-bands, brooches and pins, and lastly weapons—short swords, daggers, a curved sword, arrow and lance tips (Pl. 48*b*, Nos. 5, 7).

Particularly interesting is a rectangular copper matrix (Pl. 57, No. 2), 8½ centimetres high and 6 centimetres broad, which certainly comes from the 3rd millennium. It shows a bearded god standing with bull's horns and uplifted hands, and a goddess with the crown of feathers and hands laid on the breasts; both are shown from in front wearing a long shaggy garment or gown. The feet are turned out. Between the divinities there is standing a high sacrificial pillar bearing a bowl from which a flame is rising. By the god balls can be made out—probably some emblem—and between the heads a star. Here we most probably again have Teshup and the female divinity. The matrix must have been used for making big plaques in metal or clay. On its reverse are round pits for casting metal beads. We also found a number of small stone crucibles for casting metal ornaments.

In a room in the north-east corner of the temple-palace there was lying in the wreckage of the fire a bronze half-moon (Pl. 57, No. 5), 25 centimetres across the tips. I presume that it was set up on a high staff upon the corner tower on the east of the temple-palace façade.

The largest metal object is a low waggon in bronze (Pl. 58*b*) which we found unhurt in the main room of the temple-palace. It is 1.40 metres long, 1.20 metres wide, and (reckoning in the wheels), 0.20 metres high; it rests on four small six-spoked wheels. Its framework is ornamented with a chiselled crenellated design. The floor is of strong iron bars. In Kapara's time iron was used along with bronze. On them was a layer of bits of burned brick, the top of which was levelled so as to smooth out the irregularities. Probably the vehicle was a moveable hearth, on which the beasts slain in sacrifice at the temple-palace façade were made ready for eating. But perhaps, too, it was only a brazier of the same kind as the *mankal* used to-day in this land. Anyhow the resinous, sweet-smelling wood of the *butm*-tree was burned here, which we too used for fire-wood. The king's seat among his guests must have been in this main room, and the vehicle could easily be wheeled round on the smooth stone-paved floor.

In the Kapara and in the Guzana layer were many iron implements and weapons. As the ground is damp, they are much rusted and eaten away.

Personal Ornaments

As in all places and times, the women of Tell Halaf had a great liking for personal ornament. Only the great throned goddess wore none. However, she had holes in the lobes of her ears for ear-drops. We have seen that all the other women on our statues wear ornaments, while with men this is not so. On the other hand, in the case of the king in the 'grave tower' from the Kapara period we found a wealth of gold ornaments. The want of personal adornment on statues in the old times in the case of men is a further proof that these statues were made before the days of Kapara.

In the Painted Pottery layer we have so far not established the existence of any original ornaments, while in the Kapara layer they are in abundance. In the cult room we made great finds of ornaments. Here there were necklaces with beads of the most varied form and size and of every kind of stone: serpentine, porphyry, carneol, agate, onyx (Pl. 58*a*). The beads are round, cylindrical or elliptical in shape, sometimes only ground in the roughest way on the edges. These stones are often a centimetre thick. Often there were also beads of blue frit. Of this material we also found in the Kapara layer even bowls reminding us of fluted copper-ware; there were also beads like eyes. Often all these objects lay alternating with one another on the ground, as though they had been strung together. Sometimes between them in the row there were also very old seal-cylinders and shells. Down to the present day Beduin and peasant women are wont to wear necklaces on which besides modern beads and coins old seal-cylinders, beads from very old and Hellenistic times and other things are strung.

The bronze ornaments of the Kapara layer are of very many kinds: necklets and bracelets, brooches and rings are particularly numerous. I shall have to speak of the gold ornaments when we come to graves.

Ivory objects were found only in small numbers. The most important piece is a deer (Pl. 59, No. 5) 20 centimetres long, unfortunately much decayed, whose horns are lying over the back and whose legs with the hoofs brought together are drawn tight under the body. It may have been the crutch of a staff or sceptre for a king.

Also we found a small ivory ape, sitting upright and 36 millimetres high, the front paws being uplifted, which calls to mind our animal orchestras and the oldest representations from Egypt and Susa (Pl. 59, No. 4). It, too, was perhaps the handle for a sceptre. It was lying in a grave that we found quite untouched north-west of the temple-palace, and probably is far older than the grave. An ivory lion, 10 centimetres high, unfortunately without its head, is very old; underneath it recalls prehistoric Egyptian pieces (Pl. 59, No. 1). In the shaft-grave under the small throned goddess there were handsome ivory heads of women (Pl. 59, Nos. 2, 3) with small hammered gold plates on the hair, as also the remains of small figures of animals. These were undoubtedly brought from the west, and belong to a later period; so, too, an ivory head in Egyptian style measuring 8 centimetres. Mention must also be made of small pieces of ivory and bone with designs on them, of numerous ivory handles, pins, and spatulae,

PLATE LIX. IVORY OBJECTS

1. Underside of a headless lion lying (67 mm. long). 2. Woman's head with small gold plates laid on to the hair (20 mm. high)

and of ivory carvings measuring 8-10 centimetres, somewhat like a tortoise shell, and ornamented with ringed
designs, such as we often find in carved ivory.

Graves

Unfortunately no grave-yards have so far been found on
Tell Halaf. Graves, owing to the offerings in them, are
usually a rich store of all kinds of useful objects. The graves
of kings and great men mostly hold, besides particularly
fine clay vessels, gold ornaments, artistic objects of every
kind and often weapons as well, presuming always that
they have not been looted. In the Subaraic cultural area,
too, the graves, for example at Senjirli and Karkemish, have
yielded valuable objects. In south Mesopotamia I need
only recall the unbelievable finds made by Woolley at
Ur. In Egypt with its all-pervading worship of the dead
the graves of the eighteenth dynasty, especially Tutankhamun's and those at Dashur, yielded their well-known
and wonderful goldsmiths' work. Thus we may hope that
the grave-yards of Tell Halaf, too, will still bring us great
surprises.

From the Painted Pottery layer of Tell Halaf so far not
a single grave has been met with. From Kapara's time we
found three royal graves perfectly preserved: the shafts
under the throned goddesses and a particularly important
'grave tower' north-west of the *hilani* building. The terrace
built by Kapara rose over this 'grave-tower'. The 'grave
tower' probably holds the mortal remains of his father or
of some other forebear of Kapara's. The actual grave is
sunk into the Painted Pottery layer and roofed over with
a mud-brick cupola. At the narrow side there was an
entrance, afterwards walled up. The dead man lay on his
back with his head to the east. Only small pieces of the
skull and skeleton were still left; but the ankle-bones still
held together.

It was here that we made our greatest find of gold. The
most important pieces are a mouth-plate of gold-foil

(Coloured Pl. III, No. 5) with small rings at the ends to which the string was once fastened by which it was held before the mouth. On the plate are represented the moustache and small chin-beard, this latter being shown in two rows by perpendicular blue and a few white strips of deepened enamel ending in white dots. The lips are shown by narrow delicately worked openings. The plate was probably meant to shield the dead man from evil spirits that might enter him through the mouth. We know such mouth-plates and whole face-masks of gold from other sites also in the Nearer East and from the West.

Equally finely worked is a semi-circular embossed plate of heavy gold (Coloured Pl. III, No. 4). It was probably worn on the breast. On the well-known mountain, a motive which we have already met with on the painted pottery and on the gigantic bull of the front façade, there here stands a conventionalized palm with heavily drawn scrolls under seven leaf designs arranged fanwise. On the two sides of the palm are two gazelles standing up like a coat of arms. The motive of the mountain and the far-radiating leaves of the palm are in white and blue enamel; the whole is surrounded by a plaited band, which in turn is edged by a narrow stripe with holes. The plate therefore was once probably sewn in to a piece of leather or stuff.

The clothing of the dead man was edged with bands of chased gold (Coloured Pl. III, No. 14) in three widths (7.5, 14 and 15 millimetres); on these also are holes on both sides for sewing them on the stuff.

By the bones of the feet were still lying the gold plaques of the sandals (Coloured Pl. III, Nos. 1-3): one at the heel with a conventionalized palm and two bounding gazelles, at each of the sides a plaque with a bull behind which a tree is suggested. All this is chased work and has a row of holes at the edges; by it were lying strips of gold with pin-holes at the sides and rings for fastening the sandals to the feet.

The grave also contained some remarkable heavy gold

PLATE II. PAINTED SHERDS WITH GEOMETRICAL DESIGNS
(scale about $\frac{2}{3}$)

rings (Coloured Pl. III, Nos. 6, 10, 13). These are crescent-shaped thick lengths of wire, tapering towards the ends, which touch. On each side and below flat studs are fixed. Some gold beads made up the rest of the gold ornaments in this grave (Coloured Pl. III, Nos. 7, 8).

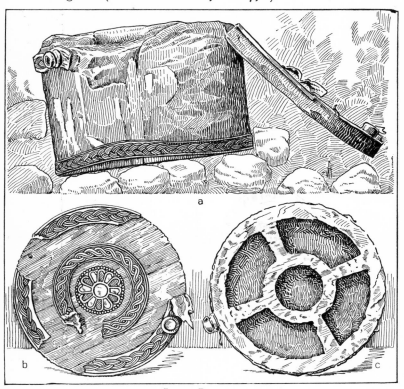

IVORY BOX
(a) As found. (b) Lid. (c) The five inside divisions

The most interesting object in the grave was an ivory box with a flat lid, 11.5 centimetres wide and 9 centimetres high. The box and the lid are decorated with chased gold bands showing the Hittite plaited band. Gold-covered ivory nails are used for fastening the parts. On top of the lid, in the middle, is a gold rosette with twelve flower petals in a star pattern consisting of alternate blue and white enamel (deepened). The inside of the box has five compartments: a round one in the middle and four ranged round it. In one compartment we found remains of rouge. By the box a silver spatula was lying: so that the king painted himself, a custom we still find to-day among men in Kurdistan. In ancient time face-painting was widespread; I would mention the Egyptian rouge palettes from prehistoric times.

A deep silver bowl was among the gifts to the dead man. Beside it was an outfit of every kind of copper bowl and kettle, some of which were beautifully fluted and had spouts. Worthy of special note was a set of copper cups widened at the top (Pl. 57, No. 7) ranged along one of the long sides of the grave and about 10 centimetres high. In one of them was still left a length of willow-wood pith; and on another the impression could still be made out of a pattern on some stuff. Probably these cups were used to hold incense.

Of pottery there were only two pieces in the grave: a red, somewhat deep, thick bowl on three heavy feet, and an ordinary yellowish one on a high foot (Pl. 55, Nos. 2, 14). These two clay vessels are enough by themselves to show that the grave belongs to Kapara times.

The two other graves are the shaft graves under the two throned goddesses. Here the dead had been burned by the grave and their ashes then buried in a clay vessel. With these ashes we found a good many bronze objects, unfortunately not with any form that could be recognized, some bronze nails and glass beads and also bits of gold foil. Under the great goddess in a pot was a gold finger-ring of fine workmanship with an onyx which undoubtedly belonged to a woman (Coloured Pl. III, No. 12). The pot also held two crescent-shaped massive earrings with a button, small hollow crescent-shaped ear-drops (Coloured Pl. III, No. 9) and a plain narrow, elliptical mouth-plate

PLATE III. GOLD OBJECTS

1-3. Sandal plaques. 4. Breast plaque. 5. Mouth plaque. 6. Earring with knob. 7, 8. Granulated beads.
9. Hollow earring. 10. Earring with three knobs. 11. Finger-ring with small lump of gold. 12. Finger-ring

of thinnish gold-foil with eyes for the string. In the shaft were also lying a much decayed ivory arm-ring, bronze bowls, small ornamented pieces of bone, more clay vessels and the above-mentioned very old three-footed bowl in limestone with a hunting relief. In the opening to the shaft grave was standing a narrow-necked clay vessel with bronze bowls. Close by the rubbish from the burning there were more clay bowls lying.

In the shaft before the small throned goddess were lying several clay vessels. In one pot were the beautiful little ivory heads already referred to and other ivory remains showing the marks of fire and also bone remains. In the shaft there was also found a hollow gold pendant with little balls in it, a silver finger-ring with a little gold ball set in it (Coloured Pl. III, No. 11) and several bronze beakers or cups widened at the top.

The offerings in the shaft graves, setting aside the old limestone tripod, likewise belong to the Kapara period. In the Old East it often happens that objects from earlier times are also put with the dead.

Between the mud-brick mass with the two throned goddesses and the citadel gate, as already mentioned, we came upon some more graves. In some there were only clay bowls and clay vessels of the Kapara time still left; the other gifts had been looted.

From the Guzana period come, as we have already said, several trough-sarcophagi of various shapes, in which the dead were laid in the Assyrian way in a crouched position. In these were found some bronze personal ornaments. To Hellenistic times belong a number of coffin graves in the town area. In them, protected by stone slabs round them, were some very fine offerings, mainly in bronze and clay.

In the Kapara times the dead were buried or burned. How they were dealt with in the Painted Pottery period we have not yet been able to make out .

In some of the pots from the Kapara layer various seeds were found, somewhat charred but well preserved enough

to be determined as being seeds of two-rowed barley and of
fenugreek, and of a weed always found among both these
—cleavers or goose-grass. Fenugreek is still often planted
in the south for fodder. The circumstance that these seeds
were well cleaned, together with the way they were kept
in narrow-necked clay vessels, seems to point to their
having a medical or a magical purpose.

Seal-Cylinders and Stamps

We also found seals and stamps on Tell Halaf. Several
are very old. The seal-cylinder shown here has by O.
Weber in his book *Altorientalische Siegelbilder* (No. 417)

SEAL-CYLINDER

rightly been assigned to the 4th millennium B.C. On it are
seated the principal personages with beaked noses facing
one another, and they are drinking from a pot with the
same kind of sucker as we saw in the two animal orchestras. Behind the drinker on the left a man is represented
emblematically in a frame with uplifted hands, and below
him an animal with bowed head and great horns. We undoubtedly have here Teshup on his holy beast. Behind the
drinker on the right two men are standing in dancing
posture; underneath them a bird is sitting. Another animal
and a tree make up the rest of the picture.

Another cylinder represents two gods leading a praying
man before a great god seated. The garments agree with

those on our copper matrix. These two cylinders come from the Painted Pottery period. Another cylinder recalls the Cappadocian seals. It shows a scorpion and above it an ox, Teshup's holy beast, before which three men stand in worship with right hands uplifted. Other representations have an Assyrian look—such as a man in prayer before a sacrificial table at which the god is seated, the fight between a god and a fabulous being, conventionalized palms with men and beasts beside them, a chariot scene, and several pictures of a god fighting with bow and arrow against a dragon with a snake's head.

On a large and beautiful seal-cylinder from the Guzana layer above Kapara's dwelling-palace we see Teshup, with the bunched lightning in one hand and some other object in the other, rushing upon a dragon with a horned snake's head. Teshup has his sword girded on. His head shows the Subaraic type.

Of the stamps most are knobs of different kinds with representations of winged sun's disks, of men with uplifted hands, and of geometrical patterns.

In the Painted Pottery layer we found along with a few small stamps in the shape of a frog a small wonderfully pretty bird in hematite with a small net design on the stamp side. The bird's neck was bored through. Some of the stamps are, as in Egypt, scarab-shaped, but their motives on the other hand are not purely Egyptian.

Most of the seal-cylinders were found in the cult room, where they had been brought as offerings with all the other things before the catastrophe.

P

VIII

Jebelet-el-Beda

IN 1913, on one of the exploring trips carried out by me from Tell Halaf during the excavations in various directions near and far, I examined the western part of Jebel Abd-el-Aziz. From its southern slopes I rode westward through a depression. In the midst of the desert a small mountain rises there of white limestone, to which therefore the name of Jebelet-el-Beda, 'The Small White Mountain', has been given. As I rode up to the highest point so as to take plane-table bearings for a geographical survey in my usual way, I saw by me from my horse just before the top on the white ground great dark stones. I dismounted and to my utmost surprise and joy I saw that I had before me basalt sculptures from the oldest times. Around me, however, there was nothing to be seen of any old ruins.

As at the time I could not think of excavating the place, which was some 70 kilometres from Tell Halaf, I had to leave my discovery there. I kept it, however, a secret, for I feared that otherwise the sculptures might come to harm.

It was not until 1927 that I could set about recovering the sculptures, a very hard task. During the season of 1929 Jebelet-el-Beda was systematically searched and dug. After I had in a preliminary expedition explored the conditions for labour and supplies, we moved there in May with all our tents and many of our best workers.

The stay on Jebelet-el-Beda entailed great difficulties of every kind. The water had to be fetched 8 kilometres on camels from a spring on the southern slope of Jebelet-el-Beda. Luckily, besides a spring Ain el-Beda known to me from before, but strongly impregnated with sulphuretted hydrogen, we had found another smaller but better one,

PLATE LVI. TOP OF THE PASS OF TELL.

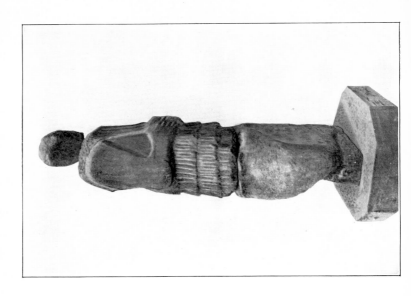

Ain Shellale, though its water was not all that it should be either. It was always a joyful event when a consignment of Khabur water reached our camp. Rice, bread and all supplies we had to have brought on motor trolleys nearly 100 kilometres from Ras el Ain, or still further from Hesseche. It was only gradually that the motor cars made a driving track through the desert and over the loose stones of the mountain slopes.

In the beginning the Baggarat ez Zor were living in tents in our neighbourhood, who though nomads, were fairly well off. They supplied us, indeed, with sheep and *lebben* (sour milk), but I am sorry to say my hopes of finding workmen among them were vain. Their head sheikh had no influence whatever over the tribe. There was no way of inducing them to do excavating work for us. There was thus nothing left for me to do but to turn once more to Ibrahim Pasha's sons. Through their good offices I then got about 100 workers from the Milli, who had already, most of them, been digging for us on Tell Halaf. I had to fetch them in trolleys, and they camped in and near our great Beduin tent. But they had no liking to be alone in the middle of the desert without their wives, children and tents, particularly as the feeding in the circumstances was a very hard task. After the Milli reached us we were able to hire twenty or thirty Baggarat besides.

Each day nearly on Jebelet-el-Beda brought with it some special surprise. A feud was declared against the Baggarat, or they were really attacked, or a Baggara was killed by one of his own tribe, whereupon regular fights between the families of the two men arose. Snakes there were in great numbers. And lastly we had to suffer several extraordinarily heavy night storms that were among the worst I have gone through on my many travels: heavy downpours of rain with thunder-storms that never stopped coming up from every side—quite an unusual thing to happen in the Mesopotamian summer. One pitch-dark night during one of these storms all our tents were blown down. The iron of our shovels and mattocks and the motor-car park were a serious danger with the lightning flashing just above us. The many *butm*-trees quite close to our camp with marks of having been struck by lightning showed that the thunder-storms were wont to discharge themselves just here on the highest point of the lonely ridge of Jebelet-el-Beda lying there in the middle of the desert.

The nearness of the Turkish frontier was the reason for the place being so unsafe. It was only too easy for Beduins to make forays this way from Turkish territory, for it was always possible for them to withdraw again with impunity and unpursued over the frontier beyond the railway. While we were at work on Jebelet-el-Beda, Mr. J. Darrous, our only French fellow-worker—so deeply mourned by us all—was murdered and robbed by Turkish Beduins near Ras el Ain.

We spent thus a month of dangerous and devoted work on Jebelet-el-Beda. The results, however, fully rewarded our pains. The topmost part of the hill was laid bare down to the living rock (Pl. 60), and was found to be a natural mass of gypsum covered with humus, partly also with burnt fragments and detritus.

We carefully examined not only this spot but also the surroundings, but nowhere did we find traces of buildings from those old times to which the sculptures belong. There never was any old town here.

The rubbish on the hill-top held from very old times only a few flint implements and very coarse sherds, corresponding with the self-coloured handmade earthenware of the lowest layer on Tell Halaf. Otherwise all that we found was Graeco-Roman and Arab sherds.

On the same ridge, about three kilometres south-east of the hill-top, were the remains of a fairly large Roman settlement with, in part, superior houses. There were the same kind of remains of houses at other places, too, on the mountain. They belonged to the time when at the southern foot of the range, at the edge of the desert, near the main spring known as Ain el Beda, there stood a great Roman military camp, whose plan we drew.

The hill-top formed a platform measuring 20 metres from west to east and 15 metres from north to south. On it we found great limestone ashlars that certainly have come down from the oldest times. They were about 60 centimetres in section and were mostly 1-2 metres long. The ashlars together with smaller, only slightly hewn stones, flattened at one side, were put together to make several roundish walls or enclosures. Inside these were heaps of quarried stones of various sizes. The whole gave the effect of a *rijm*, the name given to stone heaps serving as landmarks and as stations for look-outs. By the Beduins, therefore, the hill-top was named Rijm el-Beda, 'The White Rijm'. My workmen called it simply Ras et Tell, 'The Top of the Hill', and this name is likely to last (Pl. 61).

From the very first I suspected graves from olden times to be here, that the stone heaps were meant to protect.

After the quarried stones and the thin layer of earth had been taken away, to our astonishment eight pits in the rock came to light arranged almost in a cross. The stone enclosures but seldom fitted as walls for them. Five of the pits lay on the west side of the platform, dug exactly north to south at almost equal distances; the two farthest to the south were already on the slope from the top of the hill. Opposite the second pit in this north-south row lay one to the west and two to the east. The most westerly pit with the second one in the north-south row and the two to the east made up an almost straight line perpendicular to the other five.

The pits have in the course of thousands of years doubtless been widened through the rain-storms, of whose strength, indeed, we were able to convince ourselves. In some cases they were furthermore artificially enlarged to serve as burial places; they were turned into coffer graves with stone flags at the sides and covering-stones. In two of them we found skeletons.

On several hill-tops besides our Ras et Tell there were also the same kind of wall-like stone heaps, though without the huge ashlars. Some of them we examined and found the same coffer graves with skeletons under the stones.

All the dead lay back to earth, and always in the east-west line, the head to the west; both hands were brought up to the face. Now and again—perhaps as a result of later falls of earth within the graves—the head and arms had been displaced sideways, once to the right and once to the left. The graves had no gifts in them whatever. In all probability they belong to the time after the Romans but before Islam.

In the above six cross-wise pits on Ras et Tell there must have stood six statues, but we only found the remains of four. Of one the great lowest piece of all had been taken far off to the Roman guard-house, where it was evidently meant to be broken up so as to be used for other purposes. Probably the other missing basalt statues and many of the great limestone ashlars shared the same lot.

In 1913 I had found five stones. They belonged to three monuments: a statue in the round and two double stelae. All the pieces were about a third of their bulk in the ground. These stones must have been lying here for hundreds or rather thousands of years in the same spot.

Of the statue in the round (Pl. 62) two important pieces, which together are 2 metres high, were found in 1913. Their greatest width measures 88 centimetres; their greatest thickness 62 centimetres. They show us the cylinder-shaped body of a bearded man standing unsupported, but the head is missing. His shoulders are angular and broad, the waist is drawn in a little. The arms and hands are pressed tight to the body, resting in front on the belly opposite one another. In the right hand a club is held reaching to the shoulder, this club is made exactly like those on the Tell Halaf sculptures: a shaft with a round knob, above which the end of the shaft comes out a little. The left hand is grasping some object which can no longer be made out. The heavy beard is very broad at the top, reaching far down the chest; downwards it grows narrower to where it is sharply cut off. Perpendicular zigzag or waved lines divide it up into parallel strands. In the middle it is parted, and here the tops of the waves run together. On the right shoulder portions of the flowing hair can still be made out, which like the hair of the Tell Halaf figures, more or less follows the shoulder line.

Over the back hang two short thick bands standing away fanwise from one another and cut off sharp. They belong perhaps to the head-dress, which then must be thought of as a wig. But probably we have here the ends of a broad band that was wound round the man's head. On many of the small orthostats at Tell Halaf a band like this is to be seen, although it seems to be only put round the head, and there are no ends hanging down in the profile carvings. We might perhaps see memories of a band like this in the so-called Syrian and Mesopotamian royal fillet so feared by the Romans, such as we know it, for instance, in the case of the Abgar kings of Urfa.

In the year 1927 I found a rounded basalt stone which from its size and material must be looked on as the remains of the head of the statue. Unfortunately this object has been so damaged in the course of thousands of years that, though the form can be made out to some extent, none of the details can now be read.

The statue of the man is wearing the Old Sumerian tressed gown. It is divided up into several parallel horizontal flounces, which again are made up of many small close-set 'tresses'. Each tress ends below in a point and has a rib down the middle. The tressed garment also covers the left shoulder, the right shoulder being bare. The part over the shoulder reaches in our statue as far as the arm and has five rows of tresses. From the waist downwards there are three rows of them on the upper piece of stone forming the body. In the middle of the third row the body piece ends and the lower stone starts. On it can be seen what is left of the last flounce. In its lower part this stone is so damaged that we can no longer make out what else was carved here.

I believe that the number of the flounces did not go beyond the row of tresses still preserved on the lower piece. But the statue in all probability showed part of the legs and the feet under the gown on a stand. The cylinder-shaped stone may here have been cut away a little under the gown to leave room for the lower part of the legs and the feet. The stand must have been oval in correspondence with the shape of the stone. In the place where I suspect the recess for the feet to have been a piece of the stone was later chiselled away. Perhaps an attempt was once made to change the stone to a trough. From earliest times the nomads in waterless regions have used hollowed-out stones to pour water into from a filled goat's skin for their beasts to drink.

Feet pointing to the front on a stand would be in agreement with our Tell Halaf statues of gods and also with a great many, but much smaller, Old Sumerian statues in the round. But it may also be that the feet were shown in high relief on the surface of the stone cylinder under the tressed gown. In this case they may well have stood straddled apart in the same way as in the Tell Halaf relief figures shown from the front, as for instance in the great Teshup at the front façade of the temple-palace (Pl. 8*b*).

The second and still more important monument at Jebelet-el-Beda is a huge stela oval in section (Pl. 63*a*).

Its three parts altogether make a column 3.45 metres high, whose greatest width is 86 centimetres and greatest thickness 70 centimetres. The lowest part of the third section is unworked. But beyond all doubt both this stela and the statue with the tressed gown had once a good piece more on them below, perhaps at least $\frac{3}{4}$-metre, ending, that is to say, here in a rounded prong. It is thus that the stone monuments must have been planted in the pits

SUN-GOD ON TWO MEN

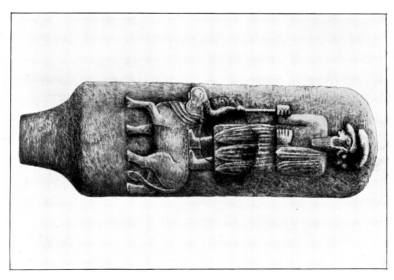

TESHUP ON THE BULL (RESTORED AND COMPLETED)

PLATE LXIII. DOUBLE STELAE ON JEBELET EL-BEDA

PLATE LXIV. IN THE TELL HALAF MUSEUM AT BERLIN, FRANKLINSTR. 6

on Ras et Tell. The limestone ashlars supported them
where they stood. Up to where the ashlars came the stelae
and the statue were not carved.

The stela shows on both sides in high relief the same
carving in every detail: a bearded man in profile walking
on a tray or table, which is borne by two smaller human
figures on their heads. On each side all the figures are
walking to the left. The narrow sides of the stone are not
worked. Thus we have here a 'double stela'.

On one side the relief is extraordinarily well preserved,
for this side by a lucky chance lay with all the three pieces
in the ground. On the other side the carving on the upper
piece has been preserved from the man's head down to the
waist, while the middle piece shows evident traces of an
attempt to turn it into a trough. Only the hanging club
has been left whole, and it corresponds exactly to that on
the other side. On the third, the lowest, piece the lower
parts of the two small figures on both sides are left in
exactly the same state as one another.

The head, legs and feet of the large figure are in profile,
the rest of the body being shown from the front. The head
has a thick beaked nose, and under it swollen, projecting
lips. The cheek is fleshy and rounded. The disproportionately big eye is almost on a level with the tip of the nose,
and is represented quite from a front view in the same
way as with the inlaid eyes of the Tell Halaf figures. The
round pupil stands out slightly from the stone. It looks as
though the artist wished to imitate an inlaid eye. The eye-
brow makes a curve that looks like the continuation of the
nose.

The ear lies lower than the lips. Behind it is an angularly
drawn tuft of hair. The chin is very retreating, and under
it a sailor's beard falls down on to the chest, narrowing
almost to a point. But this beard, remarkably enough,
is found to be looked at not as is the chin, from the side,
but from in front. It is conventionalized in the same way
as in the statue in the round.

The likeness between the representation of the beard on the statue in the round and that on the two sides of the double stela strikes one at once. In both cases the beard is drawn in parallel zigzag lines and so parted in the middle that here the wave-tops meet. The beard in the statue is, indeed, wider, and so shows more strands than it does on the double stela, whose narrower beard seems to me to be due to a kind of perplexity in the artist arising from want of space—had not the whole beard as seen from in front to find room in the space between the profile of the chin and the tresses hanging down over the left wrist ?

The head of the great figure on the stela is covered with a low cap, which, starting from the root of the nose and slightly bulgirg, goes back over the ear, keeping the same height. For this we find certain resemblances on very old Sumerian and on Cappadocian cylinders; but the cap on Jebelet-el-Beda is smaller, cut off sharply at right angles at the ends, and higher. It lies like a broad high band round the head and has almost the effect of the German student's cap without the leather peak.

The arms and hands must evidently have been rendered in the same way as on the statue in the round. The lower part of the arms are at right angles to the upper part, and held tight to the body. The hands are clenched, and held opposite one another with a small space between. The left fist shows all five fingers. While the left lower arm lies horizontally over the hip almost as far as the narrow side of the stela, the right lower arm is not seen at all. Only the right hand can be seen, whose fingers are at right angles to the upper part of the arm, which hangs down. They are holding the shaft of a hanging club, which is the same as the club in the statue in the round. The feet and legs are seen as far as the calves and set one behind the other; the toes are not carved out.

The man is wearing a gown, on which from the hip to the hem three large and very long tresses are seen. They are pointed and show two ribs within down their length,

HEAD OF THE GOD ON THE DOUBLE STELA

which meet below; between them lies a third rib. From the left shoulder hang two tresses of the same kind down to the under-side of the left lower arm. Their points hide the arm. The right side of the upper part of the body is here, as with the statue in the round, unclothed.

The garment represented on the two carvings was worn as follows: A very long shawl was wound right round the body and half-way round again under the waist from the left hip over the belly and on to the right, then the free end was drawn from the right hip across the back to the left shoulder and then thrown over this shoulder to the front, where it was left to hang down to the waist.

Wound round the body in the same way, shawls are still worn to-day in the East by certain workers—for instance, bakers and bath attendants—covering the lower body from the hips down and leaving the whole of the upper body free. They are fastened by simply putting the free end in the shawl wound often several times round the body.

There has long been a dispute over the meaning of the tresses in the representations of Sumerian garments. I cannot accept the view hitherto most widely held that the Sumerian tressed gowns were made of skins or even leaves. In Sumer there are the two kinds of gowns: that with very long tresses as on our double stela, and that with smaller tresses on flounces as in our statue in the round. In the first kind we have, I believe, long strips of stuff sewn on and coming to a point below; in the case of the tresses on flounces small bits of cloth are sewn on. On our gigantic statues this can be seen better than in the so much smaller Sumerian objects. The fleece of the golden ram from Ur and the tresses of flame on the cloak of the king on the vulture stela may well represent a skin. But it is not impossible either that the ram is wearing a royal cloak in the nature of a tressed gown. The warriors on the mosaic standard of Ur are wearing a felt cloak quite like that still worn in our day by Kurdish shepherds.

The board or slab on which the man in the double stela

is standing corresponds with the stand of the great figures of gods at Tell Halaf. On the double stela it is borne by two men on the head.

These are only slightly over a third of the size of the main figure, and like it are turned to the left. As opposed to the god they are carrying, who stands stiffly upright, they are running; their right leg is sharply bent. Their bodies, too, in contrast with the heads and limbs turned left, are shown from in front. Their faces have the same hooked or beaky noses, the same shape of the eyes and ears and the same thick lips as the large figure. The chin is strongly retreating. It almost looks as if the men had a short full beard. The tuft of hair in the large figure is lacking in the small ones, as is also the cap, which here would seem to be an emblem of the god. The hands are stretched out in front; but it certainly looks as though in the man standing behind the left lower arm were pointing upwards; it may be that he is praying. The right hand is holding an uplifted hatchet, whose edge turned to the front widens slightly, but shows no lengthening backwards. The shaft stands out above the hatchet-head. In the case of the man in front the stone is rather more weathered, so that it is not so easy to understand how the arms are held. They look as if they were both stretched out to the front also. No hatchet can be seen in the right hand,

It is hard to make out what the small figures are wearing. I believe that it was a small gown like a shirt, such as we find on the Tell Halaf figures. Below it ends above the knees and may well have covered the upper part of the body, too—at least a small furrow seems to point to this, denoting its neck.

On the rear side of the double stela the head of the large figure reaches somewhat nearer to the almost semi-circular upper end of the stone than it does on the front side. The face seems proportionately lower, the shoulders still broader and squarer, the upper arm slightly bent. The differences are, however, very small.

The representations on the two sides of our double stela correspond exactly with the god of the middle group in the relief at Yazylykaya by Boghaz Keui. It is only in unimportant details that the two carvings show any difference: on Jebelet-el-Beda the god is being borne on a stand on the heads of the two men, at Yazylykaya the two feet rest immediately on the two men's backs. In both carvings the large figure is given the same direction as the two small ones. The proportions, too, between the large and the small figures in each case are exactly the same. At Yazylykaya the large figure is the Sun god; and this is true for Jebelet-el-Beda. On Tell Halaf, too, and in the Subaraic cultural area in general the winged sun's disk, the emblem of the Sun god, is almost always borne by men or bull-men.

The fragment of the third stone carving on Jebelet-el-Beda is a large one which has broken into several pieces. It is 1.24 metres broad, 73 centimetres high and only 50 centimetres thick, the relief being worked 10 centimetres high. The basalt is much more porous than in the other sculptures.

Here again we have a double stela (Pl. 63b). On both sides the middle part of a human figure is depicted. The better preserved front side shows the lower end of a gown that narrows as it goes up. On this gown three broad long tresses can be made out, which are like those on the double stela which has been wholly preserved.

Under it to the left is seen one slightly-bent lower part of the leg ; of the other only a stump is now left. The figure is walking to the left, as can be seen from the indication of the calf.

To the left in front of it rises the upper part of a great bull's horn bent S-shape, on whose tip are still left a ball and a piece of the shaft standing up perpendicularly of a club. Undoubtedly the carving represented a god standing on a bull. As on the double stela that has been preserved, he was carrying a lowered club, whose head lay on the bull's horn.

The rear side shows the same subject, only that it stands somewhat lower than on the front.

If this object were reconstructed in correspondence with the undamaged double stela, it would in all probability be 4 metres high and 1.35 metres broad. It is the more astonishing that the essential part with the high relief is comparatively so thin. When the stela was carved thousands of years ago, the stone must have had quite another look. The basalt of the Kbise volcano often has silicious interstratifications. In our fragment there were evidently very many, and to this the high degree of decomposition shown by the stone must be set down.

On this huge stela the god Teshup is represented. As so often in the Subaraic cultural area he is standing on his holy bull.

A small but extraordinarily important find made by us in 1929 is a basalt stone of about 15 centimetres, which is exactly the same as a piece of the tress on the front of the undamaged great stela. The composition, however, of this stone fragment is not the same as that of the great double stela, and therefore cannot be part of the surface of its rear side chiselled off when the attempt was made to turn it into a trough. This basalt, too, is most certainly different from that of the Teshup fragment. We have thus a proof that there was once a third double stela on Jebelet-el-Beda, which has been lost. On it in all probability the Great Goddess was depicted, probably on the lion sacred to her. We know from old carvings that women in early times were also clad in tressed gowns.

Thus the three great godheads of Tell Halaf would also be represented on Jebelet-el-Beda: Teshup, the head god of the Subaraeans, the Sun god and the Great goddess, from whom only the small fragment of the tress has been preserved.

Besides these stone carvings, however, there must have been others in olden times on Jebelet-el-Beda. I am convinced that two more statues in the round like the statue

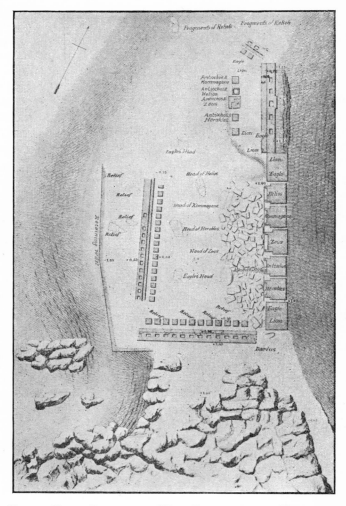

NEMRUD DAGH. PLAN OF THE WEST TERRACE OF THE TUMULUS OF
ANTIOCHUS

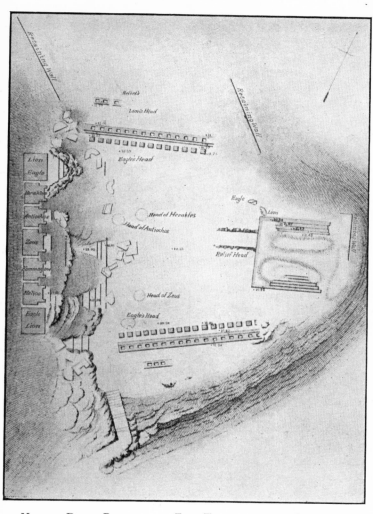

NEMRUD DAGH. PLAN OF THE EAST TERRACE OF THE TUMULUS OF
ANTIOCHUS

with the tressed gown first described are missing. The double stelae undoubtedly stood in the northernmost three pits on Ras et Tell of the five running from north to south, and with one side turned towards the east, towards the sunrise, and with the other towards the west. The order would be the same as in the entry in the temple-palace façade and in the cult room at Tell Halaf: in the middle

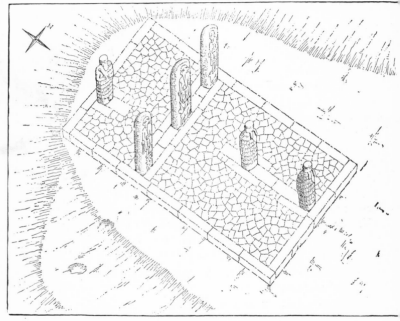

PRESUMED ARRANGEMENT OF THE STONE CARVINGS OF JEBELET-EL-BEDA
(Seen from the south-east)

Teshup, on one side his wife, in the other the Sun god. Perhaps those sides of the two stelae which are to-day better preserved were turned to the east. In this case the goddess would have had her place in the northernmost of the pits. This agrees with the way in which the carvings had fallen, as determined by me on the south-east slope of Ras et Tell. This position of Teshup between the goddess and the Sun god also corresponds to the arrangement of the figures of the gods in the entry in the great façade of the temple-palace and to that in the cult room at Tell Halaf.

The two smaller holes to the south of the double stelae are, as we said above, already on the slope of the top of Ras et Tell; they may be the result of chance, but also they may have been for smaller stone carvings of which we know nothing.

Opposite the hole in the rock for the middle stela there were, as already said, to the west one and to the east two pits one behind the other. The statue in the round with the tressed gown undoubtedly stood in one of these three holes, and, judging from the position in which we found it, I should say on the east. It was a man praying before his gods—the king. With this his holding something in the left hand fits in. It may have been a small lamb, which he was bringing for sacrifice. To the circumstance of the club being held upright by the king the fact corresponds that one of the men on the double stela carrying the god is likewise holding the axe on high. The gods on the bull and the two men as opposed to this let their clubs hang down. We cannot go into considering why the weapon was so held. On Jebelet-el-Beda this is how it was.

In the two other pits in the east and the west of the row of gods probably stood two more statues in the round of worshippers with tressed gowns.

Judging by the many ashlars and other worked stones, the top of Ras et Tell had a platform. The ashlars made up the edge; the space within was filled up and paved. Probably the platform did not take in the whole of the hill-top, but only the part where the stone carvings stood. These were planted with their prongs in the holes in the rock and were kept from falling by the heavy squared ashlar stones.

The tressed gowns on the Jebelet-el-Beda carvings correspond above all with representations in Sumer, where these gowns were the usual ones down to the twenty-seventh century for gods and mankind. From the tressed gown then grew, especially in the Gudea period, the 'plaid' or 'ruched gown', which however is as yet worn only by gods or deified kings. In Elam we know of some representations of tressed gowns from the oldest times on small terra-cotta figures and on vases of black asphalt.

In the area of Subaraic culture on the other hand the tressed gown is but seldom found; but we find it, for instance, in the above-mentioned bronze statuette of a seated bearded man from Boghaz Keui and on Jebelet-el-Beda. The wearing of the tressed gown by the man over the left shoulder as well is un-Sumerian. Perhaps this is a result of the cooler climate of Upper Mesopotamia. This kind of dress in the case of men occurs in Sumer only seldom and on very old statuettes; otherwise with the man the whole upper body is left free. The later ruched gown, however, in the case of the gods always goes over the left shoulder.

In Subartu the usual garment was above all the Cappadocian gown, which leaves one leg free: worn also was a long garment fastened up below, and lastly the short apron as we find it especially on the small orthostats of Tell Halaf.

The hooked nose faces on the great double stela of Jebelet-el-Beda exactly agree with the oldest Sumerian representations. The huge nose together with the retreating, very low forehead and the down-hanging back of the head make up an unbroken curved line which gives us the picture almost of a bird's head with a great broad beak. The eyes, rendered from in front in spite of the sharp profile treatment, are much over-stressed. Further characteristic marks are the swollen lips and the retreating chin line with the beard again represented from in front.

All this reminds us strongly of the inlaid works of Kish. In Elam and in Subartu also, beaked nose faces such as these have been found, but more seldom than in Sumer. It is, however, on Jebelet-el-Beda that the beaked nose face finds its strongest expression, and it is here that we find it for the first time on a stone carving and that moreover a mighty monument.

The beaked nose faces are too strongly marked for them not to be meant to express a racial characteristic. But what is the people that is here in mind?

It is true that in the oldest times the representations of Sumerians have beaked nose faces. These, however, link on to the terra-cotta figures found at Ur in the pre-Sumerian layer, the faces of which show the perfect bird type. In later times the Sumerians have quite another type in their carvings—the type we see best in the carvings of the Gudea period. Here there is no sign of beaked noses, and this is the true Sumerian type.

On the other hand in the area of Subaraic culture we find a racial type showing a great likeness with the beaked noses of Jebelet-el-Beda and of the most ancient south Mesopotamia. In the beaked nose faces of Jebelet-el-Beda we thus have before us, I believe, not any Sumerian racial type, but the Subaraic. The population of south Mesopotamia before the intrusion of the Sumerians belonged to the same race as the Subaraeans, as has been seen from the painted pottery belonging to their layer. The beak nosed faces of early Sumerian times are still a representation of the racial type of the original population; the Sumerians probably for some time longer kept the pattern on which men had hitherto been represented.

Many Subaraic names in the 3rd millennium in south Mesopotamia also give food for thought. It has already been pointed out more than once that they may go back to the very oldest aboriginal, pre-Sumeric dwellers in the land.

It is on Tell Halaf that the Subaraic racial type shows itself best. The depictions have a great many points of likeness with the beaked nose faces of Jebelet-el-Beda: so the throned goddess and the veiled sphinx with her retreating forehead and chin, so in the older of the scorpion-

birdmen the decidedly blubbery lips, in the full-face depictions of the relief carvings the plump cheeks. The over-
great nose of the bird faces reminds us, however, in a very
special way of the fleshy, somewhat curved nose which we
find not only on Tell Halaf but on all the Subaraic reliefs.
But to the near kinship between the Jebelet-el-Beda carvings and those from Tell Halaf and to those of the Subaraic
cultural area witness is borne by other facts as well.

The mighty size of the Jebelet-el-Beda carvings in
basalt is not Sumerian but Subaraic. The setting up of
several gods next one another is also characteristic of the
Subaraic culture. But, above all, the standing of the gods
on men and beasts is a root-element in Subaraic culture.

The garb on the figures at Jebelet-el-Beda is not the
same as on those at Tell Halaf, where we nowhere find the
tressed gown. Only in the case of the copper matrix (Pl.
57, No. 2) can there perhaps be any question of this kind
of gown.

Even if the style of the beard or the wearing of beards at
all by no means makes a characteristic of race or people,
yet the likeness shown in the finds from both places is in
this respect, too, most remarkable. So, too, the club is the
same in both places. The axe held by one of the small men
under the god on the double stela is like a copper axe that
was found on Tell Halaf. The treatment of the hands on
Jebelet-el-Beda is altogether unlike Old Sumerian models
and like that shown on the Tell Halaf carvings. In just the
same way as on Tell Halaf everything seen and known of
the man is boded forth, so the god on the double stela on
his left fist shows all five fingers one over the other. The
treatment of the arms, the outline of the muscles, the
shouldering of the weapon, especially on the statue in the
round with the tressed gown as seen from one side—all
this we find over again in the giant god at Tell Halaf.

The flint implements and the sherds which we found on
Jebelet-el-Beda point to the oldest times of Tell Halaf.
The sherds correspond with the self-coloured, thick, hand-

made earthenware; painted pottery and obsidian we did not find, but this may be only chance.

The double stelae and the statue in the round at Jebelet-el-Beda are of the same age. Everything points to there having been a carefully thought out plan, which to me has all the appearance of being the expression of a mighty king's will. This king ruled in the Khabur region on Tell Halaf and nowhere else.

The stone carvings of Jebelet-el-Beda belong to the 4th millennium. The beaked nose face is the oldest of its kind; and the tressed gowns show the oldest forms. In sculpture there is nothing older than Jebelet-el-Beda.

In those days it must have been a dreadful task to bring the basalt stones from Kbise, where they were quarried, on to Jebelet-el-Beda. Reckoning in the deviations necessitated by the lie of the land, they had to come about 100 kilometres. I think of this being particularly difficult in the case of the double stela, of which only the middle piece is left. The stones with the prongs must have been 4 metres long and more. The stone with the god on the bull was at least $1\frac{1}{2}$ metres broad. The stones were probably cut into cylinders on Kbise and then rolled through the deep wadis across country to Jebelet-el-Beda, first westwards from Kbise, where the Khabur in summer is dry, and then due south. On the north Jebelet-el-Beda does not rise up so steeply, but on the south it drops precipitously, and it would have been an impossibility to get the stones up on this side. When the sculptors had finished their work on Jebelet-el-Beda, what difficulties there must then still have been in setting the stones into their holes on the small but almost 20-metre-high crown of the hill.

When the stone carvings were overturned, and what led to it, we do not exactly know. The fact that all the fragments lay on the south-east slope of the hill-top when I discovered them would almost lead us to conclude that the destruction was due to an earthquake whose course ran south-eastwards. When the statues and stelae toppled over, the prongs by which they were planted on the hill-top may have broken off. Then perhaps in later times these old basalt blocks were got out by the people who enlarged the pits into graves, But it may be that this was done earlier for making vessels or the like from the coveted material.

When we were unable to find remains of a town or even of houses from that highly ancient period anywhere in the neighbourhood, the gigantic stones in all their loneliness made almost the impression on me of some deception. Had I not myself found the many tons of heavy sculptural remains on the ridge, I should look on the whole thing as a trick of the fantasy. But what is wonderful is that the carvings have remained so many thousands of years in the same place without being utterly broken up. It was, too, beyond all belief that through a lucky chance we should have succeeded in finding the bottom piece of the double stela quite whole in the Roman *castrum* by Ain el-Beda.

Just south of Ras et-Tell, in a rift in the precipitous cliff of Jebelet-el-Beda, we found some small remains of basalt. It is to here that some at least of the lost stones may have been rolled down in Roman times.

The many Roman sherds and a small lamp in the rubbish from a conflagration showed that the Romans set up some building, perhaps a watch-tower, on Ras et-Tell, and for this they would have used the ashlar stones also. To judge by the rubbish from the fire the building, however, must have been of wood. Last of all, the limestone ashlars and other loose stones were used to enclose and to shelter the graves that were made out of the holes for the prongs.

Geographically Jebelet-el-Beda belongs to the Khabur headwaters area. Between them lie lush pasture-lands and corn-land with many water-places. On the other hand the pasture-grounds only reach a few kilometres south of Jebelet-el-Beda and Jebel Abd-el-Aziz; and from here the boundless steppe of Upper Mesopotamia stretches as far as Belikh in the west and the Euphrates in the south. During my journey in 1911-13, 1927 and 1929, I examined this great plain in every direction. Here we find only small settlements from the oldest times, all of which I think I visited or sighted. Only far to the east of Jebelet-el-Beda, towards the Khabur, are there remains of somewhat larger settlements of man. The most important is Tell Malhat ed Deru, which in 1929 I visited, being the first European to do so. It lies far to the south-east from Jebelet-el-Beda, separated from it by the steppe.

The physiographical conditions of water and land surface do not admit of Jebelet-el-Beda being assigned to the old southern Khabur towns and princedoms. Whoever was lord of Tell Halaf held also Jebelet-el-Beda. For the Tell Halaf kings the mountain was a lookout to the south. Here at certain times in the year their herds pastured, and they themselves may well have often set their tents up during the summer on Jebelet-el-Beda or near by. In our own day Ibrahim Pasha also and his sons in the time when their power was at its height, although their abode was in Veranshehir, lived part of each summer in tents on Jebelet-el-Beda itself. In times of danger over and over again they sought here and found with their herds a place of refuge. ·

It is true that at first there is a strong inclination to take the view that the old stone sculptures on Jebelet-el-Beda may have belonged to the monument of a Sumerian king who had penetrated thus far and wished on the far-seen mountain-top to glorify his victory. This view because of the Sumerian element in the tressed gowns has, indeed, a certain attraction about it. In the Old East monuments of victory were often set up: we have only to think of the stela of Naram-Sin near Diarbekir. But they were mostly only rock carvings. In our case, however, it is not one stela only that we have, but several figures, and these in their motive and their whole treatment are Subaraic. A Sumerian king must have ruled over the Tell Halaf region for some time to make himself a monument such as this, whose setting up must have taken many years. But we have

no evidence of any kind for a Sumerian domination in the
Khabur headwaters area. So far, at any rate, we can only
look on Assur on the Tigris, and perhaps the neighbourhood of Ana on the Euphrates, as the farthest outposts from
time to time of the Sumerians.

Ras et-Tell can have been nothing else than an open
place for worship belonging to the oldest Subaraic Tell
Halaf kings—for themselves and their herdsmen. It was a
place of worship on the grandest scale.

For the understanding of this place of worship and of
the bearing of its discovery special importance seems to me
to belong to the 3000 years later monuments of the burial
mound on Nemrud Dagh. It lies 90 kilometres north from
Urfa, that is to say, still in our wider neighbourhood. Here,
too, we have the chief gods, but not as at Yazylykaya in
rock reliefs, but standing free and set up as images of gods
next to one another, and besides them, before and at the
sides, the king Antiochus, who lies buried under the mound,
and his forefathers. On the east and on the west of the
burial mound is a terrace. On both sides, that is twice over,
the same three head divinities—Zeus, Kommagene and
Helios—and King Antiochus and his greatest forefather,
Herakles, are set up one by one in a line. The gods, Antiochus and Herakles, huge separate statues made up of
several pieces from the terraces look in one case to the east
and in the other to the west, or more exactly to the north-
east and the south-west. Zeus corresponds to Teshup,
Kommagene to the great goddess Hepet, and Helios to the
Sun god of the Subaraic culture. Herakles corresponds to
Gilgamesh. On a row of smaller relief stelae opposite and
next to the main row Antiochus together with Herakles
and other forefathers are again represented along with
gods. On one stela we see Antiochus and Zeus, who is
sitting on a throne. The diadem of Antiochus has a band
with a conventional palm-leaf motive not unlike that on
the head-dress of the giant gods of the Tell Halaf façade.
The tips to the crown of the diadem of some of the gods

almost bring to mind the feather crown which also is
characteristic of Tell Halaf. The great square altar on the
east terrace opposite the statues corresponds to the enamelled brick altar before the main façade of the temple-
palace of Tell Halaf with its adornment of gods. These are
but a few of the details that on Nemrud Dagh remind us
of the Subaraic culture. What we have here is an offshoot
of this culture in Hellenistic times, an offshoot which owes
its great importance to the fact that it exactly follows
Jebelet-el-Beda in the way the statues of the gods are
arranged.

In both places the gods are ranged each apart from the
other, and look both east and west. On Jebelet-el-Beda on
each double stela the same god is always twice shown; on
Nemrud Dagh the statues, looking east and west, are
sundered by the burial mound. The king Antiochus and
his forebear Herakles are on Nemrud Dagh standing next
to the three chief gods, both being deified. The arrangement of the worshipping king and of probably two like
figures opposite the gods on Jebelet-el-Beda recalls the
stelae with the king and his forefathers set up on the west
terrace of Nemrud Dagh opposite the great gods. The top
of Jebelet-el-Beda, on which the carvings stood, was
smaller; here everything was set closer, more unified, more
primitive.

In itself the striking likeness with Nemrud Dagh calls for
an examination of the question whether on Jebelet-el-
Beda, too, there may not be a burial-place from that ancient
time to be found. We could not make out any signs pointing to such a burial-place. In four of the holes on the top
graves were indeed found, but they belonged to a much
later time. It is of course quite possible that under one or
the other stone carving the body of a king or his ashes was
laid to rest. But here there was not anything like so much
room as, for instance, in the shaft graves under the throned
goddesses of Tell Halaf. If there was ever a grave on
Jebelet-el-Beda, then it can beyond any doubt only have

been the grave of a Subaraic king of the Khabur headwaters region, who at the time of the *rabi'a* (the spring grazing) came here with his tents, or else perhaps here at the gateway to the Khabur headwaters region, in the dip between Jebel Abd-el-Aziz and Jebelet-el-Beda, was warding off a foeman from the south and in so doing fell.

But the fact of its being a burial-place would not make any change in the interpretation of the stone carvings and the way in which they are set up. The stelae represent the gods and the statue represents the king. Ras et-Tell was a place for worship; it makes no matter if it was at the same time a burial-place.

The results of our work in 1929 were so far negative that in the neighbourhood of Ras et-Tell no remains of an early settlement from the time of the stone carvings were to be found. In our hopes of making architecturally or archaeologically important new finds on Jebelet-el-Beda over and above those of 1913 we were disappointed. On the other hand, we have now recognized Ras et-Tell on Jebelet-el-Beda, lying in the dominion of Tell Halaf as an open place of worship, where in the farthest ages the sheer unbelievable stone carvings I was able to discover in 1913 once stood—and this to me seems a rich reward for the toil that has been brought to bear.

IX

The Results of our Work and the Outlook

THE most important result of the excavations on Tell
Halaf and Jebelet-el-Beda, its dependency, is the
discovery that in the old Nearer East there was besides the cultures of Egypt and Babylon a third great and
independent culture—the Subaraic; and this Subaraic
culture can be found as early as the 4th millennium B.C.
Hitherto it has been customary to call the products of the
art belonging to this culture 'Hittite'. This must be
changed, for the Indo-Germanic 'Hittites' did not come
into Hither Asia earlier than about 2000 B.C. These Hittites on their side took over the aboriginal Subaraic culture with its divinities and its art—just like the Aryan
Mitanni, who came into Mesopotamia about the same
time, and the Semitic Arameans, who became the rulers
in the twelfth century B.C. in Upper Mesopotamia and
then in northern Syria too.

As we go from the border districts of Subartu-land in
Asia Minor and western Syria the witnesses to the Subaraic culture and art become more and more frequent
the nearer we are to Upper Mesopotamia. Here it is that
for a long time past their centre, the place of their birth,
has been sought. In the Khabur headwaters region so
favoured by nature, on Tell Halaf and in its neighbourhood, I have found it. Here lies the oldest and richest
archaeological site in the great land of Subartu. Here
must once have been its capital or the capital of one of its
largest and most important divisions.

In all the sculptures of Tell Halaf from old Subaraic
times that were used over again in his buildings by the
Aramaic king Kapara there is the expression of something
utterly primitive, something childishly naïve ; the object

is to imitate nature. The personages in the Subaraic religious beliefs emanated from nature. Teshup means the
sky, Hepet the earth, and their child is the sun that rises
and sets day by day. From the phenomena of nature are
conjured up the half-gods and demons—hybrid and fabulous beings combined out of beasts and men or from forms
of the most varied beasts.

But in the carvings of Tell Halaf we are greeted by the
great art of the Primitive. It is not yet overlaid with ornament and conventionalized, but is wholly taken from
nature. Especially do the reliefs show an extraordinary
faithfulness to nature; we seem to be watching the animals
moving.

The wide range of the representations on the relief
slabs and in the sculpture in the round, the truly inex-
haustible wealth of ideas found in the carvings compel our
admiration. Moreover it is almost beyond understanding
how the men of that time could carry out such things with
such simple means.

The temple-palace façade at Tell Halaf we were able to
restore with absolute truth. It offers to even modern eye a
spectacle with an overpowering effect. The giant gods on
the animal colossi throw a spell over all. Our thoughts are
of the fear, the mystic dread, that wrapped the divine in
the Old East, of the awe felt by the faithful towards their
gods. In the Subaraic sculpture the gods are on a great
scale, great beyond all measure, they are superhuman.

In the façade of the temple-palace architecture and
sculpture are so linked together that it seems as if this were
invented here on Tell Halaf and as if sculpture had here
first been born from an architectonic need. On the other
hand the European, schooled in the thought of the classical
Greek world, cannot but see on Tell Halaf the earliest
patterns of many Graeco-Roman aesthetic forms and
works of art. I have no doubt whatever that Tell Halaf is
called upon to play an important part in the history of
art.

In much that is offered by Tell Halaf in its great monuments and carvings and in its smaller artistic objects, modern art will find points of contact without any intention on its part, as though unconsciously the art of to-day, grown weary of a useless tangle of ornamentation, has gone back again to the primitive forms that meet us in the old Subaraic art—a prelude to the Graeco-Roman. It is remarkable how, for instance, the Cubist architecture of our day—which in the sky-scrapers of the last few years in America has found its highest and fullest artistic expression—has most striking analogies with the architecture of our temple-palace and with the scheme of the cubiform parts of the great throned goddess of Tell Halaf rising in steps.

.   .   .   .   .   .

A short time ago I gathered together the Tell Halaf finds, so far as they were allotted to me, in the original, and the rest in plaster casts in a museum in Berlin (Franklinstrasse 6; Pl. 64). Here the large objects found have been given their provisional home in a machine workshop belonging to a former factory, the smaller finds being housed in the office building. In the workshop the great front façade of the temple-palace, the second gateway with the giant griffins, part of the bastioned walls and the cult room have also been set up in casts from the originals.

It is hardly likely that a complete collection of such size and with so many great and small stone carvings and most various small objects will ever again be brought to light from one hill in the Nearer East. The stone carvings of Tell Halaf belong to the 3rd millennium, those of Jebelet-el-Beda to the 4th millennium B.C., and our painted pottery belongs to the same periods.

Just as the grave of Tutankhamun and those at Ur were rich in gold objects and in splendid small examples of the arts, so was Tell Halaf overwhelmingly rich in stone carvings of the most varied kinds, some of a size never dreamed of.

My excavations on Tell Halaf and Jebelet-el-Beda are an important step to the better understanding of the finds from Ur and Kish in oldest south Mesopotamia.

But Tell Halaf still calls for several more excavating expeditions. As a result of our investigations up to now many new questions have been raised. There is much that is not yet fully cleared up. Even the names for the town and the land of old Tell Halaf have still to be found.

On Tell Halaf we shall now have to set about the systematic examination of the layers with the prehistoric painted pottery. Here the existence of remains of thick palace walls close in front of the Kapara castle has been already determined, and we shall have to follow these very ancient structures up. We cannot tell whether we may not yet find here stone carvings, or anyhow their remains, still standing in the same place where they were set up by the Painted Pottery folk. It would be a joy indeed if we could discover graveyards and kings' graves from those old times.

Besides carrying on further the excavations on Tell Halaf we have also to set to work on another great task. This task is the investigation of the second old capital of the Khabur headwaters region, Fekheria. This, too, will be an excavation on the biggest scale. The walled ruins of the town spread over more ground than the old Tell Halaf town. The citadel hill, too, is very important.

At Fekheria we may hope for finds from one of the most interesting periods, about which till now we know least for the whole of Upper Mesopotamia. It is the period that must have followed the fall of the Painted Pottery town of Tell Halaf—perhaps about 2000—and have lasted down to the fall of the Mitanni dynasty—about 1300. It is highly probable that the Mitanni rulers, as we have already shown, had their capital Vashukani here at Fekheria until chaos arose in Upper Mesopotamia and Kapara made himself a new capital on Tell Halaf. Should the Mitanni kings, who for a time were allies of the Egyptian kings of the eighteenth dynasty, really have had their palaces here, we shall beyond a doubt have to expect further great surprises: in the first place probably more stone carvings, the comparison of which with those of Tell Halaf would then be of very great importance. Any sculpture or other find from this time will be of the very greatest interest for the history of culture; for indeed from the Mitanni period we have practically no finds at all.

The new excavations will, I hope, throw fresh light on the up to now almost wholly unknown history and culture of Upper Mesopotamia and of the rest of Subartu-land, and on the history of the whole of the ancient Nearer East. If at Fekheria we were to find old Mitanni written pieces or the state archives of Tushratta, the contemporary of the great Hittite king Shuppiluliuma and of the Pharaohs Amenophis III and IV, we should have documents of the same historical importance as the Tell Amarna letters and the records from Boghaz Keui.

To reach the old layers at Fekheria and its neighbourhood we shall have to remove, anyhow in part, the remains lying above of the old Arab town of Ras el-Ain and of the Graeco-Roman Resh-aina; this holds out hopes of interesting information as to these later times also.

I am already filled with joy at the hope of shortly going back once more to the desert and the Beduins I have come to love, of making new journeys of exploration and of personally carrying through many more seasons of steady excavation on Tell Halaf and at Fekheria-Vashukani. The 'Baron Max von Oppenheim Foundation (Institute of Oriental Research)' is designed to carry on my life-work and my studies in the old and the new Nearer East after my death. The excavation concession is made out in its name. Thus provision has been made so that the further work of excavation, which will need many more years, may be continued.

R

APPENDIX I

Stylistic Investigation and Dating of the Stone Carvings
By Ernst Herzfeld

THE STONE carvings of Tell Halaf when critically analysed for style divide themselves into three great stages, which stand out clearly from one another as unities.

The first stage (T.H. I) is represented by the flat carvings of the small orthostats (Pl. 16-39). Carvings in the round from this period are wanting.

The second stage (T.H. II) is represented by the large orthostats (Pl. 8-10), and, as carvings in the round belonging to these flat carvings, the intrados orthostats and animal bases of the great temple front (Pl. 11, 12), the intrados orthostats of the inner temple room (Pl. 15), of the outer courtyard gate (Pl. 40-42a), the great bird (Pl. 14) and the torso of an animal standing clear.

To the third stage (T.H. III) belong the three divine figures of the great temple front (Pl. 13) (which are not contemporary with their animal bases), the small throned goddess (Pl. 44b), the small standing man from the cult room (Pl. 45a).

The distance in style, and so undoubtedly in time, between T.H. I and T.H. II is much less than that between T.H. II and T.H. III. Between T.H. II and T.H. III comes (and it must be put nearer to III than to II) the small double statue of the cult room (Pl. 45b). In the same way the great throned goddess (Pl. 43, 44a) comes between T.H. I and T.H. II, but very near to II.

The oldest stage, T.H. I, as we should already expect from the great number of the pieces to be reckoned to it (originally over 200), is not altogether a unit in itself. The more or less same size of the slabs, with their alternating colourings of limestone tinged with ruddle and grey-black basalt does at first sight give the impression that they were all made for one building. But a closer examination reveals differences, and at least two sub-groups (T.H. I*a* and T.H. I*b*) emerge. Finer distinctions still I would rather not make, since they would not go beyond the play that must be allowed for the individual skill of each artist, and so would not have the meaning of stages of development. But the small orthostats originally belong to at least two different buildings, different also in time.

The distinction does not simply coincide, as one might think, with the material: limestone and basalt. But it is remarkable that almost all the limestone slabs belong to the older and only a few to the younger stage, while the basalt is fairly evenly divided. This is not mere chance, for with stage T.H. II the limestone disappears once for all. In correspondence with the softness of the material the drawing on limestone is more elegant, the scale of the individual engraving is finer, and the whole picture more spontaneous and sketchy; the artistic ideas and intentions are expressed with the freshness of a first attempt. In the hard basalt something of this freshness is lost: the greater trouble demands more reflection. The works in basalt stand in the same relation to those in limestone as the finished statue of an artist to his first sketch in clay.

The oldest sub-group T.H. I*a* brings before us a wholly primitive art. It is hard to imagine that it has any presuppositions at all, and we seem to be near the birth of carving in stone, although something older still must come before this and, as we learn from the colossi on Jebelet-el-Beda, did indeed come before. It looks as if these slabs were still worked with copper, not with bronze tools. But these artists, who beyond all doubt disposed of the very simple tools only, have a creative power and an artistic boldness such as only the primitive times of an art produce that holds within it the seed of very great developments. It is outline and movement that characterize men, beasts and their actions, as on Old Stone age cave paintings. Measurements for the bodies are a secondary thing—this is especially evident in the case of human beings; they do not trouble the artist, who like a child stresses what seems to him to be essential by size also. That, too, is still represented which is known, not that which is seen—as in the feet which have always five toes. What is accomplished in this way, for instance in the carving of the individual animals, is a matter for wonder, and the design for the animal fights is simply masterly, in some ways never attained to again by the art of the Old East.

This oldest stage only knows one level in relief. The ground around the outlines, which are generally pretty well closed, is somewhat deepened and owing to the primitive tools left very uneven. The surface of the relief is quite flat, and all inside drawing is no more than scratching. Fundamentally, therefore, all these works are only drawn —they are an excellent linear abstraction from the rounded corporeality of nature. But yet these artists are sculptors and not painters, and in their carving out of the ground their conception of space reveals itself. Never do the figures stand on anything; they hover. It is the stone slab, the background, that bears their abstract corporeality: they are at once seen to be true reliefs. The slab is the space in which they move. As yet there is no abstraction of the solid ground in the shape of a basic line. These characteristics all find their counterparts only in the very earliest monuments of human artistic expression of whatever kind. Had the chances of discovery willed it that first Tell Halaf, and then Senjirli and Karkemish were to be excavated, the thought that works such as these might be 'late art', might belong to the 2nd millennium, would never have arisen.

The second sub-group (T.H. I*b*) keeps all the essential features of the older one and differs only in two characters. Firstly the relief surface is no longer quite flat. The inner drawing inside the raised outlines is no longer wholly a scratching, but begins to become a modelling. This natur-

ally emerges most clearly where heads are rendered from a
front view, also in the multiplied rows of feathers on the
wings of the many winged figures where the lower parts of
the body and of the fore-limbs that lie on the ground of the
picture are cut off in steps, and lastly in the cross-cuttings,
which throughout are only seldom found.

Secondly: The filling in of space on the slabs has an extraordinary amount of thought given it and is carried out
with great skill. This is inseparably bound up with an
advance in showing the individual figures in proportions
like the real ones; though it goes without saying that what
seems essential is still always over-stressed. But these beasts
and men are enclosed by virtual, very regular polygons,
and these yield in their grouping or their intersection sys-
tems of parallels, inclines, diagonals, triangles, even of
circles (scorpion-man, stone 141), which presuppose a careful preliminary design. There no longer prevails, as in the
older sub-group, the unhesitating, direct setting down of
the carvings, but this art has learnt much, it has become
savant. There is so much training in it that in some of the
pieces (the separate bulls, for instance stone 93, griffins =
stone 119, lions = stone 73) we might speak of routine, and
the result is that this later stage already has a less immediate effect on us than the older stage.

The second main stage (T.H. II), that of the large orthostats and of the intrados colossi and the animal bases belonging to these orthostats, is very closely linked with T.H.
I*b*. The difference in style evidently rests partly on a real
advance in the tools. Limestone is despised. The dimensions of the basalt blocks come to be gigantic. Works
such as these are unimaginable without quite hard bronze
tools.

Development goes along the lines first laid down. The
mere scratching of the inside drawing is still, indeed, there,
especially in unessential things; but the relief modelling of
the surface has made great advances. This is unmistakable
so soon as the faces of this stage II represented from in

front are compared with those of I*b*. So, too, the giving of proportions to the figures is taken further; there is much better balance between the several parts of man and beast. Yet this movement is still in its beginnings, and the culmination as shown in the god at the gate from Boghaz Keui is still very far off. But if we wish to know how a later decayed art works with untrue proportions, we need only set a Barrekub of Senjirli beside the men of T.H. II. With the giving of proportion is linked the change in fitting the depictions into the space on the slab that has to be filled. It has got beyond the experimental stage and become classical. Lastly the perception of space has changed; the earth has been found, all the figures are standing on a base line running through.

In T.H. I*a* and I*b* true carvings in the round were wanting. In T.H. II they make their appearance with the beasts of the intrados, the animal stands, the giant bird. That they go together with the large orthostats—already probable on architectonic grounds—is set beyond all doubt by the small carvings in the flat between the legs of these great beasts and on the cubes on the back of the animal bases. The relation of carvings in the flat to those in the round in this stage is exactly the same as in the style of Senjirli I. Now that the sphinxes and animal bases which were found partly shattered have been put together again this has been made much clearer still than before.

Just as the flat carvings in their design and proportions are determined by the substance of the stone slab, so, too, those in the round are wholly governed by the nature of the stone block. In the same way that virtual polygons can be described round those older figures, so round these gigantic animals can be described the surfaces of great, highly regular polyhedra. These are determined by the block, as is the cut of a precious stone by the crystal. This is what gives so remarkable an architectonic quality to the art. I said once that it is possible to believe that this architectonic character of the sculpture is older than the architecture. And of a surety these carvings in the round are not made as they are with the intention of using them in the architecture. A glance at the great throned goddess is quite enough in itself to contradict this. Rather it is the same will as makes the design of the older small orthostats be determined by the given stone slab, which here also hews the statues in the round thus out of the block. With all their angularity and flatness of surfaces they are, in the full meaning of the word, carvings in the round, which reveal to us a form of spatial perception of which we have no instance in any other art of the Old East. And while the art of the large orthostats belonging to them is already about to pass over into a classicalism, these statues in the round are still quite young and have an overpowering strength. Without any relation whatever to the most ancient arts of Sumer and of Egypt, there here stand before us the masterpieces of a contemporary, quite youthful art—masterpieces equal to those of Old Egypt and standing far above those of Sumer.

The great throned goddess in style stands quite near the works in the stage of T.H. II. This is at once shown by a comparison of her profile with that of the veiled sphinx. But the front view of the heads is not quite the same: the smiling mouth, the sharp chin of the goddess, the modelling of the cheek lines, the shape of the forehead, the eyes (which in her are worked from the basalt, not, as in the sphinxes, inlaid) have something still more primitive about them. The cube, too, of the seated body is more straitly bound, less free than the bodies of the sphinxes, not to speak of the other animal colossi. It is only with the upper part of the body that she grows outside and beyond the cube of the throne, and the will to come forth from the stone mass grows ever stronger towards the head, which gazes slightly upwards, up to where the two front locks before the cheek and neck are left quite free, and is spiritualized in the wonderful mystic smile. Thus the goddess is a little more archaic and a little older than the other works in stage T.H. II. But although she is a very early work, she is the unexcelled masterpiece of Hittite art.

The third stage of Tell Halaf shows this art essentially changed. In contrast with the older stages it is represented only by carvings in the round; carvings in the flat are wanting. These are the three colossal figures of the temple front, the small throned woman and the small standing man of the cult room. These works, too, are determined by the block from which they are made, but in quite another way. The standing figures have something of the stake or pillar. The whole outline is quite shut in, but no longer lies within the many plane faces of a polyhedron, but within one only cylindrical surface. Angularity has yielded to roundedness. Thus, too, all the details are round: shoulders, breast, arms. If it was in T.H. II that true modelling took its rise, then here in the muscles of the legs, of the faces with their thick cheeks and their wrinkled chins, a culminating point is now reached. No longer is there any groping; training has made the artists equal to their tasks. This is not only classicism; there is something over and above that: much routine. Corresponding with this—and a thing which really always betokens the beginnings of decay—is the search after decoration, the wealth of ornament shown.

Very near this third stage stands the small double statue of the cult room. It shares in all the characteristics of the giant statues, but it is decidedly simpler, not only in the lack of all ornament, but also in the modelling of the faces and the representation of the hair. It is therefore somewhat older than the other pieces belonging to stage T.H. III.

The length of time between T.H. III and T.H. II must be considerable, for, properly speaking, in neither are there any works marking the highest point actually reached by this art. T.H. II is a young art, T.H. III is the beginning of a late one. If we do wish to give figures and may be allowed to do so, I should say that T.H. I*a* and I*b* stretch over about 100 years, that they are separated from T.H. II by a gap of 100 years, T.H. II itself in turn lasting

100 years, but that in the same proportion T.H. III is separated from T.H. II by 300 years. Even if we assume shorter lengths of time, there would always be the fact that the great statues of the gods belong to a wholly different stage in art from that of the great animal bases on which they stand. And thus the conclusion can be no other than that the bases and the figures standing on them are not from the same time. So there are two possibilities. First: The great statues of the gods, when they were made, were meant to be set upon the animals. These animals are bases and have a cube—in the case of two of them worked from the same block—on the back with a mortise. They thus carried something, whether it was older statues of gods or whether it was pillars. In this case the great statues of the gods, therefore, in the T.H. III period would be to replace what was carried by the animals in the T.H. II period. Second: The gigantic figures were made without any heed to the animal bases, and were meant to be set up in the cult room. In that case they stood in their time, T.H. III, with their rather small socle slabs on some great base-block, on to which they must have been fastened with prongs. It was not until later, that is, in this case, when Kapara had the temple built which was dug out, that they would have been set on the animal bases.

The technical facts are as follows: The breadth at the shoulders and the average girth of the body of the figures of the gods are considerably greater than the width of their socle slabs. Since the figures must have been cut from an evenly-shaped cylindrical block, their ground sections may very well have been originally greater than they are to-day. They would therefore, if they did not happen to fit when the Kapara period set them upon the animal bases, have been made to fit. The cylindrical drums on the heads are pieces that have been separately set on with prongs. Whether they are a head-gear, and so part of the original figures, or whether as purely architectural elements they were only added when the façade was put up again—in either case their measurements and prongs must fit exactly. Thus the monuments themselves and their constituent parts do not yield any information by which to make a decision between these possibilities. Taken in itself there is nothing very striking in the thought of the gods on their beasts: the Moloch of Karkemish and the two Teshup statues of Karkemish and Senjirli are of the same date as stage T.H. II and older than T.H. III. What we could wish to see decided is only the age of the purely architectonic use; could true gods play the part of caryatids as early as T.H. II or T.H. III?

For we have here a very high antiquity. The relative dating of the Tell Halaf carvings lies quite open to us there. This art develops quite naturally and without disturbance. In the oldest stage (T.H. I) we have the primitive works, in the second stage (T.H. II) those that are still youthful but already ripening, and in the third stage (T.H. III) we have works before us in which the true classical high-water mark of the old Hittite art is already left somewhat behind.

The absolute dating of these stages can be found by bringing the works of Tell Halaf into relation with those from the older Hittite sites. This I have already done in the article 'Hettitica' in the *Archäologische Mitteilungen aus Iran*, II, 3-4. But there, although Tell Halaf was known to me, it was treated only very shortly as being still unpublished material. The present discussion thus supplements and extends that article, and the table here given does the same for the old table there. As something new, is now added stage T.H. III, which in the article was without importance. Otherwise there is nothing to change. All the absolute numbers, having regard to the hopeless confusion to-day in Old Babylonian chronology, may be looked on as valid, but with that vagueness that clings to all numbers in the Old Orient. With this reserve stage T.H. I falls more or less into the century 3100-3000 B.C.; T.H. II should be put at about 2900-2800, the great throned goddess at about

3400-3300	—	—	Carvings of Jebelet-el-Beda.	—	—
About 3100 Mesilim.	—	—	Ia. Small orthostats; most of the limestone slabs; half the basalt slabs.	Statue of the king of Mari in the British Museum.	—
About 3000 Urnanshe	I. Intrados lions in the Inner Citadel gate; all the orthostats of the southern town gate.	—	Ib. Small orthostats; some limestone slabs; half the basalt slabs.	—	Malatia: banquet.
About 2950 Eannatum	—	I. Water gate.	Great throned goddess.	—	All the carvings of Eyuk: Sphinx gate; religious feast; hunting pictures.
2900 Entemena	—	—	II. Large orthostats; intrados colossi; animal bases; giant bird.	—	—
About 2800 Lugalanda	II. Lions of gate Q; old statue of Hadad; all the orthostats of the Outer Citadel gate.	—	—	Teshup from Babylon.	—
About 2750 Sargon	—	II. Antithetic groups of gods; hybrid beings and beasts; Moloch, Hadad; twin animal bases.	—	—	Malatia: hunting pictures; libations; fight between gods; lion.
About 2650 Narâmsin	—	III. Two gods; two gods on lions; fighting chariots; warriors; music; women in festal procession.	Double statue of the cult room.	Lion from Babylon; warrior stela from Arslan-tash.	—
About 2600 -2550 Gudea	—	—	III. Great statues of gods of the temple front; small standing god; small throned goddess.	—	—

2950. After a gap there then follows, about 2600-2550, T.H. III, and shortly before 2600 the double statue of the cult room.

Nor are the primitive works, however, of stage T.H. I*a* the first beginnings. The carvings discovered by Baron von Oppenheim not far south on Jebelet-el-Beda—a colossal statue in the round of a man and two equally huge stelae with relief carvings on both sides (Pl. 60-63)—are older still.

The statue in the round represents a man standing. The body seems below simply to grow out of the cylindrical boss of the block. The garment is known to us from Old Sumerian depictions. Unfortunately the head is hopelessly damaged: how much or how little it stood free from the body, what was its facial type, can no longer be made out. The beard falls long and broad on to the breast, and its hairs are carefully shown by waved lines from the top downwards—not unlike the beards on asphalt sculptures from Susa—with a peculiar parting in the middle.

The relief stelae are cylinders with two sides flattened. One shows on both sides the figure of a man standing on the top of the heads of two small men; the other the remains of a man on a big bull. The garb is different, but again known to us from the Old Sumerian. The standing on a beast is a common Hittite motive; in the great festal procession of Yazylykaya by Boghaz Keui a god is standing on two men's necks. The heads are very surprising. They are profiles. The face is hardly anything but nose—of an utterly improbable shape and size—and eye, so that it is bird-like. The mouth is narrow-lipped and yet swollen out. The beard is seen from in front, though the face is in profile, which results in an impossible form of the cheeks. Around the lips and at the edge of the cheeks the beard is shaven like a sailor's fringe. Faces like this have nowhere been found up to now in the large-scale art of the Old East, though they are found in the art of small objects. For with all the difference there is in material and dimensions —colossal basalt sculpture, that is to say, and the tiniest stone carvings—we cannot but see that the facial type of certain Old Sumerian seal cylinders expresses the same thing: these are the small bird-like faces of a very numerous series of cylindrical seals, whose course of development lies wholly in the 4th millennium and finds its culmination and end in those pieces which by their inscriptions are assigned to the beginnings of the historical period—the epoch of King Mesilim of Kish, that is, to round about 3100 B.C. The colossi of Jebelet-el-Beda, according to this, belong to the same time as the last prehistoric stage of Sumerian art, the Jamdat Nasr stage—that is also, as the first Dynasty in Egypt; this means that they fall into the period about 3400-3300 B.C.

In analysing these works it is just as purposeless to start from their clothing or such details as it is to do so for Hittite art in general; this we shall only really learn from the monuments. We do not even know what these garments with their long or short tresses, in single or manifold flounces, really mean—leaves, skins, stuffs—and much less who first wore them or whence they came. But even if the dress of these gigantic stone sculptures were Sumerian, their carvers would not be. For this art is quite un-Sumerian. The idea of setting up gigantic vertical blocks of rock reminding us of European Stone Age monoliths, and giving them the form of human beings in round or flat sculpture is foreign to Old Egyptian, Sumerian, and Elamic art, but lives on in the Hittite and here in the great statues of the gods at the temple front of Tell Halaf. And just as the whole artistic idea lives on, so too the racial type of the heads, persists. How such transitions are carried out in each case can be studied from the Old Sumerian seal cylinders. The profile of the throned goddess and of the sphinxes of T.H. II has grown out of the profile of Jebelet-el-Beda; the shape of the eyes long remains the same; the lips of the scorpion-men of T.H. II are still those of the Jebelet-el-Beda gods; and their beards carry on still the great statues of the gods of T.H. III.

The carvings on Jebelet-el-Beda are a very ancient pre-lude to the old Hittite art of Tell Halaf, and these works, therefore, stretch over full a thousand years, from about 3400 to 2500 B.C.

In this study the monuments have been analysed and ranged in order only according to the characteristics be-longing to them in themselves. This method leads only to relative dating. If in spite of this absolute figures are also here given, these rest on an earlier detailed study 'Hetti-tica' published in the *Archäologische Mitteilungen aus Iran*, but also on comparisons not referred to here with Sumerian and Old Elamic monuments. For naturally there is another way of reaching the understanding and the actual chrono-logy of the Hittite monuments—the comparative method. For this again the presupposition is that the material to be compared, in this case the Old Sumerian, has been chrono-logically determined. Actually, neither the older system of Old Babylonian chronology resting on Fotheringham's astronomical investigations, and the one almost universally accepted in England, nor the newer system based by Kug-ler and Weidner on a consideration of the Assyrian chrono-logy and almost universally followed in Germany, is really proved. On archaeological grounds I hold the older figures to be nearer the truth.

There is a consideration of a general kind that is here of fundamental importance. The Old Sumerian art develops from the beginnings of a time that is pre-historic even for this land in an unbroken course up to its highest point under Sargon of Akkad. This process of growth in the fol-lowing stage under Narâmsin of Akkad has already gone beyond its highest point and it is in the following stage under Gudea that it truly falls from its zenith. After the Guti invasion that now followed Sumerian art ceases alto-gether to be productive. Already in the time of the state of Sumer and Akkad (the 3rd dynasty of Ur) 2414-2297 B.C., it is becoming purely reproductive, and in the time of the states of Isin, Larsa and Babylon it sinks into that stagnation which in the Kassite period turns to a condition without any growth or history whatever.

It is, therefore, only down to the Gudea period that Sumerian art could and did have any historical influence. And it is easy to see that the relations between Sumerian and Hittite art become closer the further we go back, so much so that the pre-historic foundations, marked by the different Painted Potteries, and from which both derive along diverging paths, are so essentially akin that perhaps they ought rather not be called two different cultures at all, but one culture only, springing from one origin. A comparative examination, however, of the individual cases shows the following correspondences:

Jebelet-el-Beda in north Mesopotamia corresponds with the last prehistoric stage in Babylonia, namely the Jamdat Nasr stage; the T.H. I*a* stage corresponds with the Mesilim stage, represented at Kish, Farah and Lagash; T.H. I*b* corresponds with the stage in Old Babylonia represented by the Urnanshe monuments from Lagash; the throned goddess corresponds with the art of the Eannatum stage; T.H. II corresponds with the art of the Entemena stage; the double statue corresponds with the Narâmsin stage; and lastly T.H. III corresponds with the Gudea stage.

These stages are what is meant by the absolute figures given in the list.

APPENDIX II

Technical Remarks on the Excavations on the Citadel Hill

BY FELIX LANGENEGGER

A. *General*

OF the surface of the citadel, which in round numbers measures 51,000 square metres, about 30,300 square metres, that is about three-fifths, was worked over, partly in extensive excavations down to the rock. In the process the following buildings were uncovered:

I. *Later times than the Kapara dynasty.*

Buildings everywhere from Arab and Hellenistic times, of small compass and without distinguishable ground plan. On the east side a complete Assyrian house with courtyard, and remains of smaller buildings with a find of tablets; lastly at various places clay coffins.

II. *Buildings of the Kapara dynasty.*

(*a*) *The North-East Palace group.*—The thick outside circumvallation with bastions, walls on the river bank and junction with the town walls; the 'Well Gate' leading into the north part of the palace with the well in the rock lying before and outside the gate; the North Gate ('Spring Gate') of the town; the North-East palace (dwelling palace), which lies about two courtyards, with its massive surrounding and extension buildings.

(*b*) *The South-East Corner group.*—The east arm of the south enclosure-wall and the south arm of the east enclosure-wall with the south-east corner bastion; the ground raised hereabouts by dumping broken stones; buildings not of a monumental kind and standing unconnected in the citadel; town houses along the outer side of the south circumvallation.

(c) *The South Gate group.*—The south gate of the citadel (an older and a newer structure); the west arm of the south circumvallation of the citadel together with the south-west corner bastion; the huge mud brick massif, a stepped sub-structure whose purpose is unknown; the graves on and in the mud brick massif, the latter with statues.

(d) *The Temple-Palace group.*—The temple-palace with terrace in two periods; the Scorpions' Gate with remains of an older gate underneath; two rulers' graves, one of them with unhurt contents; the 'north building', north of the temple-palace and standing on its terrace.

III. *Remains of oldest buildings under those of the Kapara dynasty.*

Mostly fairly small dwellings from the Painted Pottery period; under the temple-palace the lines of fairly thick walls of monumental buildings without recognizable ground plan; under the Kapara north-east palace a thick scarped stone circumvallation with cuttings along the rock, being the oldest fortification of the citadel.

B. *Inner Hill Superstructure*

The hill massif is built up within relatively simply.

Of its average height of 20 metres 8-9 metres may be taken off for the bed of rock and the layer of weathering resting on it. The remaining 11-12 metres are made up of five main layers:

1. The Painted Pottery layer of the primitive dwellers immediately on the rock or its weathering layer.
2. The layer of the Kapara dynasty with two periods of monumental building not very far asunder in time.
3. The Assyrian layer.
4. The Hellenistic layer.
5. The Arab layer.

These layers are found resting, although not uniformly, over the whole of the hill.

s

C. *Details*

I. *The Painted Pottery layer.*

A strong and extensive fortified structure—the first foundation of any permanent stronghold at all at this spot —was formed from the bed of rock at the spring and was protected to the east by the broad and deep cutting in the rock. The east cutting was shut on the north by a broad barrier of rock that had been left, over which was once the way into the citadel, and was therefore dry. It probably also went round the south and the west side of this citadel, and then in the course of a long time, through rubbish falling in, got filled up to the top more or less of the scarped wall built on the edge of the cutting. When the Kapara dynasty started building here, the old works had quite disappeared.

The east face of the wall at the cutting or ditch was at least 105 metres long, the section of the cutting was 9.30 metres above and 8.10 below with a depth of 5 to 5.35 metres. The artificial rise behind the scarp consists of a filling $3\frac{1}{2}$-4 metres high made up of the rock rubble arising from the cutting of the ditch and of masses of earth. Above the edge of the cutting the filling is faced with a rounded retaining wall of quarried grained stones in clay mortar. These oldest works show an essentially better technique and a more thorough workmanship than the same kind of buildings from the Kapara dynasty. The amount of work needed here may be measured from the fact that with a cross-section trench of 45 square metres the mass of the stone blocks to be broken up and brought away from the excavated stretch of 102 metres alone comes to 4600 cubic metres.

In the front of the cutting or ditch the traces could also be made out of an outwork. Near the west side of the hill are massed up to 5 metres' thickness many layers of dwellings with ashheaps and remains of small buildings.

II. *The buildings of the Kapara dynasty.*

All the buildings are of unfired mud bricks, the material being mixed with chopped straw. Stone substructures were found only at the river bank; they were bedded in clay mortar; hard mortar is lacking.

Besides the arch as the upper part of the door-frame wood is used for lintels and ceilings. The wooden pillar on a stone foot is used to carry wide spans. The use of the statue for carrying timber-work is the only example of the kind in all the architecture of the Old East. The very poor building materials used make a remarkable contrast with the basalt sculptures constructively associated with the buildings. Stonework and mud-brick walls are held together by wooden ties. For pegs metal is used. All the buildings are embellished without and within with mud plaster, the better ones being also limewashed. A well-executed system of drainage carries the water away from the citadel to outside or into drain-shafts inside. Privies were not recognized anywhere. Floors are hardened with layers of mud or plaster, macadam (plaster-concrete), small rubble, or a pavement of natural stone or flags.

The citadel of the Kapara dynasty has its foundations in the Painted Pottery layer on the bed of rock. Its enclosing walls are marked out more or less by the cardinal points of the compass, and at intervals are substituted by the outer faces of massive terraces that partly break their line. The measurements are (in metres):

Length on the south side from corner to corner, 282.
Length on the east side   ,,   ,,   ,,   210.
Length on the west side (only estimated, since the north-west corner is no longer to be found), 163.
Length of the west arm of the north enclosing wall, 213.50.
Length of the east arm of the north enclosing wall, 90 (making for the two arms, 303.50).
Length of the salient of the north-east part of the citadel, 55.50.

Only the north enclosing wall was a true outwork and built as a double wall with two strong corner bastions. On the other three sides the town with isolated small houses joins on to the line of the walls, which simply have turrets.

Thus the citadel was the fully enclosed core of the town-settlement. The junction of the town wall was made laterally on the east and the west side of the citadel's enclosing wall; but only the east junction could be determined.

Approaches.—The citadel could be approached on the south from the town through the south gate, and on the north through two gates lying next to one another: the narrow 'Well gate'—leading only into the north-eastern palace—with its upward slope like a shaft or gallery, and for the rest of the citadel the 'Spring gate' set at the angle of the crook in the outer circumvallation.

Division of the citadel.—The whole of the west side with the temple-palace and the south gate group, reaching to about the middle of the area covered by the citadel, is allotted to buildings whose purpose is ceremony and worship. The east side contains dwellings. As to streets, two main ways can be made out: one coming in through the south gate and forking off to the east in front of the Scorpions' gate, another coming in from the Spring gate and running along the west front of the north-east palace.

(*a*) *The North-East Palace group.*—The *Well gate*, which gives access to the palace from outside, consists of a thrice broken, very long gallery, which rises within from the foot of the bastion protecting the gate, and in so doing goes by three openings. It leads far inside the citadel and was undoubtedly formerly open above. The main part of the corridor, running north and south, is bounded on the east by the bastion wall, on the west by a thick outer protecting wall 31 metres long. The Well gate was originally the northern main entrance to the citadel, which was through the north-east palace. The gate lost this importance owing to the alterations in the palace, which shut off its north wing and necessitated a second gate being made, the

Spring gate. The entrance in this lies at the rear of a broad
fore-court defended with towers, and from this court the
north enclosure wall, which has not been preserved, was
continued to the west.

The North-East Palace, the largest building on the
citadel, in its last and mighty form is the result of very extensive alterations and enlargements. Originally it consisted only of a great middle court of a nearly square plan
(32-35 metres broad, 36 metres long), about which the
rooms were disposed in fairly small dwellings. The corridor
from the Well gate led into a room at its north-west corner.
The communication with the inner part of the citadel lay
opposite on the south side. Between the back wall of the
northern row of rooms in the courtyard and the outer
fortification there stretched an outer courtyard. At the
north-east corner an outer terrace gave communication
between the north-east corner bastion and the east row of
rooms in the courtyard.

The palace building, with an average width east to west
of 70 metres and about 54 metres deep from north to south,
stood on a foundation-floor about a metre thick of mud-
brick masonry 12-13 metres above the surface of the spring.
The considerations of firmness and height for the palace
level had weight enough with the builder for him to carry
out the heavy preliminary work of 6000 cubic metres of
brick masonry for this floor.

The rebuilding that fell within Kapara's time enlarged
the original area of the palace, 3650 square metres, two-and-
a-half times and made a thorough change in the way it was
approached and used. The independent building became
no more than a part which had to fit itself into the building
extensions in accordance with the objects of the new plan,
so far, indeed, as it did not disappear altogether beneath
them. Of the original palace was left standing a part of its
old courtyard and the out-buildings on the east and west
covering 3000 square metres.

The plan for rebuilding and enlarging had in view the

making of an independent north wing, enlarged and self-enclosed, and the building of a new south wing. The building surface was thrust about 11 metres forward towards the south over the row of rooms there and into the original middle court, and also the angle between the outside wall of the ramp corridor and the north boundary of the palace was filled in by a building extension. On the new surface of about 1950 square metres the following separate buildings were erected: the extension building at the north-west corner with three separate dwellings lying along a great corridor and with three or two communicating rooms; also a transverse building coming out 11 metres into the original courtyard, with a heavy sloping enclosure on the south shutting off this courtyard—which now has no doors— from the north wing and making a sharp division between the east wing and the southern part of the palace.

Thus the north wing could only be reached from the rest of the palace by making a round over the north-eastern outer terrace, but this way round was of small importance. Lastly on the strip left to the north up to the inside of the outer circumvallation a third new building was erected right up against the eastern boundary wall of the corridor from the Well gate, containing two bathrooms, each with a large hall-like and a smaller ante-room, and which must be called the bath building. Each of the two bathrooms has a water-tight floor, a great stone bath slab let in, and a recess with an inlet for the water, and it is carefully drained by a stone gutter down the gate corridor and so to outside.

The three buildings lie along a corridor running east and west, which communicates with the outlet of the corridor from the Well gate through a double door that can be shut. Access to the new north-west wing lying beyond the corridor from the gate was given by a bridge over the gate corridor which was a westerly continuation of the passage in the north wing. The long gallery of the gate corridor was, as it had been before, left open on top.

On the south, at the cost of the citadel area and with the

help of a widening eastward into the town area, a new part was added to the palace, having about the same area as the part already existing. Following the design of the older part, it has broad rows of buildings around a nearly square courtyard.

The new courtyard was set in front of the old on more or less the same level, and the latter, therefore, now took second place as an inner court. The two great central courtyards were separated from one another by a crosswise gateway. The surface of the old courtyard, to make up for the 11-metre wide strip lost on the north side, was widened on the south by 9 metres. The surface covering of the older courtyard, made up of two separate layers (gravel with brick slabs over it), later was raised half a metre by dumping broken limestone slabs, and so its level brought up to that of the new south courtyard, The palace was given a new approach from the west, this being from within the citadel. The new area shaped like a wide trapezium finally measured 9400 square metres.

The new south wing stands also on a massive floor of 4300 square metres with an average thickness of $1\frac{1}{2}$ metres built of mud bricks, this floor being for about 130 metres on the east and the south side edged by a strip of an average width of 10 metres, going down 12 metres deeper. It has a content for the new building alone of altogether 9000 cubic metres. To this must be added the raised mass of the north wing with 1100 cubic metres and the floor of the older part of the north-east palace with 6000 cubic metres. Thus at this part alone of the citadel for the foundation mass 16,100 cubic metres were dealt with.

(*b*) *The South Gate group.*—The main entrance on the town side into the citadel lay at about one-third of the length of the south circumvallation from its west end. The Kapara dynasty made two gates. The builder of the later and smaller south gate gave no heed to the old gate-works and the arrangement of their parts; on the west two-thirds of these works was pulled down, and on the east one-third was filled in and taken into the adjoining massif substructure of unfired bricks. The older structure with its corridor-like, broken entry (like that in the Well gate) and many small rooms on each side, and with its great size, is alone in its kind on Tell Halaf.

The parts of the wall making up its eastern third and taken into the adjoining substructure of the massif without being pulled down, in their very well preserved state up to a height of $7\frac{1}{2}$ metres—the gates cannot have been higher than 8 metres—do not by any means point to decay; rather the new construction is a result of Kapara's great building activities.

The numerous small rooms of the older structure were combined, when the new building was made, into two long rectangular gate rooms one after the other, which are crossed in a straight line by the macadamized passage-way, not along the axis, but with a westerly displacement. As a result the newer structure, measuring $22\frac{1}{2} \times 21$ metres, was smaller than the older one, measuring about $35 \times 24\frac{3}{4}$ metres. It is interesting to find in the older gate that on the inside of its front flanking towers was a cleft, interrupted at several places, which was made for a narrow wooden stairway up to the tower platform, and that in the passage room there was a cross slit in the wall on each side for a portcullis. Furthermore all the doorways in the well preserved but filled up small east rooms had mud brick arches.

The newer gateway structure lies exactly along the four cardinal points. Its front entrance has a well paved threshold, and behind this a carefully moulded entry slab together with covers from the frames of the hinge-cases for a two-sided gate.

The mud brick substructure of the massif and the broken stone heap.—This substructure in its last form stretched 55 metres long by 54 metres broad from a place east of the south-east corner of the temple-palace as far as the south enclosure-wall of the citadel right next to the south gate, and comes out beyond this wall southwards another $34\frac{1}{2}$ metres with an average breadth of 30 metres, taking the enclosure wall also into itself. The surface of the terrace lay at an average height of $4\frac{3}{4}$ metres above the neighbouring area of the citadel and of $6\frac{1}{2}$ metres above the town area. The substructure, originally smaller, namely $20\frac{1}{2} \times 5\frac{1}{2}$ metres, was enlarged to an area of 4435 square metres.

On the west side a widening of $3\frac{1}{2}$ metres was also carried out to make a way up the ramp, and on the new terrace extension was laid a not very high base running east and west about 51 metres long and 19 metres broad. The mass of masonry contained 22,500 cubic metres. Beyond some plaster remains and a drainage system no remains of buildings were found on its surface. Its purpose could not be determined.

In connection with the building extension the neighbourhood of the south-east corner of the citadel was also raised by Kapara about $2\frac{1}{2}$ metres over a width of 65 metres and a length of 117 metres, giving an area of 7600 square metres. The dumped layer consisted of shot earth with a thick top layer of large broken stones only. On this work 5700 cubic metres of broken stones and 9500 cubic metres of filling-earth were used.

The burial-place outside the South gate and to the east. In the outside angle between the gate building and the platform there lay a burial-place of the Kapara dynasty partly covered in by the rebuilding, and of which was left only two tombs and a cult room. The tombs consist of a broad ante-room and the small sepulchral chamber proper. On account of the immediate neighbourhood of the rock bottom at this spot they were laid out above ground. The slip-openings into the sepulchral cells still preserved were arched at the top and walled up. The third structure, coming from the time of the rebuilding, consists of an anteroom and a main room, which is fitted with a washing-place and an arrangement for carrying off the waste water.

Farther to the east there stood two other smaller sepulchral cells, each of which held the basalt statue of a seated woman over a shaft-like grave. The rooms, shaped as a long rectangle, at the time when the massif was built up had already gone far into decay, and lay on an east-west line alongside one another near the west edge of the salient of the massif and not far from the other tombs, with which they had once made up a common graveyard.

The sepulchral cell about the small statue standing to the north measured 3.65 metres long and 2 metres broad inside. The statue stood in a niche 79 centimetres wide, and 42 centimetres deep on the west side with its face—just like the other—towards the east. Under both statues were shaft graves of quarried stone running right down to the rock with polished walls and an inside diameter of 60 centimetres.

(c) *The Temple-Palace group.*—In it are combined: the temple-palace, the Scorpions' gate with the upward way from the citadel gate, the temple-palace terrace, the royal tombs and the north building.

The Temple-Palace with its Scorpions' gate and terrace. It represents the most important, though not the most extensive set of buildings on the whole citadel. Its importance is shown by its whole construction and its very rich adornment with sculptures.

The north and principal façade with a recess adorned with carving between the wall salients and a portico carried by sculptures stands right before the great expanse of a terrace. The south façade is divided up by five towers and from the town side stood out imposingly to the eye. It had a foot barely a metre high made up of carved orthostats alternately of black basalt and of limestone painted red. Short south pieces of the west and east fronts, decorated with this carved foot or plinth, also came out clear over the town area lying below. Their northern portions were hidden behind the structure of the Scorpions' gate and the terrace.

The temple-palace forms a long rectangle running east and west—with a length almost twice the breadth (51.70

× 30.30 metres). The main outlines and the partitions are in true right-angles to one another, if we except some slight errors in construction. They are strictly determined by the points of the compass except for a deviation in the line of the south façade. The substructure is made up by strong foundation walls, the hollows between which are filled in with shot earth, and sometimes with mud brickwork. The level surface paved with limestone flags makes up the $5\frac{1}{2}$-metres high base for the structure above ground. Its walls stand directly on the foundation walls of the substructure, and also cross them.

The line of the foundation walls follows that of the walls of a like building from the time of Kapara's forefathers that formerly stood here 6 metres lower. The older structure differs from the newer in the size and material of the mud bricks. In the older one the bricks, made of a stiff yellow clay, measure on an average 40 × 40 × 11 to 15 centimetres; in the later structure the bricks, made of a loose red clay, measure on an average 36 × 36 × 10 to 11 centimetres. The thicknesses of the walls of the newer building correspond with those of the older one. What is new in the later temple-palace is only the raising of the ground, which extended also to the neighbouring terrace, involving an immense toil.

The later temple-palace was the last monumental building of the Kapara period. It had a catastrophic end, as is shown by the fire rubbish a metre high in its rooms and the wreck of its sculptures.

The central point of the ground plan is given by a middle hall 36.75 metres long and 8.05 metres broad. The room lying before it on the north has the same length, but is only 5.22 metres broad. These two rooms or halls are linked together by a 3.90-metre wide passage, having socle-slabs in the archway and in front. The entry into the middle hall is slightly displaced eastwards from the axis of the main entrance.

The monumental entrance recess on the main front

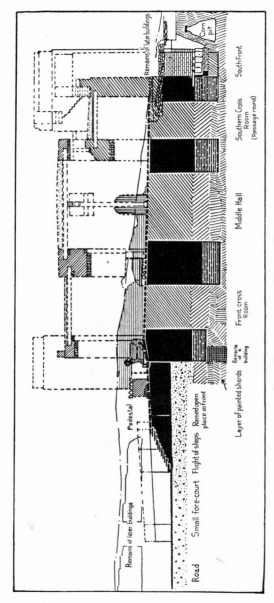

CROSS-SECTION OF THE TEMPLE-PALACE

divides it into an eastern and longer wing with a recess adorned with carvings between the towers, and a western and shorter wing. The eastern wall salient is organically united with the structure, the western was only made during the building. The recess—21.55 metres long and 2.50 metres deep—is faced with a socle of slabs over a metre high, and contains the entrance—9.20 metres broad, inside measurement, and about 6 metres high—with stone carriers (Atlantes) for the timber-work at the gate.

Cross-rooms about 3 metres wide shut in the middle hall and the ante-room on the east, south, and west. The very long room on the south side is cut by two transverse passages, wherefore its longer walls are strengthened against bulging.

In front of the entrance recess there lies a fore-terrace raised about 2 metres, and 16 metres broad, the breadth increasing at three successive levels; into this terrace a flight of steps is built to make a way up from the palace terrace. The main terrace is shut off on the south from the rest of the citadel area by the main façade of the temple-palace, on the south-east by the Scorpions' gate, on the south-west by a thick retaining wall (from the lower-lying south part of the citadel), on the west and north by the enclosing wall of the citadel and lastly on the east by a supposed, but not yet dug out, dividing wall. The last level of the terrace, when it was raised at the building of the later structure, lay some 7 metres above the nearest part of the town, but still 2½ metres below the level of the temple-palace itself. The terrace consisted of a mound averaging 2 metres high of earth and rubbish, which is clearly marked off from the 1-1½ metres thick terrace deposits belonging to the older building.

The Scorpions' gate formed the main approach to the temple-palace quarter and lies in a line with the south gates of the town and the citadel. The gate building is immediately next to the east front of the temple-palace and is like that of the later south gate with a turreted entry, gate recess, two gate chambers one after the other and a paved passage road. To the east is joined on a hall that can only be entered from without, with two ante-rooms; this hall probably was used to accommodate a strong guard, which kept a watch on the traffic in the temple-palace and to the east part of the citadel. Underneath the Scorpions' gate remains were found of an older intermediate gate structure belonging to the older south gate and the old temple-palace.

The rise in the road from the foot of the outer ramp to where the rear outlet of the gate is left behind comes to 1.70 metres in a length of 24 metres.

We have the following further measurements for the extent and area of the temple-palace structure:

	SQUARE METRES
Built over area of the later temple-palace -	1560
Outer terrace - - - - - -	6475

For the masses of masonry and dumped material here used we get the following table in cubic metres:

	MASONRY	FILLING MATERIAL
Substructure - - - -	3,200	2,700
Superstructure (about) - -	3,700	—
Raised front terrace - -	1,190	—
Scorpions' gate (about) - -	1,410	300
Terrace - - - - -	300	13,200
Total - - - -	9,800	16,200

The tombs.—On the western narrow side of the terrace square were two tombs next one another, lying more or less east and west. Of these the south one, sunk deeper into the terrace mound, is the older, the one on the north being later. The former, when the terrace was raised, was overwhelmed in the dumped material.

The southern, older, tomb consists of a single, rectangular cell, measuring inside 3.90 × 2.50 metres, and with a wall 1.80 metres thick. The top covering was a mud brick barrel-vault. The walled up slip-opening had a pointed arch. The north tomb, with an almost square plan measuring 8.40 × 8.30 metres outside, contained two chambers lying east and west alongside one another. Its enclosing wall is 1.30 to 1.40 metres thick.

The North building.—It lies to the north and opposite the temple-palace. The east façades of both are along the same line; the west façade has been lost through the whole west half of the building having been washed away. It is to be assumed, however, that the two structures were of equal length. Their main façades, more or less parallel to one another, enclosed a long rectangular open place 33 metres broad on the terrace. The north building stood clear on every side on the terrace, and had not very deep foundations in it. It comes from the Kapara period and has no earlier model. Its outline and the thicknesses of the walls show the building to have been a monumental counterpart to the temple-palace, although a modest one. The purpose of this building could not be determined. In the main room here, like a courtyard, breaking through the gypsum concrete floor, there were numerous pits for plants. The rectangular building was once made up of two nearly square equal-sized rooms in wings, which lay on both sides, east and west, of a midway passage running north and south. The length of the building, then, was about 52 metres, its average depth being about 26 metres. The east wing, which has been preserved, is 24.24 metres on the south front, on the east front 24.68 metres, on the north front 23.80 metres and along the passage wall 25.95 metres. The main entrance lay in the middle of the building and on the open square, and led into the midway passage, from which only could the two wings be entered.

The east wing, which has been left, contains four long-shaped-rooms side by side and running east and west through the outer enclosures. The principal room, measuring 19.80 × 5.45 metres, and broader than the others, must from its being fitted with a rain-tight floor and from the planting-pits in it be held to have had an impluvium in it.

All the 3-3$\frac{1}{2}$ metres wide rooms joining on to it on the south
and the north—on the north the room more or less divided
in half through the middle wall, on the south two rooms
side by side along their length—could be entered only from
the courtyard and through narrow openings. This ground-
plan of a block of long rooms side by side and parallel
differs wholly from that of the temple-palace with its
merely connective grouping of long rooms about a key
room, which likewise has a greater breadth, and which can
only be entered from an ante-room.

APPENDIX III

Technical Remarks on the Excavations in the Town Area

By Karl Müller

The town wall

THE town area (described in the third chapter) before the excavations began had already revealed the course of a town wall with moat, and this was confirmed when digging was started at several places. Since the town must have been utterly destroyed in Assyrian times, only remains from 20 to 50 centimetres high of the wall could in general be found, but these remains were enough fully to determine it. There were found on the west side 188 metres starting from the south-west corner, the whole of the south wall, 1020 metres long, and on the east side first of all, starting from the south-east corner, a piece 125 metres long and after a break of 80 metres another piece 70 metres long.

According to the time of building, three periods are to be distinguished. The core is everywhere a wall 2.80 metres thick of red heavy mud bricks. Part of the east wall, the west end of the south wall and the west wall are strengthened by an outer wall about 2.40 metres thick of bright red to white mud bricks, lightened with rock weathering. The west wall has further an inner strengthening 1.20 metres thick also of white bricks. In front of the wall was found a horizontally levelled mound made up of fragments of weathered rock, a *fausse-braye*. The wall all along its length stands on the firm red earth which throughout the town area shows the barren natural ground, and must have arisen from the strong action of water. About 6 metres before the outer wall salient the red earth takes a downward slope and leads into the town moat, which is about 5.6 metres deep and falls away at an angle of 25-30 degrees. The width right across of the moat is about 26 metres. The bottom of the moat lies 5.2 metres above the surface of the spring north of the citadel.

The town wall along its whole length and at almost equal intervals is equipped with towers projecting only outwards, there being 37 on the south side and 6 on the west as far as a deepish recess. On the east wall 5 towers were found. The towers, measured along the core of the wall, are 2.6 to 2.9 metres wide, and stand out 1.8 metres. The measurements of the towers on the outside strengthening are about 6.1 metres for the width and 1.6 metres for the salience. The curtains have an average length of 24.25 metres at the core of the wall, at the strengthening a length of 22.5 metres. On the south side some curtains measure only 17.7 to 18.3 metres at the core of the wall.

Between the 14th and the 15th tower from the western corner bastion, which are only 15 metres apart, we may suppose the south gate to have been. No remains, it is true, of a gate building were found, since owing to the caravan road that led through this spot in modern times a hollow had been made. But it was exactly in the gap between the two towers, which stand nearer together than in the other cases, that the gravelled and metalled north to south main street of the town from the direction of the south citadel gate came to an end.

We must assume at least another gate both in the west and in the east wall. The west wall at the end of 188 metres from the south-west corner bastion makes a recess 12 metres long, and somewhat farther to the north there was a street made in the same way as the above-mentioned one, pointing to a gateway.

The town wall and moat may be assigned to the oldest period of settlement at Tell Halaf, and in the later periods their line was maintained, while they were merely strengthened. In the Hellenistic and the Arab period the place was no longer fortified, since numerous, though unimportant, building remains from those times in some places pierce the town wall or even go right over it.

The buildings of the town

(a) *Dwellings.*—At all points in the town area that were explored by trial trenches there were found comparatively unimportant remains of dwelling-houses in three layers one above the other. The material in the lowest layer, resting on the natural red earth, is the same red and good mud brick that we find in the core of the town wall. The bricks belonging to the period (Kapara period) above this are not so heavy and are smaller, sometimes fairly thick, and those in the uppermost layer are usually of very poor quality. In the lowest and the middle period we find houses with one, and also several rooms, the houses lying alongside one another without any plan and not always facing the same way. Their rooms generally have the walls more or less at right angles to one another. The alleyways are narrow, most of them barely a metre wide, but with a hard floor of gravel and also coarse rubble. What is striking is a very careful draining of these alleyways; and in each one of the better houses are bathrooms. The bathrooms had a pavement either of fired bricks or of gypsum cement, and covered over with asphalt; under the floor was a channel to carry off the water, made of clay pipes starting with a knee, and the fittings were an oval clay vessel as a 'bath' and a great clay jar, both let into the floor.

Embedded in the upper layer were a great many Hellenistic cist-graves, whose walls consisted either of several smaller limestone slabs or of single ones. For the roof, too, stone slabs were used.

At the time when these graves were made the town area was as yet settled only at a few places.

(b) *Cult Room.*—West of the expeditionary house and some 40 metres behind the town wall there was uncovered a not very large building—its area was only 196 square metres—which in its ground-plan takes after the dwelling-houses and belongs to the Kapara period. It runs east and west and to the east and the north was bounded by an open square, to the west by a small alley leading to the town wall, and to the south by buildings mostly one-roomed. From the east side we come first to an ante-room 4 metres broad and running back 3 metres, and out of this through another door we come into the main room, lying along the same axis and with a breadth of 4.5 metres and a depth of 15 metres. Both doors had basalt hinge-stones, and so could be shut. In the west of the south wall of the main room a door in a recess leads to a side room 4.6 metres broad and 2.8 metres deep, a kind of sacristy, connected with the front chamber on the east (2 × 2.8 metres). The room on the west (1.4 × 2.8 metres) has no communication. The building material is made up of good, almost white mud bricks measuring 40 × 40 centimetres. The walls were decorated and washed with plaster. The floor was of fired bricks 33 × 33 centimetres in size. The threshold of the door between the ante-room and the main room was a large limestone slab.

At the western end of the main room, that is of the cella or shrine, stood an altar of fired bricks with a surface measuring 75 × 75 centimetres. It is plastered on each side up to 6 centimetres thick in several layers, which were laid on from time to time one after the other when an earlier one had become damaged. The top of it, too, was plastered, but was much blackened and battered, and in the rifts remains of ashes were found. In one corner two bits of brick were still left on the top with the plaster standing up on them. They lead us to suppose there were small brick supports at the four corners carrying a baldachin or a gridiron; brick remains fitting in with this suggestion were found at the foot of the altar. Before the altar there was lying a rectangular basalt stone with two pits of different depth with a pipe-like connection between them—the sacrificial stone. Behind the altar was the double statue of a seated pair, 80 centimetres high, and left of this the metre-high statue of a man standing. Both figures were resting on one and the same base of mud bricks, which was coated with plaster 1-3 centimetres thick on an average. Before the north wall was built a bench or table, behind which the wall plaster was carried down, its height being about 50 centimetres.

(c) *Town Temple.*—On the highest ground in the north-west of the town area was uncovered a building with an area of 2000 square metres—an Assyrian temple. It was just below the surface and was the last settlement at this spot. As early as Hellenistic times the temple ruins, probably already by then covered with rubbish, were used as a burial ground. On the other hand under the Assyrian building there lies an older one, whose walls, anyhow on the south side, have about the same outline. The line of direction is more or less east to west.

Two main portions are to be distinguished: the true temple, ornamented on the east front with towers, and the fore-court enclosed by rooms. The temple consists of a rectangular courtyard, the cella adjoining it on the west and raised six steps above it, two small side-rooms north of the courtyard, and the gate-room with a chamber adjoining. From the gate-room we come not only into the courtyard, but also through the adjacent smaller room on the south into the passage going round all the temple rooms.

The architectonic details of the whole temple are carried out with the utmost care and are remarkably fine: the pavement of carefully cut limestones with narrow gaps, the two stairways and the landing between them all covered with neatly worked stone slabs, the walls plastered and lime-washed and on the west walls of the small side-rooms, which have astragals or rounds, even a treatment in two colours, yellow and red. By the stairways were standing in the corners of the courtyard basalt socles with shallow round hollows. The mud bricks are 40 × 40 × 11 to 12 centimetres, 10 layers with joints rising 1.3 metres.

The fore-court is an irregular quadrilateral with rooms

along each side; its north side is more or less in line with
the temple enclosure, while the south front stands out
southwards by the whole length of a row of rooms. The
paving of the court is irregularly laid without any particular care. A drain leads outside from the middle of the
court midway through the east front, the gate lying
somewhat north of it.

APPENDIX IV

On the Smaller Finds

By Hubert Schmidt

IN the case of the smaller objects found at Tell Halaf a distinction must be drawn for the several cultures between the objects of stone, bronze, iron or clay based on the layers in which they are found. As in all excavations it is the clay vessels that are here the most numerous and most important. Taking the whole, three great complexes may be distinguished in the layers: (1) the prehistoric layer with the painted pottery; (2) the palace layer with the main buildings and the stone carvings; (3) the latest and uppermost layer from Hellenistic times.

I

Of special interest is the *Prehistoric layer*, which is characterized especially by the painted pottery—called N-ware. On grounds of technique, forms and ornamentation it is made up of three groups standing in close connection with one another, and so representing a continuous evolution. Everything is made by hand without the potter's wheel.

The older group is that with glazed painting (N 1), to use the term which since Furtwängler and Loeschke after the Mycenae finds is usually applied to 'varnished' painting (Pl. 51, 52, 53). With it is associated a perfected firing technique: vessels are of well washed clay and usually baked ringing hard, sometimes of a yellowish colour or, where the heat is sharper, red. The painting colours have as fundamental tones black, brown, red, orange, but show many gradations, according to the accidents of the firing or the strength with which the colours are laid on. The peculiarity of glazed painting lies in the fact that the colours laid on become glossy or lustrous in the firing.

The designs are geometrical, simple elementary forms being combined into the most manifold figures or variations. The elementary forms consist of horizontal lines—zigzag, curved, waved; strips filled in variously (as with hatching or with lattice-work); rows of points, rows of triangles, hanging and standing, rows of rhombs variously filled; rows of angles; rows of slant lines. These elementary forms are set one below the other in horizontal belts, or in a vertical arrangement they lead to fields of metopes.

FIG. I. PATTERNS OF THE PAINTING ON THE PREHISTORIC PAINTED POTTERY
The upper five rows are in one colour; the lower three in two colours.

Rows of circles are less often found; particularly noticeable are chess-board patterns, fields of rhombs or net-like figures. Special motives also are the four-leaved clover and the so-called Maltese cross, the so-called spring-oyster (thorn-oyster, water-clam), the fiddle motive, together with rings of points and star-like combinations. Compare the five upper rows in Fig. I.

The wealth of forms shown by the pots is very remarkable. Usually the forms have a broad, sharply cut-off base. The following may be distinguished (Fig. 2):

(*a*) Funnel-rimmed beakers, the shape by far the most affected, and one showing an extraordinarily great number of variants, most of them with a broad sloping rim, but others also where it is more upright and quite flat, so that the shapes are almost those of the basins and dishes. The decoration on the outside of the rim is confined to simple motives; the main decoration is to be seen on the inside of the rim, as a rule parallel belts, but also a vertical arrangement with a division into metopes. A special part is played by the bull's head painted inside or out (Fig. 2, *1*).

(*b*) Beakers in various sub-kinds with conical shapes— with the rim sharply under-cut, with the rim curved, with the wall curved, or with a sharp break (Fig. 2, *2*, *7*, *8*; Pl. 51, *5-7*, *9*; Pl. 52, *7*, *10*). The designs are as a rule on the outside; much favoured is a self-contained ground design made up of numerous belts or zones.

(*c*) Basins: especially favoured with a broad rim and a sharp break near the bottom. Other shapes like the beakers with a rim, but mostly wider and with a sharp profile to the rim and the wall (Pl. 51, *8*; Pl. 52, *1*, *2*, *6*, *8*, *9*). A special form is that with a wide, slightly projecting rim, and a high, tapered lower part. The designs are in zones or belts and fields of metopes.

(*d*) Bowls: usually wide, sometimes calotte-shaped, sometimes with a break, and a rim turning either inwards or outwards (Fig. 2, *5*; Pl. 52, *11*). Particular forms are the deep and wide bowls with a sharply stepped rim bending outwards, that is funnel-rimmed bowls (Fig. 2, *3*). In the widely open shapes the designs are on the inside, the middle being most usually left unpainted. The usual decoration is of zones.

(*e*) Pots: mostly with out-turned rim; variants with a break in the wall. A special form is the loop pot with upright rim (Fig. 2, *4*, *11*; Pl. 52, *5*). Variants of it have a double break in the wall. The designs are mostly of the zone kind, on the shoulder of the loop pot a division into metopes is often found.

(*f*) Jars with a narrow neck: this may be sometimes straight, sometimes bulging, sometimes spherical; funnel-rimmed jars, too, are not unusual (Fig. 2, *12*; Pl. 51, *1*, *2*; Pl. 52, *3*, *4*). For household purposes a rounded jar with a double neck is used. The designs are mostly simpler than they are on the smaller shapes.

(*g*) Cauldrons with a wide belly: also loop cauldrons

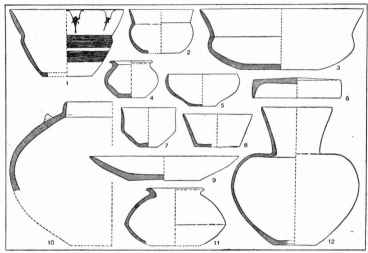

FIG. 2. FORMS OF THE PREHISTORIC PAINTED POTTERY.
All belonging to N1. Scale about ⅛.

with a low rim are found, analogous to the forms of the smaller pots (Fig. 2, *10*). The loops bring about the vertical division of the designs. The heavy forms are used for household purposes and are decorated more simply.

(*h*) Dishes: mostly large with a thick wall, some with a slanting rim, some with a rim bending outwards, and some with a funnel-rim (Fig. 2, *3*). The decoration as usual inside runs round in zones, but large chessboard patterns also are found.

(*i*) Plates: mostly with a slanting rim, and generally distinguished by elaborate inside designs (Fig. 2, *9*; Pl. 52, *8* behind).

(*k*) Covers and Lids: as a rule flat lids with straight edges, but also bell-shaped (Fig. 2, *6*; Pl. 51, *4*). The decoration is of cross-patterns.

(*l*) Special forms: With bowls and beakers a hollow foot is sometimes added; household vessels have a special spout for pouring out, particularly cauldrons and dishes.

In the two-colour, less often three-colour painting (N 2) three cases may be technically distinguished (see Coloured Plate I, II):

1. As a rule the vessels have a white or yellowish-white coating. The two-colour technique first arose by chance in the firing and is already to be seen in good varnish technique, when on the same vessel a brown or a black strip of colour gradually or suddenly comes out red. The same painting colour therefore gives different shades and different lustres according to the effect of the wood fuel or of the heat when fired in closed ovens.

2. This experience leads to a deliberate two-colour technique (cp. Fig. 1); thus on the same vessel two different colour shades or even colours are applied alternatively in the same design or in different designs. As a result the two-colour technique is found in the best glossy painting. Here the red is either a thin coating or a separate colour, but in most cases a dull red beside a glossy black. The three-colour technique arises through white being added, when white may appear as a covering colour over the glossy painting. The carrying out of the designs in fine lines leads to the highest development of glossy painting.

3. The ordinary N 2 ware makes its appearance in black and red as dull colours (Coloured Pl. I, II). It is significant for progress that the old forms change and new ones come into use (Pl. 54, *2-11*). The funnel-rimmed forms and the pots are disappearing; changes come in in the profile, the wall becoming curved and the lower part drawn sharply

in. Changes like these are to be seen in the jars, cauldrons and bowls. The pot is given a rounded bottom and so goes the way of decay; so, too, in the case of the beakers and basins a gradual disappearance can be noted; the bowl on the other hand is what is most favoured in their stead (Fig. 3).

The *bowl*. By far most often it is with indrawn lower part that the bowl is found, usually with a good white coating

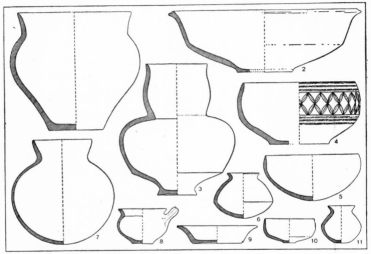

FIG. 3. FORMS OF THE PREHISTORIC PAINTED POTTERY
N 1: *1*; N 2: *2, 3, 4, 8, 9, 10*; N 4: *5, 6* (transition), *7*; N 6: *11*. Scale about ⅙.

(Fig. 3, *2, 4*; Pl. 54, *6, 8, 9, 11*). Among designs very frequent is the zigzag strip of metopes in black and red variants alternating with spring-oysters (thorn-oysters); then there are rows of rhombs, rows of four-leaved clover, strips of curves and an arched ridge alternating one above the other in several belts, and separated by a horizontal line and alternately black and red. More seldom do we find rows of triangles, ladder designs, lattice-work strips, rows of angles, and so on; occasionally there is seen also in the open field of metopes a small spring-oyster, alternating with vertical lattice-work strips. Rarer is the form with the sloping or level rim, so that the whole of the inside can be seen (Pl. 54, *8*, *9*); hence the designs are here also painted on the inside. Among them stand out the chess-board pattern variously filled in—especially with the four-leaved clover—and the Maltese cross in red with latticed squares in black. Particularly striking, too, are the arrow-head motive and the eye pattern in rows. The motives we have mentioned are set above one another in belts to make extended designs. Cp. Coloured Plate I, II.

Among the *cauldrons* new forms appear. One has a sloping side and upturned rim, another a steeper outline, and lastly there is a bellied cauldron that closes in above with a narrow opening and a high rim slightly bent outwards on top. On the wide bellies of the cauldrons there is a great fondness as elsewhere for decorations of zones and metopes. A striking feature on the free ground are patterns of eight-fold stars of the same kind as the four-leaved clover, red edged with black; quite alone in their kind we see here large skins of beasts spread out next to one another with neck and tail, and dotted black; in the gaps are long-drawn tree or bough designs, usually black, with red strokes for leaves. On cauldrons and jars we also sometimes find drawings of faces in two colours with a naturalistic representation of the eyes; so, too, the trees are given leaves like those in the leaf motives, painted black and red.

Among the *plates* we find a basin-like variant richly painted on the inside, with a great fondness for hanging garland motives (Pl. 54, *4*; cp. also *10* here).

A special group is made up by the painting in white (N 3) in combination with polychromy. At first white makes its appearance as secondary only on a black varnish, for instance as a circle of dots, but also in the form of dotted fillings for large surfaces—white dots, for instance, on a black ground. More seldom are found white wave lines on a red strip, as also in a few cases white groups of zigzags and rows of dots on black varnish. Lastly white combined with red and black leads to the rare polychromy, as in Coloured Plate II, 5.

Naturalistic representations are especially to be noted in the above-mentioned three groups; we may here distinguish beasts, human beings and plants (Pl. 53). Horses are shown whole figure on the belly of large vessels in a long row one behind the other. The conventionalization here is characteristic: on the head the ears set forwards (the length of the ears on the analogy of other cases does not stand in the way of the above interpretation), the profile of forehead and nose with a sharp bend downwards and the exaggerated jaw-bones. Horses like these are to be seen behind one another, too, at the rim of the inner surfaces of funnel-rimmed bowls. These depictions seem to have a definite racial type as their basis, but it is hard to fix which it is; horses like these are found also on the oldest seals from Susa. What differs is the ears falling limply backwards; it is impossible to say whether it is meant in this way to mark another race, or even another animal, an ass, say, or a mule (Pl. 53, 7).

Quite a stereotype representation is given us by the horned beast with bent legs and head thrown back, likewise shown one after the other in rows, the space between being filled in with small dots. Judging by how the horns are shown, some kind of cattle (a bull?) seems to be meant (Pl. 53, 3, 13). The same beast is found as a partial picture with head and neck but no body. The horned head seen from in front is also used purely as a geometrical ornament, usually on the rim of a funnel-rimmed bowl; less often on the belly of larger vessels (Pl. 53, 4, 5). In a few cases, as the inner picture of a bowl there is a ring of bulls' heads looking like a rosette.

Other horned beasts are at once seen from their horns to be ibexes; so, too, the sheep are characterized by two curving horns. The ibex with the head lowered is found sometimes on the belly of the larger vessels, sometimes on the inside of the larger open bowls.

There is a fondness for birds, which are shown in various

ways (Pl. 53, *6, 9, 10, 14, 15, 16*). On large surfaces is drawn
a bird with a long neck and outstretched wings, evidently
in flight. This motive leads to a light sketch of two wings.
Clearly the birds are shown during flight, just before settling on the ground: the wings are seen to be bow-shaped,
the neck and head stretched downwards, as also the legs
and claws. This bird has always a long beak and a tail
whose feathers stand away from one another; according to
Professor Hilzheimer we have here a crane. Less often there
are birds standing at rest next to one another and with a
long neck and legs, probably a small stilt-bird (according to
Hilzheimer). The motive may be given a varied treatment.
The ostrich, too, according to Hilzheimer is clearly marked
by a small head, long neck and high-arched tail-portion.
In other birds of this kind the beak is strikingly long—probably a stork or perhaps a swan (according to Hilzheimer).
Particularly striking is the long-necked bird with back-
turned head.

Among the human figures we are struck by one drawn in
profile in lively movement towards the right with an especially long and high head-covering or perhaps fluttering
hair, seemingly a mythological figure. The arms are bent
at the elbow; on the foremost, anyhow, of three figures
hastening one behind the other a tail can be clearly seen,
so that it may be a Silenos (in the Greek meaning) (Pl. 53,
18). Very often we have the stereotype drawing of a dance,
figures set side by side and reaching hands to one another
(Pl. 53, *17*); there is a particular fondness for this on the inside of the rim in bowls. In one example (Coloured Pl. II,
5) the treatment is polychromatic, a black-latticed garment with red dots at the neck (a necklace) within a decoration of zones with white lines between. On large thick-
walled vessels are found some scenes with more figures than
one; thus we have clearly (Pl. 53, *11, 12*) a squatting man
and by him one standing with lifted and bended arms.
Alone in its kind is a conical deep basin with several scenes
lightly sketched and set side by side like metopes (Pl. 51, *8*):

(*1*) a man standing with uplifted arms before a wheeled design, perhaps in connection with a fragment beside it that might be read as the breasting of a chariot, that is, perhaps, a man in front of his two-wheeled chariot; in that case, too, certain lines above the breasting could be taken as a horse. The same kind of representations of a chariot on the earliest seals from Susa are indeed just as primitive in their perspective; (*2*) A thing like an armchair, and in front of it a horned four-legged beast, in the upper left-hand corner a lattice-like drawing; (*3*) on the right side of the picture is again a man with uplifted arms, next to him on the left a smaller representation of the same man with uplifted arms; (*4*) An incomplete and ill-preserved representation: on the right possibly a human figure seated, before which is an object whose upper part only is preserved, perhaps a musical instrument of the same kind as the like primitive representations on seals and reliefs.

Of plants there is in the N 1 group on larger vessels a tree, alternating with fields of lines and zigzags. The trees themselves are found in two types of a geometrical kind with parallel strokes as boughs, or when carried out on a larger scale they are found so that the long boughs are given parallel lines on one side; in the latter case the top of the tree may also be given a tufted form.

The four-leaved clover, cannot be characterized at once as a naturalistic motive; in the two-colour N 2 group both, the tree and the four-leaved clover alike, are taken over, the tree in a simple line treatment alternating with metope fields as before. The leaves of the four-leaved clover are also used purely geometrically for boughs in black and red painting.

In the nature of objects are occasional comb-like motives in a long and a triangular form, which may also point two ways as a double comb.

The decay of this wealth of ornament came about gradually (group N 4). In the forms of the vessels this process shows itself in a spherical formation of the bottom; this is found already in the pot, but also shows itself in the jars and cauldrons (Fig. 3, *6*, *7*; Pl. 54, *1*). It is the bowls that occur oftenest in this spherical form (Fig. 3, *5*). In the same way we also now see a retrogression in the technique of the painting and in the designs, both in the ordinary painting in black and in the two-colour technique.

Particularly striking in the case of the jars is a thickening on the inner side of the rim for fixing on to it a loop on the inside, which is probably also a device for hanging up the vessels.

Special designs belonging to the decay are large curves put side by side on jars and pots where the wall is at its widest. Out of all the wealth of geometrical ornament only a few designs are now left, which are repeated over and over again: rows of zigzags, of curves, of strokes, and sometimes of triangles, and lattice-work patterns or fields of rhombs. Cp. Pl. 54, *1*.

Besides these four groups of painted pottery discussed at length, there is a plain unpainted group of vessels, which seem to be made by hand in the same shapes (N6; Fig. 3, *11*).

There are certain cases which may be noted as unusual. Very remarkable are the basket-vessels, in which the walls are divided up by hollows arranged like ribs or by clay ridges made at the same time as the pot. Sometimes these vessels are even painted, some of them in a good glossy technique (Pl. 51, *3*). So, too, there is something particular about vessels with finger-prints like shells (shell vessels). Some designs, such as maeander-strips opened out by rectangles filled with dots and set oppositively, as also stepped designs opened out by oppositive long rectangles between parallel strips, call to mind pottery of Samarra and of Tepe Moussian just as forms like the pots with a sharp break remind us of the pottery of Susa. These likenesses, however, may also arise out of a parallel development, for the true Susa forms, especially the typical beaker, are wanting. One piece only of this form was found on Tell Halaf and carried out in a very bad technique of decay.

U

Thus taken altogether the painted pottery of Tell Halaf is seen to be an independent and self-contained field of art. In the four groups of vessels above-mentioned it embraces the whole process of growth of which at other cultural sites such as Samarra, Susa, Tepe Moussian, Kazinch and Aly Abad, we find only the single stages in separation. So much the more important must this painted pottery be for the oldest culture of Tell Halaf.

For this reason another pottery must be mentioned in this connection, the Old Monochromatic variety—N 9— in a primitive technique with remarkably thick-sided forms (Pl. 50). It is made from roughly washed clay, and is grey, seldom black or yellowish-brown, or is coated red, and is mostly well polished. Its forms are not those of the painted pottery: clumsy cauldrons, basins, dishes, plates, jars and larger storage-vessels. They are only occasionally decorated—with lines scratched in; so that it is the more surprising to find painting on some of the pieces, which can only be explained by influence from the painted pottery. Thus, too, we find once only a glossy black strip of paint, that is, varnished painting; and with the same rareness do we find in the primitive technique of this group in imitation of the painted pottery forms the funnel-rimmed beaker (Pl. 50, *11*) and the funnel-rimmed dish. Under this same influence the vessels are found with an improved firing technique, even with a red varnish-painting.

There can be no doubt that at Tell Halaf the makers of the Old monochrome vessels must have belonged to another and older population than the Painted Pottery folk, but that both of them for some time at least lived peacefully side by side and in the end fused into one.

The Old monochrome pottery in this time gradually lost all its importance and the painted pottery on the other hand went on developing down to decay and final disappearance. It is interesting to find that in both these techniques what is the earliest form of the lamp makes its ap-

pearance (Pl. 51, 5, 7): a small conical basin with a notch
in the top of the rim on which lay the wick.

While the pottery is decisive for characterizing this oldest
culture at Tell Halaf, there are also other important marks.
Thus, in the same layers great quantities of simple implements in flint and obsidian have been found: knives,
scrapers, scratchers and the like (Pl. 48b, 1-4, 6). Among
the rare objects is a longish arrowhead, finely worked from
a narrow flint splinter and with a short tang (Pl. 48b, 3).
From these productions we have to draw the conclusion
that the oldest culture was Neolithic. To it belong also axes
or hatches of rock-stone in various forms and sizes, small
flat chisels and simple forms of the hammer, often with
boring started, from which we may draw the conclusion that
they were made here on the spot. To this same cultural
stage, however, may be also assigned a flat hatchet and a
lance- or dagger-head with a tang, both of copper and
found during the deep digging in 1929 in the north part of
the south gate of the citadel (Pl. 48b, 7, 8). Perhaps we may
add here a flat copper arrow-head with a long tang, coming from the layer in front of the Kapara building at the
depth of the orthostats (Pl. 48b, 5). Anyhow the copper
forms along with the stone weapons and implements already mentioned would thoroughly fit in with the general
character of the Susa I culture as we know it from the
results of the French excavations in Susa; we may call both
cultures—that of Tell Halaf and that of Susa I—chalco-
lithic in accordance with the usual terminology in European prehistory.

To Painted Pottery times also belong clay figures of men
and beasts with glossy painting (Pl. 56). A persistent type
is represented by a woman's figure in a squatting attitude
with strongly developed breasts and arms folded together
on the body (Pl. 56, 1, 2, 3, 5). The head is narrowly com-
pressed with the profile-edge standing forward, and on it is
a separate object, probably as a head-covering. The knees
are drawn to the body and the tips marked by triangular

small lumps of clay put on separately, probably to show feet. The figure is painted from top to bottom, the eyes are shown as two small dots, and above and below them on the head is a horizontal line, broken behind, to which small vertical strokes are applied. From these lines, whose meaning is hard to see, are to be distinguished two parallel lines running round as a necklace. The arms and breasts, as also the legs, are covered by parallel strokes, while two lines go round the hips as a girdle. It would seem that the figure is to be looked on as fully clothed, with head-dress and neck-ornament (Pl. 56, *1, 2*). Of painted figures of beasts there are some fragments, apparently horned cattle, the painting on which is done in largish spots and strokes (Pl. 56, *4, 7*).

As to the above-mentioned representations of horses in the painted pottery the following remarks should be added. Clay chariot wheels, and their fragments, are also found with felloes and spokes painted on. Here belongs the clay body of a two-wheeled chariot, on whose axle-sockets are still left the traces of glossy black paint of the same kind as on the painted vessels. For the bent shaft, presumably of wood, a slanting hole is brought down right through the structure of the body of the chariot. We may therefore assume that two-wheeled chariots also of this kind belong to the Painted Pottery culture, that the horse, therefore, and the chariot are a mark of the carriers of this culture. This is of the greatest importance, for in southern Mesopotamia the Sumerians, to whom originally the horse and the chariot were unknown, received these cultural gifts from their neighbours of another race, who may have had their abode equally well to the east as to the north; that is to say, these were either the carriers of the Susa culture to the east or the carriers of the Tell Halaf culture to the north. This question can perhaps be decided in accordance with the Sumerian name for the horse: 'ass of the east'.

The picture of the Tell Halaf prehistoric culture would be left incomplete if no mention were made of an important result of the excavations in 1929: the scarped citadel

wall of stone—a fragment of it is still to be seen under the
north-east dwelling-palace in D 1-3, VII 1—which is to be
completed by a top structure of unfired mud bricks (the so-
called air-dried bricks) belongs to Painted Pottery times,
that is, it must be looked on as the work of the carriers of
the culture thus marked off.

II

From the Palace layer the pottery—D ware—has altogether the character that belongs to historical times, and
corresponds with the Babylonic-Assyrian pottery; it comes
from the time of the Kapara dynasty and its Assyrian successors (Pl. 55 and Fig. 4). Three main groups can be distinguished, which are all highly turned on the wheel: an
undecorated ware for daily use, a smaller ware painted
with simple stripes, and a one-coloured red polished
ware.

1. For ordinary use were cauldrons with handles and
ears, dishes and large amphora-like jars (Fig. 4, *1, 2*; Pl. 55,
1, 3). Especially characteristic for both larger and smaller
forms are the vessels with a pointed or rounded bottom,
some of which also end in a knob (Fig. 4, *9, 13*; Pl. 55, *4-6*).
Here especially belong finer pots and flasks with an egg-
shaped or rounded belly (Fig. 4, *10, 11*). As palace ware in
the narrower meaning we may look on beakers with a
pointed or knobbed bottom, and finely outlined bowls and
plates (Fig. 4, *3-8, 12, 14-18*; Pl. 55, *5, 8, 9, 10, 14*). A particular
kind of bowl inclines to the forms of the well-liked stone
bowls of the time (Pl. 55, *10*). With the pointed-bellied and
the round-bellied vessels are to be reckoned the ring-shaped
stands so often found.

2. The group of painted vessels links up with the above-
mentioned palace ware in the narrower meaning, and consists of finer plates and bowls, beakers, especially knobbed
beakers, small flasks, jars, dishes and basins, also cauldrons
(Fig. 4, *19, 20*; Pl. 55, *1, 9*). The colour painted is a dull
blue-violet. The painting consists of simple parallel hori-

zontal stripes in the case of the smaller vessels; the pots
have also a metope-like pattern on the shoulder with large
motives like spring-oysters, also hanging triangles and
other and more naturalistic patterns, such as hanging
pomegranates in rows under one another. Especially striking are concentric circles, apparently drawn with com-
passes, side by side in rows. The cauldrons are decorated
particularly at the rim and show the same sets of patterns;

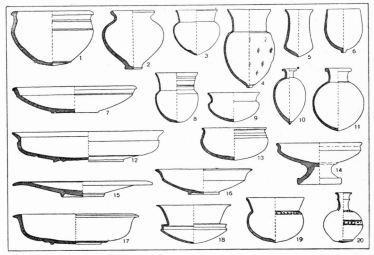

FIG. 4. FORMS OF THE POTTERY FROM THE KAPARA PERIOD.
Palace ware (D). Scale about ⅛.

occasionally we find broad vertical stripes side by side,
reaching down over the belly of the vessel. Particularly remarkable is the painting in white on a violet-red and red
ground in a horizontal or a vertical arrangement, with
rows of large curves, zigzags, groups of vertical lines, and
lastly spiral motives such as entwined spirals and patterns
like plaited ribbon thus arising. The dotted circle, too, is
used as a filling for these.

3. The one-coloured red well-polished ware seems to be
linked with coloured stone vessels (Pl. 55, *2, 10, 12*). Besides

the red vessels we find elegant yellow and also grey-toned ones. As a rule it is more elegant forms of plates, bowls and dishes that are so treated. A fine bowl, polished black, seems to be actually an imitation of a stone bowl; in the same way the three-footed bowl is made in a red mono-chrome to imitate stone implements (Pl. 55, *2, 10*). It is especially important to note that from all the three groups we named examples are found as burial-gifts in the kings' graves, namely, in the tomb-building (Pl. 55, *2, 14*: three-footed bowl and bowl with stem) and the burial-places under the 'throned goddesses' (Pl. *42b*, 43, 44; among the gifts a tun-shaped pitcher and a navel-shaped bowl, Pl. 55, *3, 12*): thus we have the pitcher in shape of a cask, the ele-gant bowl with a high hollow stem, on which (the bowl) traces of red paint are to be looked on as remains of the polished red monochrome technique, the red monochrome basin with a turned omphalos inside and a large red mono-chrome three-footed bowl (Pl. 55, *2, 12, 14*). It is worthy of note in this connection that it is to these very forms that parallels are found in the graves of Gezer in Palestine to-gether with late Mycenaic imports (late pitchers with ears and bronze weapons).

To this period at Tell Halaf, so far as we can make any inference from a few fragments, also belong remarkable imported pieces.

To the Hittite complex must be assigned pitchers with a clover-leaf mouth and ruffed neck in a refined yellow-brown and reddish-brown monochrome technique. From the Asia Minor-Aegaean productive complex come geome-trically decorated vessels with varnished painting (for in-stance, concentric circles drawn with the compass), which doubtless invited imitation in the home workshops. Special mention must be made of a deep basin with two horizontal handles; on the free ground are concentric semicircles cut-ting one another. From the same manufacturing centre, but at a somewhat later time, comes a pitcher with broad stripes and, falling on to the shoulder, great lotus blooms and rays with rosettes in dots between them, corresponding to the stage of the Greek-Orientalized style.

As an Assyrian import we may consider the glazed clay vessels, and also some with painting in colour. The glazing on them is whitish with a green-yellowish sheen; the colours of the paint are whitish-yellowish, and the designs do not go beyond simple geometrical motives. Compared with the productions found at Assur by Walter Andrae, they are wholly inferior technically and decoratively.

Characteristic for the culture of this great palace layer are the frequently occurring stone bowls, which probably were used for purposes of worship (Pl. 49*a*, *2*, *3*). With them are to be reckoned, too, the rectangular stone tables with four or three feet; in accordance with their purpose they are ornamented with bulls' heads as emblems (Pl. 49*a*, *4*). To the same culture belongs the great bulk of the copper and the bronze objects found on Tell Halaf. Among the rare objects found is a small broad dagger-blade with a broad tongue to the handle and one or two rivets—a fairly old type from the Bronze Age. Of the same rareness is an axe with a shaft-socket of the ordinary Sumerian form, as found at Susa in the upper layers of the hill. With it are linked leaf-shaped arrow-heads with a stepped tang. To a later period belong three other types of arrow-heads: that with two winglets and a long tang, that with two winglets and a shaft-socket and barbs, and that with three winglets and a shaft-socket. The two latter were found in Assur in the fortifications, especially near tower C. From the Kapara building comes the top-piece of a standard shaped like a sickle-moon (Pl. 57, *5*). Personal ornaments are very numerous, above all, the arm-rings with ends in the form of animals' heads; there seems to have been a particular liking for the slender heads of gazelles. The usual shape of earrings was that with a thickened curve below. Among the above-mentioned grave finds are also some smooth bronze bowls like skull-caps or bosses, as also cauldrons with curved handles put on. Particular mention should be made of the small cylindrical beakers, which are also found among the clay-ware as imitations. Small bronze figures with a prong for fastening into something were used for purposes of worship; some are standing, some sitting, and always they are wearing long gowns (Pl. 57, *1*, *3*, *4*, *6*, *9*). In one of the main rooms of the Kapara building stood a four-wheeled chariot's framework of iron rods with bronze wheels (Pl. 58*b*). To the time of the Assyrian dominion belong the many clasps (fibulae) of the ordinary Hither Asiatic type, which is derived from the simple bowed and bent clasps of the Aegean culture-complex.

Lastly, mention may be made of the lamps of this period. They are found in two types: firstly, basins narrowed at the top with a long spout standing out (Pl. 55, *13*), such as are very often found in Babylon in New Babylonian dwellings, and such as are there represented on the so-called *kudurru* (boundary-stones) with a flickering flame, and secondly, bowls in the shape of clover (Pl. 55, *11*)—also known as shell lamps—mostly with the outline of the rim richly marked, as known to us in manifold parallels from Palestine in the fourteenth to twelfth centuries. Belonging to the same time as theirs are probably the high massive stone bowls (Pl. 49*a*, *1*) called stand-lamps, for which parallels, too, can be found in Palestine from 1400-1000 B.C., but also earlier than this. Furthermore these stone lamps are also copied in clay on a high cylindrical stem.

III

Above this palace layer inferior buildings of a far later Hellenistic period spread themselves out. The pottery—B ware—is characteristic for them. As to the smaller part it is the fine Hellenistic varnished ware, as known to us from culture centres in Asia Minor, especially in the Mediterranean coastal lands. Of this ware may be mentioned as a rare specimen a deep basin with pointed bottom and an elegant moulding and proportioning of the inside of the rim carried out in an intensive red varnish technique; it is the imitation of a silver vessel that is often to be found in the centres of this culture. Among others particularly striking, too, are the gleaming black cantharus forms with a high moulded stem, fluted belly and delicate white painting on a yellow leaf decoration treated in relief. Constantly occurring also are the small beakers with a ring handle on which a plate is fastened, made like costly metal shapes, or with disk-handles or with a bearded mask in relief. In the main it is an ordinary earthenware with the characteristics of the technique and with the forms of the same time; like the finer kind it has been imported from those far-off workshops.

The great bulk of the pottery consists of coarser vessels in the usual forms with a hasty varnish painting, probably coming from the same workshops in Asia Minor, in contrast with the former groups, therefore, ordinary household implements. There are long series of plates, basins, bowls, beakers, amphorae, pitchers, flasks and the like. Worthy of notice are very large amphorae with stamped ornamentations, some of which are imitated from cut glass or show special designs for stamping. Other ornaments painted on are found to be motives from ornaments for the neck or breast. There is a smaller group which may be called coarse kitchen crockery; it has only simple coloured stripes and spots. A fourth group is made up of what are probably imitations of Hellenistic forms, likewise often painted and made, we may suppose, in native workshops; to them belong the fish-plates—found also everywhere else—with the channel in the middle where the sauce collects. In large household and storage vessels there is a great fondness for deeply stamped ornamentations through which the surface is plastically enlivened—among them are triangles, circles, spirals, angles and especially conventional palm-leaves. It is interesting to find that here, too, Greek amphorae with stamped handles were imported, and, we may assume, with the wine or oil also, just as they were spread by trade throughout the whole of the then known world. Thus in this layer a whole deposit of tall pointed amphorae—we called it the 'wine-cellar deposit'—was laid bare; they were not those we have just mentioned with stamped handles, but had no handles, and some had Greek letters painted on them in black. With these extensive groups of vessels correspond the many clay lamps that were found in this layer. They have the usual Hellenistic forms, with the long spout, as we know them from the centres of this culture— Greek lamps with knob or handle, some of them turned out of moulds and with plastic embellishments of every kind. It was not everyone that could afford such lamps, for there are a great many rough imitations of this imported ware, which are a long way behind their originals.

To the import trade we must also assign bronze vessels— bowls in the skull-cap shape and a ladle, as also a bronze lamp with a twisted handle. Among the rarest objects is imported glassware, such as a Greek aryballos (bucket) with a faceted ornamentation.

A special part is played by the glazed pottery from Seleucid-Parthian times (A group). It has the forms of the Hellenistic pottery, such as plates, basins, (in some cases with stamped Hellenistic palm-leaves), bowls and dishes (in some cases with tall hollow stems) and jars with disk-handles. In part this pottery is of the same kind as was found at Susa in the uppermost layers of the hill.

APPENDIX V

Remarks on the Cuneiform Texts

By Bruno Meissner

THE cuneiform documents that have come to light on Tell Halaf are highly varied, from the point of view alike of the material on which they are found, of their content, and lastly of the time to which they belong.

I. *Cuneiform inscriptions on orthostats and stone statues.*

They are wholly made up of Kapara's inscriptions, which, to judge by the character of the writing and by various peculiarities in the language and in the views uttered, would seem to have been composed in the twelfth century B.C.

The usual inscription on most of the orthostats says only:

'Palace of Kapara the son of Khadianu'.

On the statue of the giant goddess to this usual short inscription are added a short building report and the words of a curse:

'Palace of Kapara, the son of Khadianu. What my father and my grandfather, who (have become) gods (that is, are dead), did not do, I have done. Whoso blots out my name and puts (his) name in—seven of his sons shall be burned before Adad (the thunder god), seven of his daughters shall be dedicated (?) to the goddess Ishtar as hierodules. Abdi-il has written the name of the King'.

Another inscribed stone fragment would, were it well preserved, give the name of the land whose capital was Tell Halaf. To-day only the following can still be read:

'Palace of (Kapara, the son of Khadianu), the King of the Land of Pa-li-e . . . (what my father, my grandfather . . .) did not do, I (have done it). Whoso blots out my name and puts his name in—(seven of his sons) shall be burned before (Adad). Abdi(-il has written the name of the King).'

To the same effect, but very much defaced, are the inscriptions on the statue of the giant god and on the sphinx on the east side of the entrance.

II. *Cuneiform inscriptions on seal-cylinders and stone amulets.*

Some of the seal-cylinders coming from Tell Halaf also show remains of inscriptions; but they are so scanty that no meaning can be got from them. A stone amulet gives a formula calling on the gods Marduk, Irra, Ishum, Namtar and the Seven Spirits.

III. *Clay cuneiform texts.*

From the time soon after the conquest of Guzana by the Assyrians we have from Tell Halaf several royal decrees to the governor of the province, whose name was Mannu-ki-Assur, and who, as we know, in 793 b.c. also held the dignity of eponym. As we learn from inscriptions, the Assyrian king gives heed to each and every small matter in the provincial capital, so that the governor was left little room to act on his own account. When, for instance, he was to serve in the field, he was given the following order from head-quarters:

'Decree of the King to Mannu-ki-Assur. Raise (?) thy forces for the King's campaign. On the 20th of the month Tammuz be thou in the town of Sare'.

Or when an atonement ceremony is to be held in the land, he is simply told:

'Decree of the King to Mannu-ki-Assur. Thou and the people of thy land, ye shall for three days before Adad (the head god), wail (?), weep and pray. From sin purge your land and your fields. Burn burnt-offerings. Let the purging from sin of the house of . . . be carried out. Do thou make the sacrifice (?) before Adad. On the 1st day let it be carried out'.

To the same time also belong some lists, containing mainly names.

The other cuneiform texts on clay tablets are from the time shortly before the fall of Nineveh (between 648 and 612 B.C.). They contain business and law documents, mostly from the house of the merchant Ilu-manani. As an example I will give the translation of an agreement between this Ilu-manani and his opponent Shamash-shum-kin:

'Lawsuit that was carried on by Ilu-manani, the son of Sagib, from the town of Mekhini, with Shamash-shum-kin, the son of Nani, from the town of Zamakha, anent sixty sheep. (Here follow impressions of seals). Record of an agreement as to the action which Ilu-manani brought against Shamash-shum-kin. Ilu-manani has thus spoken to Shamash-shum-kin: "My sheep that are with thee bring thou hither". Shamash-shum-kin has spoken as follows: "I do not owe the sheep". Then they have come to the following agreement before the god Adad. Shamash-shum-kin is before the god Adad to withdraw and (renounce) the sixty sheep. After Shamash-shum-kin had given Ilu-manani (the sixty sheep) peace was made between them. The one shall not go to law against the other. Which ever breaks the agreement is to set down and give ten minas of refined silver and ten minas of refined gold upon the knees of the god Adad, that dwelleth in Guzana. Shamash (the Sun god) be the lord of his lawsuit. On the 1st of the month Sivan in the eponymate of Sin-dui.

(Witnesses)
Before A'uni, the son of Adad-suri
Before Si-nuri, the herdsman of Adad
Before Adad-rapa, the herdsman of Adad
Before Adad-khari
Before Mate'-Si'
Before Adad-Shakni
Before Kiri. . . .
Before Bariki, the messenger
Before Abi-eriba.'

Some of these documents from Ilu-manani's house, that mostly deal with loans of corn are written on clay in Aramaic writing and speech.

Of literary texts on clay there has so far been found only a small fragment, which is a duplicate to the series 'of the evil spirits' written in Sumerian and Assyrian. While the piece of clay tablet is only a small one, it shows that the religious ideas on Tell Halaf at this time were the same as in Babylon and Nineveh. The fragment (with completions) reads:

'Heaven and Earth bring hurt,
a bull demon, that doth harm to the land,
a bull demon, that doth harm to the land,
whose strength is mighty,
whose strength is mighty, whose gait is mighty,
a devil, a goring neat, a great death demon,
a death demon that cometh into every house,
a devil, that hath no fear, are the Seven (evil spirits)'.

APPENDIX VI.

On the Aramaic Documents

THE few Aramaic documents found at Tell Halaf are by no means the least important of the results, and among them a special interest belongs to the Aramaic business documents referred to in Appendix V as counterparts and supplements to the Assyrian business documents dealt with in this same section. They, too, are written on clay, but not on small tablets of the well-known shape, but on heart-shaped lumps. Since they are ill- (in part very ill-) preserved, we cannot reach much certainty as to their content. They seem, mostly anyhow, to refer to barley.

A comparatively well-preserved document among them reads *more or less* as follows:

1. Barley, 4 (measure)
2. (in debt) to Il(u)manānī, (putting debt) on
3. Nabū-dalā. And Hadad-d-m (?) -?-j,
4. see (he is) the supplier to him of the barley,
5. which (is) on the threshing-floor.
6. [The] barley [D-b] will
7. from Q-r-b-n (Qurbān?)
8. supply to the suppl[ier] of the barley.
10. [The?] witness[es] (are):
11. Q-?-r-kh. 12. Z-r-c-l. 13. Kh-z-g. 14. R-c-d-d.

It will interest students of Aramaic and Hebrew to learn that in our documents we find the word 'sh'āhid' for 'witness', for which word, as we know, what was till now the oldest duly attested derivation is found in Genesis xxxi. 47 in the explanation of the name Gilead.

INDEX

x

PRINTED IN GREAT BRITAIN BY ROBERT MACLEHOSE AND CO. LTD.
THE UNIVERSITY PRESS, GLASGOW